Pitt Series in Policy and Institutional Studies

Bert A. Rockman, Editor

Regulation in the Reagan-Bush Era

The Eruption of Presidential Influence

Barry D. Friedman

University of Pittsburgh Press
PITTSBURGH AND LONDON

Published by the University of Pittsburgh Press,
Pittsburgh, Pa., 15260

Manufactured in the United States of America
Printed on acid-free paper

Library of Congress Cataloging-in-Publication Data

Friedman, Barry D., 1953–
Regulation in the Reagan-Bush era : the eruption of presidential influence / Barry D. Friedman.
p. cm. — (Pitt series in policy and institutional studies)
Includes bibliographical references and index.
ISBN 0-8229-3878-2
1. Deregulation—United States. 2. Trade regulation—United States. 3. Administrative agencies—United States. 4. Administrative procedure—United States. 5. United States—Politics and government—1981–1989. 6. United States—Politics and government—1989–1993. 7. Exchange theory (Sociology) I. Title. II. Series.
HD3616.U47F75 1995
338.973'009'048—dc20 95-8654
CIP

A CIP catalogue record for this book is available
from the British Library.
Eurospan, London

Contents

Acknowledgments

This dissertation was made possible in large part by generous institutional support from the University of Connecticut and Valdosta State University in Georgia. For their consideration in allowing me time away from my teaching duties and for other forms of support, I express appreciation to Dean John C. Upchurch and department head James W. Peterson at Valdosta State.

The current and former officials of various government offices and bureaus and of various interest groups who participated in interviews made a vital contribution to this research. I am deeply grateful for their sacrifice of a substantial amount of their valuable time.

While I have benefited from the advice of many scholars during this research effort, I would especially like to recognize the contribution of Louie A. Brown, Robert S. Gilmour, Howard L. Reiter, Harold Seidman, and David B. Walker, whose imaginative ideas were pivotal in shaping the development of this work. I am fortunate to be able to bound ideas off of my fellow UConn alumnus, Akira Hayama. My students at North Georgia College who enrolled in the seminar entitled "the Presidency" used an earlier draft of this manuscript as a textbook and provided useful perspectives and suggestions. Daniel P. Franklin and two anonymous reviewers offered extremely perceptive, helpful comments on my University of Connecticut dissertation, which made it possible for me to revise it and prepare it for publication. Lylia C. Lorrin, Kathy McLaughlin, Jane Flanders, and Jane Todd of the University of Pittsburgh Press devoted their noteworthy talents to improving the manuscript. Any errors that remain in this work were resistant to the heroic efforts made by those individuals to alert me to them.

Although I had a long involvement in politics as a hobby, it was Robert S.

Gilmour, professor of political science at the University of Connecticut, who converted me from a political activist into a political scientist. I am indebted to him for believing that I had the potential to contribute to our discipline as a researcher and teacher. My beloved wife, Cynthia Landis Friedman, has also believed in me and has endured without complaint the hours and days I spent away from home to conduct and complete this research. I dedicate this volume to Bob and Cindy in recognition of their contribution to whatever merits may be contained in the following pages and to my career.

Regulation in the Reagan-Bush Era

Introduction

The Reagan era was less than a month old when, on February 17, 1981, the Executive Office of the President (EOP) announced the promulgation of Executive Order 12291, "Federal Regulation."[1] The order instructed executive regulatory agencies to submit proposed regulations to the Office of Information and Regulatory Affairs (OIRA) in the Office of Management and Budget (OMB), a component of the EOP. OIRA would then submit proposed regulations to a cost-benefit analysis to determine their fitness . Proposals that failed this economic test would presumably be repudiated by OIRA, leaving the executive regulatory agency with the Hobson's choice of either aborting its own proposal (in many cases the fruit of years of development) or promulgating it over EOP objections, thereby risking presidential reprisal. The potential for friction in this dilemma was reduced somewhat by the placement of Reagan loyalists in positions at the highest levels of the agencies.

The Reagan administration's intervention represented a substantial expansion of the regulatory reform program conducted by the administration of the preceding president, Jimmy Carter. Although the councils under Carter that specialized in regulatory review—notably, the Regulatory Analysis Review Group and the Regulatory Council—were committed to promoting regulatory analysis and efficiency, they were moving through relatively uncharted territory and were unprepared for the inevitable attempts by bureaucrats to evade or overcome the involvement of the president's agents. Knowing history and resolving not to repeat it, Ronald Reagan's aides designed a program that (1) required that a cost-benefit criterion be applied to proposed regulations, (2) mandated that proposed regulations be submitted to the powerful OMB for approval, (3) appointed Reagan loyalists to top positions in the agencies with the understanding that these officials would cooperate with the regulation review mechanism, and (4) created a presidential Task Force on Regulatory Relief to oversee the review of existing and contemplated regulations with the objective of relieving the business community of some of its mounting compliance costs. Unlike the Carter program, which lost momentum, the Reagan program secured a foothold in government-wide rule making. Indeed, as the president's second term was about to begin, he promulgated a second key order—Executive Order 12498, "Regulatory Planning Process."[2] The order required agencies to disclose the proposed regulations that were "planned or underway" and to evaluate how consistent the regulations were with the president's standards.

When EO 12291 was issued in 1981, agency staff members immediately recognized the threat to traditional regulatory autonomy. They and the advocates of regulation (especially of social regulation) objected to (1) the apparent bias of the EOP toward the predilections of business and against social regulatory programs, (2) the EOP's methods, which included delay of regulations, secrecy, and coercive pressure, and (3) the disruption of the guarantees of due process that had been developed pursuant to the Administrative Procedure Act of 1946. Members of Congress—the institution that had created the agencies and delegated rule-making authority to them—expressed alarm over unprecedented interference by the presidential establishment. They demanded certain but limited protections against the most egregious violations of the principle maintaining that every participant admitted into the regulatory arena should find a level playing field. While conceding to the president the constitutionally based privilege of directing the political decisions of his appointees, the judicial branch demonstrated its resolve to ensure that agencies delegate rule-making power in accordance with applicable laws, and that, in cases of conflict, these laws take precedence over the president's preferred policies.

This book evaluates the behavior—primarily reactive—of the executive agencies, Congress, the courts, and interest groups as they gained experience with Reagan's regulatory relief program. The sociological approach of exchange theory, discussed in detail in chapter 11, supplies the framework for the analysis, explaining the surprising degree of cooperation, compliance, and comity among entities that might have been expected to act with determination to overcome and defeat Reagan's advisers and to eliminate the centralized review process. The significance of this study is that it offers a portrait of how political institutions, confronted with an initiative for power from a competing institution, do not necessarily devote their resources to blocking the initiative. Rather, they may evaluate the possible legitimacy of the initiative; classify the concessions required by the ambitious institution's initiative into those that are acceptable, those that are negotiable, and those that are intolerable; and look for opportunities to exploit the new capacity of the competing institution. Exchange theory supports the contention that participants in the same associational system routinely make sacrifices if there is a reasonable expectation of a pattern of rewards; it is uncommon for these participants to reflexively reject other participants' solicitations of cooperation. Accordingly, the participants in the regulatory arena adapted to some of the ambitions of the EOP to establish a regulatory review process—accepting some aspects but setting limits on *all* aspects. For example, executive agencies established rather elaborate policy analysis structures and procedures, but successfully resisted OMB's decisions in cases where the core values and missions of the agencies were threatened. Members of Congress showed some interest in legitimating the review process through legislation, joined in the process by writing letters to OIRA asking for changes in proposed regulations on behalf of constituents, and repeatedly rejected movements to defund OIRA and terminate the process. But they also extracted procedural concessions from OIRA and shone a spotlight on some of OMB's most egregious violations of due process. The federal courts, which for years had shown a determination to play a key role in defining the rule-making process through decisions on administrative law, legitimated presidential involvement that reduced the judiciary's prominence. But the courts also refused to tolerate EOP procedures that ran afoul of the letter of laws delegating rule-making authority. Many interest group leaders conceded that the president was entitled to guide executive agencies in their rule-making function and that such management might be desirable, but they invested many resources in defeating EOP actions that deprived them of due process and of the opportunities to secure desired policies that had been guaranteed by the array of laws establishing social regulation.

This book shows, therefore, that the president's demand for influence in the regulatory process was accepted with a measure of respect, and that executive agencies proceeded to make accommodations. These accommodations included some limitation on the compliance costs to be imposed, a delay in promulgation of proposed regulations, the preparation of regulatory analyses, and negotiations with OMB. When the sacrifice reached a level where the agency could not possibly anticipate any commensurate reward, agency heads would engage in direct confrontation, risking OMB's wrath, or agency employees would resort to acts of sabotage and leaks to interest groups and news media. Such acts of resistance attracted support from the other entities that had a stake in the viability of the executive agencies and in the rule of law.

1 Regulation

The term "regulation" refers to government control over certain actions and decisions by business managers. Early regulation in Great Britain and the United States was designed primarily to control prices of and prescribe accessibility to privately operated essential services. The tenet of *justum pretium*—"just price"—was a facet of Roman law and a component of English common law. Sir Matthew Hale, Lord Chief Justice of England, wrote an essay on rates for wharf services in 1670, defending the necessity of public regulation of private industries that affect the public interest. He explained:

> If the King or subject have a public wharf unto which all persons that come to the port must come and unload their goods... because they are the only wharfs licensed by the King... or because there is no other wharf in that port... there cannot be taken arbitrary and excessive duties... but the duties must be reasonable and moderate.... For now the wharf and crane and other conveniences are affected with the public interest.[1]

Upon adoption of the federal Constitution, the United States Congress quickly entered the arena of regulatory activity. In 1789, the First Congress enacted laws to provide licensing and rate-making authority to port collectors.[2] More formal regulation was instituted in 1837, when the Steamboat Inspection Service was established in reaction to repeated incidents of steamboat explosions.[3]

State governments specialized in the regulation of public utilities, empowered by the United States Supreme Court's decision in the 1877 case *Munn v. Illinois*. Chief Justice Morrison R. Waite wrote:

> Property does become clothed with a public interest when used in a manner to make it of public consequence, and affect the community at large. When, therefore, one devotes his property to a use in which the public has an interest, he, in effect, grants to the public an interest in that use, and must submit to be controlled by the public for the common good, to the extent of the interest he has created. He may withdraw his grant by discontinuing the use; but, so long as he maintains the use, he must submit to the control.[4]

The national government's regulatory activity advanced to a higher level of formality when Congress enacted the Interstate Commerce Act in 1887. The law prescribed regulation of the railroads and created the Interstate Commerce Commission (ICC), originally a component of the Department of the Interior. The delegation of regulatory authority to the ICC established a precedent that Congress would imitate frequently in the twentieth century, creating agencies and commissions whose purpose would be to regulate many industries and corporate activities.[5] Another aspect of the Interstate Commerce Act that established a pattern was its appeal to numerous constituencies, including the regulated industry itself. As Wilson wrote, "the act... provided something for almost everybody: for railroaders, a ban on paying rebates to big shippers; for shippers, a ban on price discrimination against short-haul traffic."[6] Railroad officials anticipated that regulation might prove to be a valuable resource. By 1892, a railroad lawyer realized the opportunity, prophetically observing:

> The Commission, as its functions have now been limited by the courts, is, or can be made, of great use to the railroads. It satisfies the popular clamor for a government supervision of railroads, at the same time that that supervision is almost entirely nominal. Further, the older such a Commission gets to be, the more inclined it will be found to take the business and railroad view of things.[7]

The ICC was the first of the major economic regulation agencies, which would dominate the regulatory arena until the 1960s. After that time, social regulation agencies would come to share the spotlight.

ECONOMIC REGULATION

Public utility regulation established the pattern of economic regulation. Economic regulation was typically established to address problems relating to monopolistic control of a market (including, but not limited to, natural monopoly control characteristic of public utilities), excessive or discriminatory prices, destructive competition, quality control, employee or consumer safety, or nondisclosure of financial information. Meier identifies six categories of regulations that were commonly applied: (1) price regulation, (2) franchising and licensing, (3) standard setting, (4) direct allocation of resources, (5) operating subsidies, and (6) promotion of fair competition.[8] Economic regulation, then, may control prices, govern entry into or exit from a market, establish minimum levels of service quality, and require workplace safety. The ICC was established in 1887 chiefly for the first purpose—price regulation.

Typically, Congress would establish a regulatory commission to regulate a specific industry. Congress would delegate rule-making ("quasi-legislative") authority to the commission, and the commission presumably would develop "official expertise" in developing policy relating to the industry. The ICC was supposed to be expert in the area of railroad regulation. (Later, regulation of interstate trucking, interstate water carriers, interstate telephone [until 1934], and interstate oil pipelines [until 1977] was added to the ICC's purview.)

Another kind of economic regulation is antitrust regulation, which prohibits certain mergers, price fixing, and other activities that undermine and discourage competition. The rise of the colossal trusts and the demise of thousands of small firms attended the severe recessions of the 1870s and 1880s. Populist candidates for seats in Congress and state legislatures promised to restrain big business. The Sherman Act of 1890 prohibited arrangements and conspiracies that would restrain trade or commerce or that would establish a monopoly. Doubts about the efficacy of the Sherman Act motivated Congress to enact the Clayton Act and the Federal Trade Commission Act, both in 1914. The Clayton Act was more specific than the Sherman Act in identifying unacceptable business practices, and it was designed to abort the development of a monopoly by prohibiting mergers and acquisitions that would imperil competition. The Federal Trade Commission Act established the Federal Trade Commission (FTC) and empowered it to issue orders to cease and desist. The Antitrust Division of the Department of Justice exercises its authority to pursue antitrust litigation pursuant to the Sherman and Clayton Acts. The FTC's authority was established by the Clayton and Federal Trade Commission Acts.

The 1930s brought the creation of a number of agencies devoted to economic regulation, including the Federal Communications Commission (1934), Federal Power Commission (1935), Federal Maritime Commission (1936), and Civil Aeronautics Board (1938).

Much of the literature on economic regulation, especially from the 1950s to the 1970s, focused on the question, "Why does the government regulate?" The simplistic answers—for example, "to protect the public" or "to correct market failure"—became unsatisfying to increasingly critical and cynical political scientists and economists. In 1952, Samuel P. Huntington reported on the "capture" of regulatory agencies by their respective regulated industries. The plausible claim that the decisions of administrative agencies were "extremely likely to be[come] impregnated by the environing atmosphere"[9] undermined the legitimacy of the agencies. A 1964 study by George J. Stigler demonstrated that regulations of the Securities and Exchange Commission were ineffective in improving efficiency in securities markets.[10] In 1955, Marver H. Bernstein concluded that, although regulatory agencies are founded with legitimate public interests in view, each agency conducts day-to-day business with its particular industry, gets to know industry officials, and perhaps loses some of its staff to the industry or hires away some industry employees for its own work force.[11] With so much interaction, the regulators lose their taste for conflict with industry, Bernstein explains. At this point, the capture is complete.[12]

The United States Court of Appeals for the District of Columbia Circuit became a vocal critic of regulation that protected the regulated industries. In the 1970 case of *Moss v. Civil Aeronautics Board*,[13] the circuit court adjudicated a case concerning Civil Aeronautics Board (CAB) procedures for determining air fares. Judge J. Skelly Wright said that the operative issue was "whether the regulatory agency is unduly oriented toward the interest of the industry it is designed to regulate, rather than the public interest it is designed to protect." The CAB was horrified by Wright's conclusion that its processes fit that severe description. The decision in this case was typical of findings in the 1970s that economic regulation was serving the interests of some minority, an outcome inconsistent with the original objective.

SOCIAL REGULATION

The origin of social regulation can be traced to railway safety laws, the Pure Food and Drug Act of 1906 (amended in 1938 and 1962), and airline safety regulation dating back to the 1930s. Other social regulation programs prior to the 1960s were essentially the exclusive domain of state and local governments. David Vogel reports that, between 1900 and 1965, only one federal regulatory agency—the Food and Drug Administration, established in 1931—had as its primary responsibility the protection of consumers, employees, or the public from physical danger caused by corporate activity.[14]

Social movements in the 1960s became influential enough to secure congressional legislation for regulation in such areas as environmental protection, consumer protection, occupational safety, protection against discrimination, and promotion of health, welfare, and safety.[15] For example, in 1965 Ralph Nader published *Unsafe at Any Speed*,[16] which criticized design deficiencies in General Motors' rear-engined Corvair. Nader's increasing prominence gave him influence, which contributed to Congress's enactment of the Motor Vehicles Safety Act of 1966, the Wholesome Meat Act of 1967, the Natural Gas Pipeline Safety Act of 1968, the Coal Mine Health and Safety Act of 1969, and the Occupational Safety and Health Act of 1970.[17] Economic regulation had moved off stage, as Congress proceeded to catch up on long neglected issues of health, safety, and quality.

Advocates of social regulation offer several justifications. First, consumers often obtain inadequate or faulty information from producers, and rely on government compulsion to coerce producers to disclose essential information about safety concerns, nutritional value, product quality, and so forth. Second, innocent bystanders who are not a party to the vendor-customer transaction may be adversely affected by externalities, such as pollution generated in the manufacturing process or injuries sustained by third parties when dangerous products are used. Third, in a society characterized by consumerism, where quality of life is often defined by how much one can buy, it can be difficult for consumers to resist demand manipulation by firms. Government intervention may be needed to protect customers from being lured into transactions by rhapsodical advertising of products that are worthless or even harmful. Fourth, producers may be willing to endure the risk of being inadequately insured, leaving customers vulnerable to insufficient compensation for their losses if a product malfunctions or if malpractice occurs. Fifth, some advocates of social regulation propose as a matter of principle that the health and safety of consumers and employees should not be protected solely through the threat of civil lawsuits and damage awards—which makes health and safety a commodity to be bought and sold. Rather, health and safety should be safeguarded through compulsory preventative programs that reduce the risk from the outset.[18]

DIFFERENCES BETWEEN ECONOMIC AND SOCIAL REGULATION

The purposes of social regulation differ markedly from those of economic regulation, and so the results differ as well.

While every old-style agency for economic regulation governs a single industry and usually falls victim to the "capture" phenomenon, the new-style agencies of social regulation regulate a function in *all* industries, thus defying any "capture" attempt.[19] Observers agree that the Environmental Protection Agency (EPA), the Occupational Safety and Health Administration (OSHA), and the Consumer Product Safety Commission have not been and cannot be captured in a frontal assault by industry. On the contrary, as Allewelt explains, agencies can dominate a company's activities with regard to the function being regulated, and—in the absence of the more intimate relationship that arose between the old-style, economic regulation agencies and their regulated industries—the new-style agency has little sympathetic concern for the health of the firms it regulates.[20]

Accordingly, the "capture" theory is inapplicable to social regulation, and the generalized interpretation of regulation as a response to industry demands is misleading. Social regulation, says Meier, is "more likely to be forced on [the regulated industry] by a Congress that respond[s] to nonindustry groups."[21]

This leads to another difference between the two kinds of regulation: While economic regulation was often established with the approval and encouragement of the regulated industry, social regulation has rarely been created at the demand of industry and has usually been thrust upon industry following demands by public interest groups.[22]

Social regulation is not concerned with control of entry, prices, and quality of service; according to Edward Paul Fuchs, this explains the term "social regulation." "This prompted economists erroneously to label them as social regulations, or not essential to the conduct of the marketplace, even though they were directly related to the production of goods and services."[23]

Paul H. Weaver points out another distinction between economic and social regulation, which does not seem to be inherent in the concepts of these two forms. While the acts of Congress that established economic regulatory agencies were notorious for delegating extremely broad powers to the agencies without providing specific policy guidance "save to enjoin the regulators to act in the public interest," the acts establishing the newer agencies tend to be "extraordinarily lengthy and specific." Weaver takes note of the environmental protection statutes, which fill hundreds of pages in the United States Code. "The Clean Air Act is so specific that it spells out precise pollution-reduction targets and timetables and leaves the EPA virtually no discretion whatsoever."[24]

One limitation regarding this phenomenon ought to be noted: As Fuchs observes, the complex, technical nature of social regulation has occasionally restricted Congress's opportunity to define the issue, leaving regulators with *more* discretion on such occasions.[25]

Unlike economic regulation, which tends to concentrate on the relationship between the seller and the buyer, social regulation is apt to protect other parties, such as employees, third-party victims of malfunctions or accidents, or members of the general public who may be subjected, for example, to polluted air or water.[26]

While the focus of economic regulation on case-by-case resolution of a firm's application for rate increases or other changes in operations tends to generate adjudicatory proceedings, social regulation involves more generalized rule making applicable to the entire corporate sector.

> The rules governing these procedures are much less rigorous. The whole structure of the federal administrative process, under the legislation that has governed it for thirty years, depends to a great extent on the notion that many types of rule making (and especially those that affect a broad range of enterprises) follow the procedural model of legislation rather than that of litigation.[27]

Another difference involves the public's commitment to the two kinds of regulation. While the public has been indifferent to economic regulation, surveys have indicated public support for the objectives of social regulation. The public had little reaction to deregulation in economic regulation matters, but has been hostile to attempts to dismantle social regulation.[28]

The two kinds of regulation are also distinguished from each other by social regulation's focus on risk management. While economic regulation tends to be oriented toward the elimination of certain categories of managerial practices (e.g., restraint of trade, overcharging, and disseminating misleading or false information), social regulation tends to divide categories of managerial practices into those that are essentially free of risk, those associated with tolerable risk, and those fraught with excessive risk. Michael D. Reagan explains: "In an era characterized by acid rain, smog, ground water toxicity, and near meltdowns of nuclear power plants, any set of ideas that gets us beyond simple emotionalism in dealing with hazards to our persons would seem to have much to recommend it."[29]

Much legislation dealing with social regulation can be distinguished from economic regulation legislation by the source of authority that underlies its enactment. While Congress generally and principally justified laws establishing economic regulation by citing its own constitutional power to regulate interstate commerce (hence the ambiguous title "Interstate Commerce Commission" for the commission established to regulate the railroad industry), it has been just as likely to justify delegations of power to promulgate social regulations by citing the legislature's constitutional power to promote the general welfare and its power of the purse.

Finally, old-style, economic regulation has usually been carried out by independent regulatory commissions (IRCs). The new-style, social regulation is carried out within the executive branch.

INDEPENDENT REGULATORY COMMISSIONS AND EXECUTIVE AGENCIES

The entities of the national government that implement most regulatory policies can be classified into three categories: IRCs, freestanding agencies of the executive branch, and regulatory agencies contained within cabinet-level departments.

The ICC was established in 1887 as a component of the Department of the Interior. Two years later, the ICC was lifted out of the department, becoming the first IRC. The change in status is attributed to the efforts of Senator John H. Reagan (D-Tex.), author of the Interstate Commerce Act, who feared undue influence from newly elected President Benjamin Harrison, a former railroad lawyer.[30] Congress seemed greatly pleased by its invention, because for years afterward it relied on the IRC form when additional industries were targeted for regulation. Because this period coincided with the dominance of economic (as opposed to social) regulation, economic regulation and the IRC form became inextricably linked.

Frustrated by holdover Republican members of the IRCs (as well as of the Supreme Court), President Franklin D. Roosevelt notified a Republican member of the Federal Trade Commission, former Rep. William E. Humphrey (R-Wash.), that his services were no longer desired. Commissioner Humphrey sued to keep his job. The case was decided in Humphrey's favor after his death, in the 1934 Supreme Court decision of *Rathbun ("Humphrey's Executor") v. United States*.[31] The court reasoned that commission members who adjudicate cases, and who thus wield quasi-judicial power, should be free from fear of the reprisal of removal if their decisions displease the president.

Thus, it was established that the commissions were to be relatively free from the most potent presidential influence of all—removal. Meanwhile, Congress indicated a determination to maintain exclusive custody of the IRCs. For example, in 1910, a debate on ICC amendments contained numerous references to the commission as an "arm of Congress" and even as a "committee of Congress." Over the years, members of Congress have asserted repeatedly that the legislative powers of the IRCs inevitably make them extensions of Congress, not of the presidency.[32] At the same time, the regulated industries learned that their day-to-day interactions with the commissions could result in advantages to the industries. Indeed, much regulation was established at the demand of the regulated industry. For example, the railroads were hopeful that the newly created ICC might avoid future price wars.[33] The relationship often resulted in the "clientele capture" described earlier in this chapter.

The other regulatory forms, which involve locating regulation within the executive branch, similarly arose out of congressional authority. "Agencies are creatures of Congress," the Supreme Court declared in 1961. "... The determinative question is not what an agency thinks it should do but what Congress has said it *can* do."[34] In this regard, there is an element of congressional control that resembles the control over IRCs. But the president appoints his own agency heads for the executive branch agencies, and these administrators are more likely to be sensitive to the president's policy preferences. Eads and Fix speculate that the president's higher profile in these agencies creates the impression that the president can "do something" to manage their operations and thus shape regulatory policy.[35] But the major factor usually cited in Congress's shift toward executive branch agencies beginning in the 1960s is the disrepute into which the IRC form slipped when the "capture" phenomenon was identified in the literature of regulation. The executive branch agencies that carry out social regulation have been less vulnerable to clientele capture than have the IRCs that carry out economic regulation. Nevertheless, the organizational location of these agencies and commissions is not the most likely explanation, as noted earlier. The fact that each social regulation agency regulates a function of *all* industries makes it difficult to capture; in contrast, the assignment of one economic regulatory commission to a single corresponding industry facilitated capture. Therefore, the preference that emerged in Congress for executive branch agencies did, indeed, coincide with the alleviation of the capture effect, but the two developments were for the most part merely coincidental.

There are two varieties of executive branch agencies: the freestanding agency that reports directly to the president, and the agency that is located within a cabinet-level department. EPA is of the first variety; its administrator reports only to the president. Examples of the second variety are OSHA, a component of the Department of Labor; the Office of Surface Mining, a component of the Department of the Interior; and the National Highway Traffic Safety Administration, part of the Department of Transportation.

THE RISE OF THE DEREGULATION MOVEMENT

The 1974–75 recession motivated business leaders to seek out the root cause of the setback to the economy. They concluded that social regulation programs instituted in the late 1960s and early 1970s in the areas of consumer protection, environmental protection, and workplace safety constituted the best explanation for the recession and for the declining fortunes of United States businesses in international markets. A study by the Committee for Economic Development concluded that, in 1974–75, indirect costs of environmental, worker safety, and health regulations reduced the annual change in efficiency (output per unit of input) by 0.5 percent. "This is equivalent to about one-fifth of the nation's average annual rate of growth since the end of World War II," the study complained.[36] The business leaders' vocal criticism of regulation as a drag on the economy effectively countered the calls from regulatory advocates for more regulation, which had been made in the mid- and late 1970s. According to this argument, regulators were imposing compliance costs on business enterprises, but were not ensuring that a commensurate level of benefits was accruing to society. Politically and otherwise, no regulator had any incentive to contain compliance costs.

Bolstering the claims of business representatives were studies estimating the total compliance costs necessitated by federal regulation. The most famous study was conducted by Robert DeFina and Murray L. Weidenbaum at the Center for the Study of American Business at Washington University (St. Louis), in 1979. The study estimated and projected these costs, in billions of dollars, by fiscal year.[37] (See table 1.1.)

Purchasing magazine conducted a similar study, and concluded that 1979 costs would amount to $134.8 billion. Thus, the estimated annual cost was about $500 per capita.[38]

(More recent studies include a 1992 study by Thomas Hopkins of the Rochester Institute of Technology, who estimated that the annual compliance costs would amount to $564 billion, including costs associated with economic and social regulation. Of that amount, $164 billion was attributed to environmental, work safety, and health regulations (excluding such regulation as FDA rules). Robert Litan pronounced Hopkins's estimates "in the ballpark.")[39]

Just as private business felt overburdened by the growth in federal regulation, so too did state and local governments, which nearly buckled under the weight of a stack of regulations concerning accessibility to public buildings and transportation systems by handicapped individuals, availability of unem-

Table 1.1
Cost of Federal Regulation (in billions of dollars)

	Administrative Costs	Compliance Costs	Total Cost
1977	$4.1	$ 82.0	$ 86.1
1978	4.9	98.0	102.9
1979	5.8	116.0	121.8
1980	6.0	120.0	126.0

ployment compensation to public employees, wastewater treatment, environmental impact, and clean water standards. New York's Mayor Edward I. Koch complained that federal regulations "threaten both the initiative and financial health of local governments throughout the country."[40] Conditional grants-in-aid have offered state and local governments the choice of implementing federal regulations or losing subsidies for various projects in the respective policy area. While some "partial preemption" laws mandate that state governments implement certain federal regulatory programs (see, e.g., the Clean Air Amendments of 1970), "softer" partial preemptions have offered the state governments the choice of implementing their own regulatory activities (provided state standards match or exceed the federal standards in stringency), or of being bypassed by federal regulation, which is then imposed directly on industries within the state. (Under the Constitution's supremacy clause, no third option is available to state governments.) The "softer" preemptions have been common in the case of occupational safety regulations. Through conditions and partial preemptions, a trend developed whereby state and local governments took on the appearance of administrative districts of the national government.[41]

Vogel observes that the election of a Democratic president in 1976 was followed, ironically, by the 1977 defeat of the two most important legislative goals of the labor union and consumer movements—labor law reform and the creation of a Consumer Protection Agency. Vogel sees Ronald Reagan's 1980 victory as the culmination of the decline of the leftist liberal politics of the 1960s and 1970s.[42]

The period of the mid- to late 1970s provided the backdrop for unexpected deregulatory initiatives. Weidenbaum describes some of them:

> In January 1974 the federal government terminated the interest equalization tax on American holdings of foreign stocks and bonds, as well as the

> five-year-old program of controls over direct investments abroad by United States corporations. Simultaneously, the Federal Reserve System ended its guidelines limiting lending and investments overseas by United States banks and other financial institutions. Under the Airline Deregulation Act of 1978 entry and price regulation of domestic airlines [was] ... phased out by 1982 and 1983, respectively.[43]

The decade of the 1970s introduced systematic presidential involvement in the regulatory process. President Richard M. Nixon's administration developed the "quality of life" review process, which—insofar as its primary objective was to control EPA regulations—established a pattern for subsequent Republican administrations. President Gerald R. Ford established the "Inflation Impact Statement" program, requiring assessments of the effects of major regulations on inflation. As economists published compelling studies indicating that regulation was counterproductive and generally a drag on the economy, President Jimmy Carter established the Regulatory Analysis Review Group and the Regulatory Council, which conducted a collegial process of regulatory analysis and review. Recalcitrants could ignore this process with few or no consequences. Also, social regulation agencies dramatically accelerated the pace of rule-making activity. These precedents were well known to the Reagan transition team, which prepared to roll out a systematic regulatory review program coordinated by the powerful OMB. Agencies could not safely evade this process, which guaranteed that Reagan's imprint would appear on the government's regulatory policies.[44]

Weaver uses the example of the deregulation movement to dispute the prevailing view among political scientists that the public is indifferent to the activities of government agencies, and that only a subgovernment—consisting of the "iron triangle"[45] of the relevant executive agency, the corresponding congressional committees and subcommittees, and related interest groups—is concerned about and dominates any given government policy. According to that popular view, the movement for deregulation "simply shouldn't exist." And yet, the movement does exist, and has won support from the Council of Economic Advisers, the Antitrust Division of the Department of Justice, elements of OMB, other agencies, Presidents Ford and Carter (and we may now add Reagan, George Bush, and Bill Clinton), and progressive Democratic and conservative Republican members of Congress. Nearly all of the deregulators, Weaver argues, should have opposed deregulation if the subgovernment ("iron triangle") model were accurate. He concludes: "The truth is that the 'iron triangle,' where it exists, was and is a political coalition like any other—sometimes successful, at other times not, and always dependent over the long run on the good opinion of the people."[46]

Another "truth" of public administration and organization theory is that every institution devotes itself to its survival, to the exclusion of other objectives if necessary. However, Alana Northrop notes that civil servants have been observed dismantling their jobs and agencies in the service of political officials. "Civil servants do in fact help to end their own programs and even do so willingly." She continues:

> Serving your boss is a professional value held by many civil servants. So when policy directives change, the career bureaucrat continues to do his or her job even though it may have a new content or direction. This aspect of administrative professionalism may help explain why bureaucrats work dedicatedly to end or alter their own agencies' programs.[47]

Martha Derthick and Paul J. Quirk consider other social science models similarly imperiled by the evidence of deregulation, claiming that deregulation contradicts the likely conclusions of organization theory and role theory. They cite cases of regulatory commission chairmen who overcame their own vested interests by advocating radical adjustments in the scope of authority of their agencies.[48]

These ironies and theoretical inconsistencies that have surfaced in recent deregulatory efforts can probably be accounted for by the public policy explanation of Benjamin I. Page and Robert Y. Shapiro. They found that public opinion is most likely to influence public policy in those cases where collective public opinion sustains a dramatic, durable change.[49] Because, during the post-recession period, the public was sold on the notion that regulation was a contributing factor to the slowdown; because presidential candidate Reagan was able to uncover a number of so-called nonsense regulations (to be discussed in chapter 5) and to package them rhetorically in a manner that effectively held them up to ridicule; and because public mistrust of the bureaucracy has deepened in the past twenty-five years,[50] public consensus lasted long enough for the deregulatory movement to make inroads. But the Reagan administration's assault on environmental, consumer protection, and workplace safety regulation created discomfort among the public, provoked dissension in the agencies, and may have resulted in the defeat of new regulations. Organization theory, role theory, and the theory of the "iron triangle" have not been disproved as useful models, but have, perhaps, been stripped of their appearance as immutable laws. In any case, few social science theories can escape this fate in the long run.

2 The Regulatory Oversight Role of the Presidency and Vice Presidency

PRESIDENTIAL CONTROL OF REGULATION

Until the 1980s, the role of the presidency in federal regulation was limited. In 1971, Roger G. Noll wrote, "Although the President could exercise authority over regulatory agencies, there is little evidence that he or his administration makes much of an attempt to do so."[1] As Morton Rosenberg observes, the Administrative Procedure Act of 1946 reserves no place for presidential involvement.[2] Other sources note that the ICC was given independent status in 1889 for the express purpose of putting railroad regulation policy out of the reach of Republican President Benjamin Harrison.[3] The recent trend toward presidential control, which will be traced later in this chapter, would suggest that only recently has there arisen a demand for such control by a sufficiently influential number of participants in the public policy-making process. Pfiffner has attributed this demand partly to the decline of political parties in recent decades.[4] In this section, I propose to review political science literature to identify perspectives on three questions that constitute a logical progression. They are: (1) Is there a need for involvement by the president in the regulatory process? (2) If there is a need, then is the president in an opportune position to exert suitable control over the regulatory process? (3) If he is in an opportune position, then does the president possess legitimate authority to exert this type of power?

Need for Presidential Control

Calls for centralized control of federal regulatory policy predate the 1970s, and, in fact, are prominent in some of the landmark documents in the literature of public administration.

The celebrated Brownlow Committee, commissioned by President Franklin D. Roosevelt, denounced the independence of the independent regulatory commissions (IRCs) as bringing about a "headless 'fourth branch' of the Government, a haphazard deposit of irresponsible agencies and uncoordinated powers." The committee considered "confusion, conflict, and incoherence" to be the result of uncoordinated regulatory policy.[5] The Hoover Commission reports of 1949 and 1955 criticized the quality of regulatory commission personnel and the rule-making process itself. The Landis report, prepared for the incoming Kennedy administration, expressed concern about the impact of uncoordinated economic policy on the economy. President Richard M. Nixon's Ash Council on Government Reorganization echoed the Brownlow Committee in finding disharmony between the policies of the IRCs and national policy goals.[6]

The IRCs were an inviting target for criticism by blue-ribbon panels, apparently because of the peculiarity of their organizational placement outside the executive branch. But as we study the IRCs and the executive branch regulatory agencies, many distinctions in rule-making process, policy objective, and policy impact become blurred. By the late 1970s, many critics of the regulatory process were focusing their attention on *all* regulatory agencies, irrespective of organizational location. The calls for reining in the regulatory agencies and commissions shared the premise that these institutions were producing results that were inefficient or that contradicted the public interest. Regulatory agencies and commissions were accused, first, of producing policies and compliance requirements that duplicated or contradicted those of other agencies and commissions; second, of creating high compliance costs, which harmed individual businesses and the economy in general; third, of perceiving regulation and compliance as ends in themselves to the exclusion of other values; and fourth, of tending to devote resources to advancing their own institutional interests at the expense of the public interest.[7]

The evidence suggests that regulatory commissions and agencies cannot necessarily be relied upon to act in the public interest. While it is not my intention to condemn the regulatory process, I offer the foregoing observations to indicate the possibility that some correction may be necessary on certain occasions in the face of irrational regulatory policy, whatever the cause.

Opportunity for Presidential Control

Advocates of presidential control of federal regulatory rule making cite a number of characteristics that, they claim, make the president particularly (even uniquely) suited to exert such control. First, the president is considered the *manager of the bureaucracy*. Both Harold Seidman and Richard Nathan identify the president as the only holder of "institutional authority" and "programmatic incentives" that would permit coordination of bureaucratic activities.[8] "Without presidential managerial leadership," Dwight A. Ink warns, "The huge and unwieldy Executive Branch will not be managed."[9] While Ink calls for the strengthening of the "M" (management) side of the Office of Management and Budget (OMB), Ronald C. Moe observes sadly that recent presidents have pursued no comprehensive organization strategy and have supervised the continuing decline of the "M" side of OMB.[10]

Second, the president is *leader of a national constituency*. West and Cooper see the national constituency as providing the president with "the motivation to act as a counter to the parochial tendencies of agencies."[11]

Third, the president is a *source of balance*. James L. Sundquist has cited the necessity of having a government official who will weigh costs and benefits to individuals when the regulatory process operates. He concludes that the president is the appropriate holder of power to reconcile conflicting regulations and to allocate resources. Sundquist asserts that this applies to coordination of regulations.[12]

Fourth, the president is *holder of the appointment power*. Use of the appointment power to place ideological partners of the president at top levels of regulatory agencies is part and parcel of the trend toward institutionalizing presidential efforts to place capable and ideologically compatible executives in all agencies.[13] This presidential appointment power applies forcefully to the IRCs, insofar as the president can dictate the designation and removal of commission chairmen.[14]

Fifth, the president is an effective *persuader*. As the politician who has most recently commanded a majority of the nation's votes, the president possesses a unique level of persuasiveness. Meier describes how President Jimmy Carter influenced consumer protection agencies to adopt his approach to consumer matters and how President Ronald Reagan's criticism of OSHA led to a cutback in its enforcement activities. "No federal regulatory agency, not even the Board of Governors of the Federal Reserve, can resist the pressures of a president who devote[s] full time and all presidential resources to that pressure."[15]

Sixth, the president has a *natural adversarial role relative to the bureaucracy.* Many authors have taken note of the natural animosity that arises between the White House and the bureaucracy, and a number of them draw the conclusion that the president—locked in this adversarial role—might as well use the occasion to control regulatory agencies.

Paul R. Verkuil attributes conflict between the president and the bureaucracy, at least in recent decades, to inevitably differing perspectives on the need to stabilize the economy. In 1980, he claimed that inflation had compelled recent presidents to make attempts to achieve reductions in compliance costs. Thus, White House advisers, concerned with economy, struggled routinely with agency officials committed to health, safety, and environmental rules that were contributing to inflation.[16]

Seventh, the president is an *established holder of centralized control.* The literature calls attention to the indisputable fact that the president and certain entities in his cabinet and the Executive Office of the President (EOP) already exercise a panoply of mechanisms of centralized control, so that regulatory control is merely one more entry in the repertoire of a well-established apparatus. Significantly, many of these mechanisms apply as much to IRCs as to executive agencies; this indicates that "independence" need not always indicate freedom from all restraint. The mechanisms include central coordination of litigation at the Department of Justice (this applies to agencies and commissions alike, in most cases);[17] central coordination of the executive budget in OMB;[18] central coordination of paperwork requirements in OMB's Office of Information and Regulatory Affairs (OIRA), pursuant to the Paperwork Reduction Act; and central clearance of legislative proposals in OMB before they are transmitted to any member of Congress (this applies to agencies and commissions alike).[19]

This enumeration of preexisting presidential powers suggests that the president does have the opportunity to control the federal regulatory system. The president's management tools and restructuring capacity (through executive orders and reorganization plans) place him in a unique position to coordinate, direct, and balance federal bureaucratic policy. It would be suboptimal to forgo the use of the president's coordinating capacity when the sprawling regulatory establishment has a clear need for coordination.[20] Lloyd N. Cutler and David R. Johnson wrote in 1975:

> If what we need is more flexible, coordinated and politically acceptable regulatory policymaking, it can be argued that the President should be given much more extensive power and responsibility to intervene in the regu-

> latory process—whether he wants it or not. Even the critics of expanded presidential power would probably admit that the President is capable of acting more quickly than can the Congress in formulating and articulating national policy goals. In addition, the President and his immediate staff have an overview of government management—and a constitutional responsibility for executing all the laws—that is not shared by a single regulatory agency, by any specialized congressional committee or by the Congress as a whole. The President is the only nationally elected officer, and thus, at least arguably, our most politically accountable official. He is uniquely situated to intervene (at least in a limited number of instances) in order to expedite, coordinate, and, if necessary, reverse agency decisions.[21]

Legitimate Authority for Presidential Control

We now arrive at the third question, relating to the president's possession of legitimate constitutional and statutory power to exercise central control. Scholars, politicians, and interest group leaders disagree, vehemently in many cases, over whether the president has any such role. Michael E. Kraft and Norman J. Vig were troubled by Reagan's approach: "Reagan's regulatory review process . . . fares poorly in the criteria of both legitimacy and technical rationality. It has no statutory foundation. . . . [It] violates all norms of openness, fairness, and accountability to the public. . . . [It] is [not] grounded in credible cost-benefit analysis."[22] As noted earlier, Rosenberg has insisted that the Administrative Procedure Act is written in a manner that clearly excludes the president from involvement in rule making.[23]

On the other hand, James R. Bowers offers a "shared powers" interpretation that suggests that the president's veto power, established in Article I of the Constitution, provides conclusive evidence that the president is vested with an indeterminate amount of legislative power, which arguably justifies his supervision of regulatory rule making.[24] Harold Seidman also argues for a presidential role, countering Rosenberg's interpretation of the APA.

> The Administrative Procedure Act is silent on the issue of presidential intervention in informal rulemaking. To the extent that the OMB review process makes available to the rulemakers the comments of the affected agencies and the White House, the OMB review process is consistent with and supports the letter and spirit of the Administrative Procedure Act. The availability of such information does not in and of itself limit the discretion of responsible decision makers in reaching informed judgments.[25]

B. Dan Wood and Richard W. Waterman recognize the president's opportunity to control regulation, but they worry whether it is fair for him to take advantage of the opportunity.

> If one democratic principal—say, the president—is more effective than others, we might ask whether it is appropriate for policy implementation to reflect executive preferences over those of the Congress or the courts[.] Some would argue—though certainly not without opposition—that the Congress reflects the public will better than the president because of decentralized constituencies, and more frequent elections.[26]

Nevertheless, Kraft and Vig recognize that the argument about whether the president may be involved in regulatory oversight is academic: "The issue . . . is not whether a president may intervene in regulatory decisionmaking, but how, and for what purpose."[27]

The question of whether the president possesses legal authority to control regulatory activity persists only because of Congress's silence in the matter. It is difficult to conceive of any statute that Congress could enact to legitimate presidential intervention that would not be deemed equally conclusive by the judicial branch. In the failure (or, some might say, the prudent hesitation) of Congress to take a firm stand, the issue remains in the "zone of twilight" that Justice Robert H. Jackson described in a concurring opinion in the 1952 case of *Youngstown Sheet and Tube Co. v. Sawyer*.[28]

Because Congress has rarely enacted legislation establishing presidential oversight of the regulatory process, recent presidents have relied on the executive order to activate regulatory reform. Joel L. Fleishman and Arthur H. Aufses observe, "executive orders have become the most important means of presidential legislation."[29] An understanding of the president's power to make "ordinances"—i.e., orders having the force of law—is impeded by the ambiguous language of Article 2, §1, cl. 1, of the Constitution, which vests the "executive Power" in him while providing few clues concerning the nature of that power. "The question which has arisen is whether the term 'Executive Power' refers merely to the specifically enumerated powers in article 2, or whether it is an affirmative delegation of some all-pervasive independent power."[30] This ambiguity has left the interpretation of the constitutional concept of executive power to each president (as well as to the other two branches that monitor his use of that power). It appears to many observers that presidents have used executive orders to create laws in circumstances where Congress clearly would not have enacted legislation for the purposes desired by the presidents. Phillip J. Cooper observes, "President Johnson's

Executive Order 11,246 [which in 1965 established affirmative action requirements for government contractors] marked the rise of the contemporary use of executive mandates as... tools to get around a recalcitrant Congress."[31]

A statute that specifically grants authority to the president is a reliable source of authority for an executive order (assuming that the statute itself is constitutional). An executive order is a viable instrument that the president may use to fulfill his obligation to enforce the statute. It has the same validity as the act from which it derives its authority.[32] In the 1952 case of *Youngstown Sheet and Tube Co. v. Sawyer*,[33] the Supreme Court determined that the Constitution limits the president's involvement in lawmaking to the "recommending of laws he thinks wise and the vetoing of laws he thinks bad." In a District Court case relating specifically to delegated lawmaking authority, Judge Harold Leventhal maintained that the Constitution does not prohibit delegations of legislative power by Congress to the president.[34] The resulting executive orders are indistinguishable from law, except that the civics textbook formula of "how a bill becomes a law" does not happen to govern their transformation into binding rules of authority.

The Constitution grants the executive power to the president and confers on him the duties of commander in chief. These grants of power are vague, and the framers of the Constitution assigned their descendants and successors the task of resolving the ambiguity. The clause concerning the duties of commander in chief provides relatively clear authority for the president to regulate the affairs of the military in time of declared war,[35] but attempts by various presidents to extend their ordinance-making ability to the civilian population during wartime have met with mixed success. President Abraham Lincoln suspended habeas corpus during the Civil War, established military courts, and exercised other extraordinary powers, many of which were subsequently approved by the Supreme Court.[36] The vague grant of executive power has left a "zone of twilight" in some circumstances and there remains some doubt about whether Congress or the president has jurisdiction.[37] If Congress remains silent or inactive in cases of concurrent authority, a president will be tempted to occupy the field by using executive orders.[38] These orders might be perfectly legitimate and defensible in court. Congress can prevent or stop the president's involvement in areas of concurrent authority simply by taking the initiative and occupying the field. This will normally crowd the president out of the picture.[39] Reviewing executive orders issued outside of statutory authority, Justice Hugo L. Black commented acidly that such orders "look more like legislation to me than properly authorized regulations to carry out a clear and explicit command of Congress." He added that "the Constitution does not confer lawmaking power on the President."[40]

While presidents have experienced frustration in seeking to have their desired legislation enacted, their executive orders, intended to have roughly the same effect, have survived largely unscathed, with neither the Supreme Court nor Congress exhibiting much desire to void them. "The growing power of the Presidency in domestic matters makes the Executive order potentially one of the most significant sources of public law," wrote Ruth P. Morgan.[41] It may be appropriate to reverse the statement and say that the use of executive orders has contributed to the growing power of the presidency.

The use of executive orders is becoming increasingly significant as presidents find executive orders effective for purposes never before envisioned. Once a president has occupied a given field, he and his successors will tend to attempt to continue to govern that field with additional executive orders until some event interferes. This so-called decree inertia has been observed in such fields as civil rights, loyalty and security matters, oil imports, and regulatory reform.[42] Even though presidents since Franklin D. Roosevelt have issued fewer orders than was once considered common, the scope of these orders has been broadened and their impact has increased.[43] Civil rights and security are two areas where, by using orders less frequently but making each one more influential than its predecessors, presidents have increased the importance of executive orders as tools of federal administration.

The president's use of executive authority to institute and expand his control of regulation relies on ambiguous legal authority and has been tolerated, thus far, by an ambivalent Congress. The best explanation for the continued use of this practice is the initiative of a determined presidential staff and the failure of detractors to mount a sufficiently effective opposition that would lead to the termination of the practice.

A HISTORY OF PRESIDENTIAL INVOLVEMENT

"For as long as the federal government has been engaged in regulation," write Eads and Fix, "presidents and their aides have occasionally taken an interest in the outcome of regulatory proceedings."[44] They note that economic and political rights may be enhanced or abridged through regulation, and that "politically well connected people" have interests that may be promoted or imperiled in regulatory proceedings. Thus, they reason, "sporadic White House attention is all but inevitable."[45]

In 1971, the Nixon administration became the first ever to institutionalize regular, systematic regulatory oversight. In this case, the target was the new Environmental Protection Agency (EPA), established in 1970 and headed by William Ruckelshaus.[46] The business sector and Secretary of Commerce

Maurice Stans expressed alarm at the rapid flow of ambitious regulations being promulgated at the EPA. OMB officials grew concerned about the supplementary budget requests from EPA and about EPA water quality regulations that compelled expansion of federal grants for sewage and water treatment plants.[47] On May 21, 1971, OMB director George P. Shultz wrote a letter to Ruckelshaus asserting his authority to review and clear proposed regulations of several executive branch agencies.[48] In June 1971, John D. Ehrlichman, assistant to the president, created the Quality of Life Committee. The committee included members of the Domestic Council, among them, Russell Train, chairman of the Council on Environmental Quality, Ruckelshaus, and other White House staff members. Its mission was to design a high-level council to review proposed regulations that could disrupt the balance between "consumer and environmental interests, industrial requirements, and safety aspects."[49]

According to a memorandum from Shultz activating a presidential executive order of October 1971, the Quality of Life Review process was purportedly designed to apply to several agencies, but in fact only EPA's rules were reviewed. Budget examiners of other agencies, knowing that EPA was the target, did nothing to comply. The Food and Drug Administration's budget examiner recalled that he "simply ignored" Shultz's directive.[50]

The review process remained in operation until acting EPA administrator Charles Elkins notified OMB in January 1977 that his agency would curtail its participation. But EPA's structure and procedures had been affected in an enduring manner by its development of a regulation analysis staff and by its habit of consulting with industry and other agencies earlier in the regulation design process.[51]

After assuming the presidency from Nixon on August 9, 1974, President Gerald R. Ford recognized inflation as the major problem of domestic policy. The White House arranged a series of economic "summit" meetings, attended by prominent Americans, for the purpose of formulating possible solutions. There was a consensus among the economists who participated in these meetings that regulatory policy was a culprit. Hendrik Houthakker, former member of the Council of Economic Advisers (CEA), prepared a list of "sacred cow" regulatory policies, such as the prohibition of privately operated first-class mail services and minimum wage laws, which were exacerbating inflation.[52]

On November 27, 1974, President Ford issued Executive Order 11821, "Inflation Impact Statements,"[53] initiating the Inflation Impact Statement (IIS) program. The order required every executive agency proposing major legislation or a regulatory policy to prepare an evaluation of its inflationary impact. OMB was designated as the implementing authority to develop standards and criteria and to either review the evaluation statements or delegate the review to other administration officials. This delegation often involved the Council on Wage and Price Stability (CWPS), created by an act of Congress in 1974, which proved to have an important role in the IIS program. "Virtually all regulatory agencies came under the purview of [the council], where a small group of economists reviewed newly proposed regulations and supporting documents."[54]

Comments submitted for the public record by CWPS became a welcome symbol, signifying that the administration was "doing something" to combat inflation. In response to questions about the legality of CWPS's involvement in rule-making proceedings, Congress enacted a law authorizing the council to "intervene and otherwise to participate on its own behalf in rulemaking, ratemaking, licensing, and other proceedings before any of the departments and agencies of the United States, in order to present its views as to the inflationary impact that might result from the possible outcomes of such proceedings."[55] CWPS assistant director James C. Miller III observed that the quality of IISs varied from agency to agency, with some agencies providing detailed, sophisticated statements, and others providing inadequate, poorly developed statements. Estimates of costs tended to receive more thorough analysis than did the assessments of benefits. Alternatives to the selected regulatory policy were rarely enumerated.[56]

On December 31, 1976, the lame-duck president issued EO 11949, extending and renaming the IIS program, thus creating the Economic Impact Statement (EIS) program, in the hope that regulatory review would be perpetuated in future administrations.

President Carter pursued regulatory reform more vigorously than his predecessors did because he was committed to bureaucratic reform generally and because he agreed with prevailing opinion that overregulation was damaging the economy.[57]

Carter turned to a collegial mediative procedures for evaluating proposed regulations for redundancy, waste, and other forms of inefficiency.[58] In early 1977, the Economic Policy Group (EPG) directed CEA chairman Charles Schultze to develop a new regulatory review process. Late that year, based on recommendations from Schultze and other officials, the president authorized creation of the Regulatory Analysis Review Group (RARG), chaired by the CEA chairman and comprising representatives of OMB, the Office of Science and Technology Policy, the Department of Health, Education, and Welfare, and the Departments of Agriculture, Commerce, Energy, Housing and Urban Development, Interior, Justice, Labor, Transportation, and Treasury, as well as the EPA. RARG activity was limited to reviews of between ten and twenty regulations per year (and no more than four from any one agency), with reviews prepared by the staffs of the CEA and CWPS. These reviews were filed in the respective agency's rule-making records during the sixty-day public comment period.[59]

The RARG procedure, though it contributed very substantially to the evolution of a presidential role in the federal regulatory process, is remembered as a relatively ineffective instrument of regulatory reform in and of itself. RARG was hamstrung by the constraint on the number of regulations it could review in any given year. Because RARG needed to comment before the public comment period expired in sixty to ninety days, its analyses tended to be rushed and incomplete. RARG decisions were not legally binding on agencies, although provisions of the Administrative Procedure Act necessitated *some* kind of response to RARG's criticisms by agencies. Carter's economic advisers hoped that intervention by high-level administration officials would induce agency heads to withdraw or modify proposed regulations that "got RARGed," but observers such as Christopher C. DeMuth saw participants in the RARG review process as "kibitzers" trying to extract concessions out of each other across a bargaining table.

On March 23, 1978, Carter issued Executive Order 12044, "Improving Government Regulations."[60] Regulations involving costs of at least $100 million were classified as "major," necessitating an economic analysis. A summary of the analysis would be printed in the *Federal Register*, inviting public comment. Fuchs describes the results.

> The president gave OMB the task of implementing the executive order. The order, however, neither clearly defined nor enunciated OMB's authority or its specific responsibilities. The reason was simple: The constitutional basis of presidential authority was unclear. The president, in effect, did not know the precise boundaries of his purview in regulatory matters. The Justice Department had issued a statement earlier, claiming that the [cost-benefit analysis] program might be legally binding on all regulatory agencies. The department based its argument on the rightful duty of the president to enforce the laws, or to see to it that all agencies performed their functions "efficiently and without undue delay." It was concluded that the president, in exercising his rightful duty, may "require agencies to weigh the economic impact of their decisions." Congress clearly would have none of this. It was

> politically expedient, then, to forego offering definitive statements about executive office evaluation staff authority.[61]

In October 1978, President Carter created a new group called the Regulatory Council. The council included representatives of many of the executive agencies represented in RARG, and also representatives from most of the independent regulatory commissions. EPA administrator Douglas Costle chaired the council. The Regulatory Council was given the task of coordinating the regulatory activities of agencies with overlapping responsibilities. It was also ordered to prepare "calendars" of major regulatory proposals developed in federal agencies. The council conducted studies describing how regulations impacted certain industries, such as steel and automobiles. No representative of the EOP sat on this council, "a guarantee," according to Litan and Nordhaus, "that nothing truly important would be entrusted to the Council for resolution."[62]

The most enduring instrument of regulatory reform crafted during Carter's presidency was the Paperwork Reduction Act of 1980. The act transformed OMB's Office of Regulatory and Information Policy into the Office of Information and Regulatory Affairs (OIRA) and charged it with administering the paperwork reduction program. The OIRA would rise in significance early in the term of President Reagan.

TRANSITION TO REAGAN

Ronald Reagan became president in an atmosphere already characterized by pressure for regulatory reform. Laws for economic deregulation in several industries, such as airlines, railroads, and trucking, had already won passage in the 1970s. Eads and Fix offer a list of three "important intellectual and political developments" that paved the way for Reagan's regulatory review program: (1) recognition of regulation's effect on the performance of the American economy; (2) evolution of presidential involvement in regulation; and (3) legislative sympathy toward the concept of deregulation.[63] Peter M. Benda and Charles H. Levine identify three legacies Reagan received from Carter:

- Lessons about what *not* to do (such as not being drawn into the political quagmire of executive-branch reorganization campaigns and not attempting to reform the budget-making process through format and process revisions).
- Lessons about what *to* do (such as the creation of special councils

like the President's Management Improvement Council which could identify methods of modernizing and improving administrative processes).

Mechanisms for better control of the executive branch, including inspectors general, regulatory review, and civil service reform.[64]

The political acceptability of deregulation was founded on growing skepticism about previously unquestioned "principles" of regulation. The "technocratic model" visualized administrative policy making as an empirical process "in which 'experts' reach a uniquely correct result derived from logical analysis of objective and accurate data." Cutler finds this technocratic model, which sees the "experts" as free of "political" inclination, to be "gravely flawed," because it fails to account for the competition for resources that results when worthwhile social goals collide.[65] Government officials, including prominent Democrats, joined in expressions of concern about the expansion of the bureaucracy's power. Carter's attorney general, Griffin Bell, had advocated a shift of power from bureaucrats to "directly accountable public officials."[66] Senator Thomas F. Eagleton (D-Mo.) objected to "unrestrained regulatory power."[67] Senator Lloyd Bentsen (D-Tex.) ruminated about the failure of the legislative branch to place a ceiling on the compliance costs imposed on the private sector by regulatory requirements.[68]

There could be no question, in the presence of this policy consensus, that the Reagan administration would unveil a plan to move deregulation forward. A number of regulatory agencies were notified by OMB of the new administration's determination to impede the many regulations drafted in the waning days of the Carter administration. In early 1981, 110 planned regulations were killed, 16 of which were proposals developed in EPA. OMB also recommended legislation that would cancel a number of pending and existing EPA regulations.[69] A presidential executive order was prepared, instituting cost-benefit analysis for proposed regulations pertaining to the operations of private business and state and local governments. In its determination to establish the new process quickly and at all costs, the administration disregarded the formal procedure of circulating proposed executive orders among affected agencies for review and comment. Instead, when agency lawyers visited OMB to discuss plans for the new regulatory reform process, they were surprised to find that Executive Order 12291 was a fait accompli, already signed by President Reagan (see chapter 5). For Reagan, there was no room for negotiation because reduction in the regulatory burden was a sacred promise made during his 1980 campaign. "During the Presidential campaign, I promised quick and decisive action. Since taking office, I have made regulatory relief a top priority. It is one of the cornerstones of my economic recovery program."[70]

Seidman and Gilmour characterize Reagan's design for bureaucratic reform as one of centralization—of the budgetary process, of the appointments process, of decision making, and of the control of regulations.[71] These centralization measures all struck the regulatory agencies, with substantial force in many cases. Budget restructuring was used to slash the budgets of numerous regulatory agencies, leaving many of them "bereft of resources, and struggling to maintain a minimum level of operation."[72] Reductions in force (RIFS) followed, all but destroying the capability of some agencies to maintain a competent work force. The savings and loan association fiasco has been blamed on, among other things, staff cutbacks that may have doomed the Federal Savings and Loan Insurance Corporation.[73] The centralized appointments process placed at the helm of many agencies managers who had little regard for the objectives of regulation and questionable loyalty to the agencies they headed. Fuchs reports the results:

> The Anne Gorsuch-led EPA approved only 3 of the 130 rules proposed by the [Carter] administration. Nancy Steorts halted the production of rules to protect consumers at [the Consumer Product Safety Commission]. The [Federal Trade Commission] initiated a drive to restore the free market, cutting back on the flow of information to consumers and ceasing the pursuit of antitrust policy. The [Interstate Commerce Commission] befriended big trucking interests, and the [Federal Communications Commission] moved to cut competition among broadcasters. The new regime[,] then, was moving to stop the production of all liberal rules when legally possible.[74]

Reagan did not overlook the opportunity to install deregulation instruments in the EOP. He appointed a presidential Task Force on Regulatory Relief chaired by Vice President Bush and delegated day-to-day oversight responsibilities to OIRA, the office created by the Paperwork Reduction Act. The cost-benefit standard, only hinted at by the Carter program, became an almost rigid economic canon for the Reagan team and formed the central methodology for Executive Order 12291.

In that order, the president directed every executive agency to refer all proposed regulations to OIRA, including a cost-benefit analysis for proposals involving compliance costs of $100 million or more. A cost-benefit analysis would need to demonstrate that the benefits of the regulation would exceed compliance costs.

The president's staff presumably realized that the IRCs were legally immune from this sort of oversight, and so the order was addressed only to the executive agencies.[75] The commissions were urged to consider voluntary participation.[76] Furthermore, the president's staff realized that enabling statutes and the Administrative Procedure Act vested rule-making authority in the regulatory officials, not in the president or OMB. Thus, any provision maintaining that a negative evaluation of a proposal by OIRA would preclude promulgation by the agency would clearly be illegal. As a result, no such provision was included in the order. Many observers worried that Executive Order 12291 had created a new procedure that would be recognized as a right to due process among parties in regulatory dockets, which could open the door to excessive litigation. OMB's solution was to attempt to conceal the process under a veil of secrecy so that no party would have evidence to present in court. Finally, those who drafted the order sought to immunize the order, in a somewhat paradoxical way, by including a provision that the order would not have any effect prohibited by law. By this circular reasoning, the order could not be illegal because it acknowledged it was limited to legal purposes only. The structure was clearly a radical departure from the rule-making model, but a memorandum produced by Assistant Attorney General Larry Simms pronounced the order to be in harmony with the Constitution and with the statutes enacted by Congress.[77]

The resulting presidential effort to control the activities of the regulatory agencies was "more self-conscious in design and execution, and more comprehensive in scope, than that of any other administration of the modern era," write Benda and Levine.[78]

Goodman and Wrightson distinguish Reagan's regulatory policy from that of his predecessors by the degree of purposefulness that marked the Reagan approach. "In the seriousness with which it has taken the issue of regulation, the Reagan presidency is unprecedented. Most past [presidents] interceded in regulatory affairs only rarely and with little enthusiasm. In sharp contrast, under Reagan, executive office intervention in regulatory affairs has been vigorous and sustained."[79] While some wrote the epitaph to Reagan's regulation relief program as early as 1983,[80] the fact remains that the OIRA process survived throughout the Reagan administration and continued under President Bush. In a June 1987 message to Congress, Reagan indicated an irreversible resolve to maintain the pressure to limit regulatory burdens on business and private citizens. "It has been, and remains, a basic tenet of my Administration that there is too much regulation of American life and that true regulatory reform must involve regulatory reduction."[81] The administration's determination helped it to weather the formidable storm of partisan literature, congressional hearings, and litigation aimed against the centralized review process, and accounted for the survival of the process throughout the next administration.

OFFICE OF MANAGEMENT AND BUDGET

To command the attention of the bureaucracy, Reagan's EOP placed the centralized review process under the authority of OMB. This was strategic, because OMB already possessed an impressive array of instruments of authority. OMB director David A. Stockman and OIRA administrator Miller wanted bureaucrats to recognize that if they circumvented OMB decisions disapproving proposed regulations, OMB's other powers could be brought to bear to punish the recalcitrants and to discourage imitators.

OMB's powers—including central coordination of the executive budget and of paperwork requirements, and central clearance of legislative proposals—applied to executive branch agencies and to IRCs. However, OMB had applied these powers with restraint until the arrival of the Reagan appointees.[82]

OMB succeeded in amassing an intimidating set of review powers across the spectrum of agency actions and prerogatives. According to Frank B. Cross, at least ninety-four statutes assigned management responsibility to OMB.[83] OIRA deputy administrator Jim J. Tozzi said, "The Government works using three things: money, people, and regulations; the agency must get all three through OMB."[84] Thus, when asked whether OMB could succeed in its effort to compel agencies to promulgate only those regulations approved by OMB, OIRA administrator Miller boasted, "You know, if you're the toughest kid on the block, most kids won't pick a fight with you."[85] In 1990, Anthony J. Principi, deputy secretary of veterans affairs, acknowledged OMB's capacity to interfere in his department's operations. "They control everything I do," he lamented.[86]

EVOLUTION OF OIRA

OIRA, a component of OMB, was founded under authority of the Paperwork Reduction Act of 1980.[87] This law assigned to OIRA the job of monitoring federal agency rules that created paperwork obligations for private parties. Insofar as the act was scheduled to take effect on April 1, 1981, the promulgation of Executive Order 12291, which established centralized review of federal regulations, meant that OIRA was carrying out two functions beginning in 1981. As Miller, who served as OIRA administrator and later as OMB director, explained the logic, the paperwork and regulatory review processes were "highly complementary," and so it was natural to put OIRA in charge of the regulatory review process also.[88] A later OIRA administrator, Wendy L. Gramm, described OIRA's regulatory oversight as a facet of OMB's expanding role as coordinator.

OIRA pursued the paperwork reduction objective vigorously. Between 1981 and mid-1987, OIRA reduced paperwork burdens by 44 percent, or about 600 million labor hours annually.[89]

To Robert Gilmour and Roger Sperry, it was the regulation clearance process that distinguished OIRA in its impact on federal regulation. "The Reagan Administration's designation of [OIRA] as its central clearance arm for regulatory policy capitalized on a national mandate for regulatory relief and set in motion—administratively—the most sweeping reform of the regulatory process in 35 years."[90] Benda and Levine find an irony in the combination of paperwork reduction and regulatory oversight in OIRA. The Paperwork Reduction Act that established OIRA was carefully drawn up to limit OMB's capacity to influence the regulatory policies of federal agencies.

> In its report accompanying the bill [which became the Paperwork Reduction Act], the Senate Governmental Affairs Committee noted that provisions had been added to guard against this possibility [of inordinate OMB influence over regulatory policy], and emphasized, with respect to OIRA, that it did "not intend that regulatory reform issues which go beyond the scope of information management and burden be assigned to the office."[91]

OIRA undoubtedly made its mark on federal regulation. Although many of its original members used their tour of duty at OIRA as a "springboard" to loftier jobs in government and in the private sector, their replacements had a professional commitment, in many cases, to the cause of government efficiency and reform. Senator William V. Roth Jr. (R-Del.) offered this high tribute: "Mr. President [of the Senate], I have often questioned the vigor and effectiveness of the management side of OMB. The Office of Information and Regulatory Affairs is perhaps the singular exception."[92]

THE VICE PRESIDENT AND THE TASK FORCE

The Institutional Vice Presidency

The growth of presidential involvement in regulation happened to coincide chronologically with the evolution and expansion of the institutional vice presidency. Originating as a consolation prize for the runner-up in the presidential election, the vice presidency was converted into the inconsequential and often frustrating position of minimal authority and minimal accomplishment. This was the hallmark of the position for most of the history of the United States. To keep busy, Martin Van Buren's vice president, Richard M. Johnson, managed a hotel on the side; William McKinley's vice president, Theodore Roosevelt, had time to finish law school.[93] Nine vice presidents have succeeded to the presidency upon the death or resignation of the president. Otherwise, the vice presidency has been so inopportune as a stepping stone to the presidency that from 1837 to 1988 no sitting vice president was promoted directly to the presidency by virtue of the electoral process. Vice presidents were "errand-boys, political hitmen, professional mourners, and incidental White House commissioners."[94] Ever since Benjamin Franklin wondered aloud whether the vice president ought to be known as "His Superfluous Highness," the vice presidency has been an object of disdain, the vice president a target of ridicule in many cases, and few accomplishments have been attributed to the nation's second-highest elected official.[95]

The only function assigned to the vice president, apart from the role of understudy to the president, is to preside over the Senate and cast a tiebreaking vote there. Although the presidency of the Senate might have secured for the vice president a position of legislative importance comparable to that of the Speaker of the House, the elected senators chose to relegate the offices of president and president pro tempore of the Senate to ceremonial triviality. Instead, the Senate majority leader casts the longest shadow in the upper house. In 1973, Senate Majority Leader Mike Mansfield (D-Mont.) instructed Vice President Ford, "Here, presiding officers are to be seen and not heard, unlike the House where the Speaker's gavel is like a thunderclap."[96]

Nevertheless, the vice president's constitutional role as president of the Senate created a convenient excuse for the nation's chief executive to confine his running mate to an office in the Capitol, one and one-half miles away from the two loci of executive activity on Pennsylvania Avenue—namely, the White House and the Old Executive Office Building (OEOB). In 1960, fewer than twenty staff members were assigned to the vice president's office.[97] The next year, Vice President Lyndon B. Johnson was given an office in the OEOB by President John F. Kennedy.[98]

Several developments led to the enhancement of the vice president's administrative functions beginning in the 1970s. According to Paul C. Light, these developments include the decline of the national political parties, longer election campaigns, and the proliferation of new policy issues.[99] Vice Presidents Ford, Nelson A. Rockefeller, and Walter F. Mondale solicited and secured an expansion of vice presidential resources and authority, coming to fill the role of senior adviser. President Ford placed Rockefeller in charge of the Domestic Council. Vice President Mondale was a key policy adviser for Carter. The vice president's staff has grown rapidly since 1974. The office now has a separate line in the executive budget, with a value of $2 million. The vice president has office space in the west wing of the White House and in the OEOB as well as at the Capitol. The result is the "institutional vice presidency," the fifth largest agency in the White House and a key component of the EOP. "The Vice-President's office is now a replica of the President's office, with a national security adviser, press secretary, domestic issues staff, scheduling team, advance, appointments, administration, chief of staff, and counsel's office."[100]

The Task Force on Regulatory Relief

Unlike his predecessor, Mondale, Vice President Bush expressed a willingness to accept line assignments in the EOP. President Reagan appointed Bush to chair the Task Force on Regulatory Relief. Insofar as Bush deemed it inadvisable to undertake long-term duties that would entangle him in interdepartmental struggles, he delegated day-to-day supervision of the task force to his counsel, C. Boyden Gray.

The task force was created on the first full working day of the Reagan administration—January 20, 1981. It was intended to be a visible center of regulatory relief activity. The task force would monitor regulatory activity and review regulations already in effect, and—if any such regulatory instruments conflicted with the Reagan deregulation plan—would call for the cancellation of the offending measures.

The task force and administration officials prepared five lists of regulations targeted for review and possible repeal. On March 25, 1981, the task force issued a list of twenty-seven existing regulations that would be "reassessed." Vice President Bush's office estimated annual savings of $1.8 to $2.1 billion and a one-time investment savings of $6 billion. On April 6, President Ronald Reagan announced a list of thirty-four regulations affecting automobile manufacturers, whose repeal would save consumers $9.3 billion in a five-year period and save the industry $1.4 billion. On August 12, the vice president announced a list of thirty regulations to be reviewed for possible regulatory excess and nine areas in which paperwork burdens seemed excessive. In February 1982, Bush published a list of eleven regulations considered burdensome to small businesses. In August 1982, the task force advocated a list of eight regulations to allow state and local governments more freedom to set clean air standards, to develop land in floodplains, and to save or destroy historic buildings.[101] About one-quarter of the regulations that the task force designated for review involved intergovernment relationships.[102]

These lists resulted from research by administration officials and also included controversial regulations denounced by certain interest groups. The administration left the door wide open to the groups that wanted to express objections to certain regulations. In this process, both tactical and public relations errors were made. In a speech Gray delivered to a business audience in the Capitol Hall of Flags on April 10, 1981, an address that attained some degree of notoriety, he urged: "Well, if you go to the agency first, don't be too pessimistic if they can't solve the problem there. If they don't, that is what the Task Force is for; . . . the system does work if you use us as sort of an appeal."[103] The invitation set off alarms for those who were working for personal, professional, or ideological reasons—and in accordance with the legitimate "rules of the game," such as the Administrative Procedure Act—to secure regulations favorable to their interests or ideologies. The message seemed to indicate a new and perhaps decisive point of access for business groups, which would make political participation by social interest groups a lost cause. As an additional source of frustration for advocates of social regulation, the information obtained from business groups by the task force was referred to the OIRA but not to the regulatory agency involved. That the OIRA should then make decisions against proposed regulations based on information never possessed by the rule-making agency enraged interest groups advocating such regulations. The anger persisted for years; in the closing days of the Reagan era, one OMB official said, "A lot of anger of the interest groups is left over from the Task Force days."[104]

For those regulatory agency officials who might perceive the task force as a viable place to appeal adverse decisions on their regulatory proposals by OIRA, a surprise awaited them. The task force's executive director was none other than the administrator of OIRA. One House subcommittee staff counsel was left to wonder: "Since [Christopher C.] DeMuth, who heads the OMB office [OIRA] which makes the final determination [on proposed regulations], is also the Executive Director of the Task Force, is the appeal to the Task Force a meaningful one?"[105]

By the summer of 1983, criticism of the regulatory relief program was raining down on the Reagan administration. In order to limit the public relations damage, Vice President Bush's office announced, on August 11, 1983, that the task force—by saving society $9 to $11 billion in one-time investment costs and $10 billion in annual recurring costs[106]—had accomplished the task given to it and was thus suspending its operations. Most scholars writing on the subject wrote epitaphs for the task force, assuming it would never be heard from again.

Instead, the task force was reconstituted in November 1986. The existence of unfinished business was proclaimed. Vice President Bush resumed his role as chairman. He was joined by the attorney general, the secretaries of labor, treasury, and the interior, and the director of OMB. White House staff people and other staff (such as the director of cabinet affairs, the chairman of the CEA, the counselor to the vice president, and the administrator of OIRA) also attended, and attendance averaged fifteen or sixteen persons. The OIRA administrator continued to serve as executive director of the task force.

The propensity for list making that characterized the early days of the task force was not evident in the post-1986 period. Vice President Bush's deputy counsel, John P. Schmitz, explained, "The 'unfinished business' requires a legislative change as likely as an administrative change." The new focus of the task force involved regulatory matters that could not be legally tampered with unless Congress enacted, amended, or repealed certain laws. "The Task Force is looking at major areas of change, such as fuel economy standards for the automobile industry. You can't send that to [the Department of Transportation], because they'll say they have no statutory authority."

In the final years of the Reagan administration, the task force was meeting not quite once a month, and was considering from two to four discrete legislative proposals oriented toward deregulation. For instance, S.1518 on fuel economy legislation in 1988 was a response to a task force proposal. The task force recommended repeal of CAFE (corporate average fuel economy) standards; Congress decided to amend the requirement, to the delight of task force members.

The task force suggested a number of legislative changes to the president's Office of Legislative Affairs, which transmitted proposals to the vice president (as president of the Senate) and to the Speaker of the House. Each transmission was reported in the *Congressional Record*. An individual member of Congress would introduce the proposal. "Almost all Task Force business operates this way," Schmitz said.

The process by which agencies could appeal adverse OIRA decisions to the task force was resumed. Vice presidential counselor Gray had the pivotal role of deciding whether to leave the ball in OIRA's court or bring the matter before the task force. The door remained open to regulated parties to object to proposed regulations deemed unduly burdensome. "That's where the Task

Force makes its mark," said Schmitz. Agencies would press their cases only if they were willing to see their arguments posed directly to Vice President Bush. This would motivate them to amend their proposals in many cases to avoid potential embarrassment at that level.[107]

CABINET COUNCILS

Imitating similar initiatives by Nixon and Ford, Reagan divided the cabinet into seven separate cabinet councils. These were the Cabinet Council on Economic Affairs (CCEA), the Cabinet Council on Commerce and Trade (CCCT), the Cabinet Council on Human Resources (CCHR), the Cabinet Council on Natural Resources and Energy (CCNRE), the Cabinet Council on Food and Agriculture (CCFA), the Cabinet Council on Legal Policy (CCLP), and the Cabinet Council on Management and Administration (CCMA). These councils tended to concentrate on the details of implementation and rarely dabbled in broad policy making.[108]

In April 1985, the seven cabinet councils were abolished, giving way to two policy councils—the Domestic Policy Council (DPC) and the Economic Policy Council.

President Reagan sent word to his cabinet members that he wanted disputes to be resolved in the cabinet councils, and not argued for his benefit in the Oval Office. The cabinet council system and the president's demand that disputes be resolved in that forum made it more difficult for cabinet members to press their particularistic constituency interests with the president. A proposed policy to advance a constituency "would have to survive 'the scrutiny and criticism of cabinet peers and White House staff members' before making its way higher up the chain of command."[109]

This structure and the norms that grew up around it impacted directly upon disputes over proposed regulations. Cabinet members involved in disputes could have gone to the task force, but they seemed no more inclined to argue the matter in front of Vice President Bush than in front of the president. "No Cabinet official wants to sit in front of the president or vice president and argue with another Cabinet member—[he] might lose," said Schmitz. So the disputes were often brought before the DPC, chaired by Attorney General Edwin Meese III, or the Economic Policy Council, chaired by Secretary of the Treasury James A. Baker III. "Once the issue goes to the Domestic Policy Council, it has gotten to the same people who would have seen it at the Task Force," said Schmitz—except that the vice president would not attend DPC meetings.

Formally, the task force and the DPC had separate jurisdictions, with rules of thumb deciding which issues went where. A rare overlap involved the United States–Canada acid rain issue. The DPC was responsible for coordinating the response of the United States, but it asked the task force to develop a regulatory proposal. The task force called on the National Acid Precipitation Advisory Council to issue a report and on EPA to perform a cost-benefit analysis on strategies to control acid rain. The State Department arranged for a Bilateral Advisory Consulting Group to report to the DPC on its negotiations with Canada. The Task Force would design a Clean Coal Technology Program and other emission reduction measures. Schmitz observes that the DPC "stood between the Task Force and the president," and that the incident confirmed that "controversies that need to be resolved at the Cabinet level should go to DPC" whenever possible.[110]

3 Processes of Regulatory Relief

COST-BENEFIT AND RISK ANALYSIS

Students of public administration and public policy are familiar with "incrementalism" as an explanation for how public policy is made. As described by David Braybrooke and Charles E. Lindblom, incrementalism is the making of next year's policy by applying small, incremental changes to this year's policy.[1] The traditional line-item budgeting process, in which each agency's budget is increased by some modest percentage from one year to the next, is characteristic of incrementalism.[2] The alternative to incrementalism is the approach of rationalism, or the "comprehensive" method, in which an exhaustive list of alternatives is prepared, each evaluated thoroughly, and the most attractive selected. It is apparent that the incrementalist approach is more conservative and rationalism more progressive.

Although Ronald Reagan is a conservative Republican, he perceived little advantage in conserving many of the government's policies, practices, and methods that he inherited from his predecessors. Despite the Republican presidencies of 1969 to 1977, Reagan and his aides saw Washington, D.C., as a center of unremitting, excessive government intrusion into the private sector, orchestrated by an overactive Congress and a bloated, left-leaning bureaucracy. Accordingly, they deemed incrementalism counterproductive, and Reagan opted for the methodologies of rationalism—in particular, cost-benefit analysis. Although in theory rationalism appears to be a progressive approach, in practice it involves costly, time-consuming analyses and deliberations that slow down the decision-making process. Reagan's aides—conservatives who delighted in the notion of impeding the progress of regulation—

settled on cost-benefit analysis as a ritual that every substantive regulation had to undergo. Thus, the Reagan Revolution was riddled with contradictions, with conservatives generating a whirlwind of activity. Terry Eastland observes:

> The idea of a strong presidency may be unappealing to conservatives taught by Ronald Reagan that "government is not the solution to the problem" but the problem itself. But Reagan ironically proved that government can be the solution; indeed, Reagan demonstrated that the strong presidency is necessary to effect ends sought by most conservatives.[3]

The prescription of the elaborate analytical tool of cost-benefit analysis—the centerpiece of Executive Order 12291—was combined, ironically, with a cut in the work force of the regulatory agencies. Therefore, deliberately or not, the administration had designed a system destined from the outset to cause the agencies to fail. As Paul Portney wrote: "If the Reagan administration wants to see good cost-benefit regulatory studies, then these research budget cuts ... make it virtually impossible to do it. ... You will not get the enhanced analysis the administration says it wants if at the same time it slashes the research budget needed to do it."[4] Executive Order 12291's prescription of cost-benefit analysis, though historically important in its scope, did not pioneer the use of cost-benefit analysis in the national government. The Flood Control Act of 1936[5] is the first known record of any government's attempt to apply cost-benefit analysis. The *Proposed Practices for Economic Analysis of River Basin Projects* (better known as the "Green Book") published by the Inter-Agency Committee on Water Resources in 1950 "was the first significant attempt to codify CBA principles and techniques for use by government analysts."[6] The Planning, Programming, and Budgeting System (PPBS) introduced in the early and mid-1960s under Secretary of Defense Robert S. McNamara called for cost-benefit estimates to be an integral part of the programming stage of the process.[7]

The Consumer Products Safety Act required the Consumer Products Safety Commission to consider the risks of injury; the number of products subject to the rule; the public's needs for such products; the projected utility, cost, and availability of the projects; and the possibility of adverse effects on competition that would result from any rule making. Congress's Office of Technology Assessment determined in 1977 that similar considerations of compliance and indirect costs were required under provisions of such laws as the Federal Insecticide, Fungicide, and Rodenticide Act; the Federal Hazardous Substances Act; the Toxic Substances Control Act; the Federal Food,

Drug, and Cosmetics Act; the Occupational Safety and Health Act; the Clean Water Act; and the Clean Air Act.[8]

In testimony at a 1979 hearing, Environmental Protection Agency (EPA) administrator Douglas M. Costle, then serving concurrently as chairman of the Regulatory Council, reported that his agency had been experimenting successfully with regulatory analysis. "EPA has been preparing... regulatory analyses for some time now, and I can report that they do help me try to find the best regulatory approach."[9] The stream of legislative and administrative precedents for the use of regulatory analysis did not escape the notice of the judicial branch when the Reagan administration policy of requiring cost-benefit analysis was challenged in the courts. In the Supreme Court's opinion in the 1981 case of *American Textile Manufacturers Institute, Inc., v. Donovan, Secretary of Labor*—popularly known as the "cotton-dust" case—Justice William J. Brennan wrote: "When Congress has intended that an agency engage in cost-benefit analysis, it has clearly indicated such intent on the face of the statute.... Congress uses specific language when intending that an agency engage in cost-benefit analysis."[10]

Representatives of the business community became very vocal in their demands to circumscribe federal regulators' license to impose compliance costs indiscriminately. The Business Roundtable's Task Force on Government Regulation demanded the use of economic analysis.

> We frankly do not understand why requiring an economic analysis as part of the process of developing major regulations should even be a matter of controversy. The economic resources available to our society are limited. If they are employed for one purpose, they cannot and will not be available for another.
>
> The determination of priorities in the use of resources is as essential to intelligent decisionmaking in Government as it is in private business. And even the advocates of regulation ought to be interested in assuring that scarce resources are appropriately employed.[11]

Cost-benefit analysis involves five steps: (1) identifying costs that the proposed policy would entail and the benefits it would generate; (2) quantifying costs and benefits in dollars; (3) analyzing probabilities and risks associated with certain costs and benefits; (4) discounting, to take the time value of money into account; and (5) calculating a measure (e.g., the ratio of benefits to costs) to determine the acceptability of the proposed policy.[12]

Like other social science techniques, cost-benefit analysis is an imprecise method. The House Oversight and Investigations Subcommittee declared that "the most significant factor in evaluating a benefit-cost study is the name of the sponsor."[13] Rarely can a cost-benefit analysis be free from methodological criticism, for three reasons.

The first problem is that *costs and benefits are difficult to assess accurately*. Outlays by a regulated entity to comply with a regulation may merely displace other costs, such as those that have heretofore been externalized. For example, transfers of wealth are often classified as costs. As a result, when wealth is confiscated from the affluent class and transferred to the needy class, a shift that could actually be classified as a benefit, the transfer may fail to score well in a cost-benefit analysis and may appear irrational. Yet the transfer itself may be justified in terms of equity. Michael D. Reagan declares, "Cost-benefit analysis is useless on distributional questions, which are often at the heart of the politics of policymaking."[14]

Another aspect of this first difficulty is risk assessment. One of the benefits of regulation, by intent, is the reduction of certain kinds of risk. However, since risk is not an expression of what *has* happened but rather of what *might* happen, the effort to estimate risk and to place a value on it is somewhat illusory and often provokes debate. For example, Senator Albert Gore Jr. (D.-Tenn.) and Office of Management and Budget (OMB) director James C. Miller III had this heated exchange on the topic of risk:

> [Q. Gore] You said in your testimony just a moment ago that OMB concluded that the grain dust standard as submitted to OMB for review was deeply flawed because, for one thing, this risk was "grossly overstated." Do you think the risk to the three workers who were killed in Knoxville was grossly overstated?
>
> [A. Miller] That is not the appropriate use of the term risk. I don't know what you mean by the term risk when you see someone suffering an accident.
>
> [Q.] . . . My question to you is, *in retrospect*, do you believe that the risk faced by those three workers, when they walked into that grain elevator was grossly overstated by those who recommended the removal of that risk? . . . You just testified that the risk was grossly overstated. The question is a very simple one. Do you think that the risk that was faced by those workers as described by the analysis of this accident was grossly overstated or not?
>
> [A.] Senator Gore, you are shouting at me, and I don't think that that is conducive to a reasonable exchange of information.[15]

Furthermore, knowledge about benefits is undeveloped. Dr. Nicholas A. Ashford, assistant director of the Center for Policy Alternatives at the Massachusetts Institute of Technology, told a Senate committee that the benefits of regulations—especially in the areas of health, safety, and the environment—cannot be accurately determined by current methods. "The state of the art in estimating the numbers of cancers or cases of chronic disease prevented—or even injuries—is in its infancy."[16] No "safe" exposure level to a carcinogen is known. Ashford noted that no organized interest group devotes much effort to estimating benefits, while much research has been dedicated to estimating compliance costs. Therefore, no sophisticated methodologies for benefit estimation are available.[17]

In addition, health and safety considerations tend to defy quantification.[18] One of the most rancorous sources of controversy in cost-benefit analysis is the problem of placing a monetary value on human life. The problem arises because the purpose of some cost-generating regulations is to create, as a benefit, a lower incidence of loss of human life. Benefits can only be compared to costs if a common unit is used, and the unit inevitably is the dollar.[19]

Thus, any cost-benefit analysis is subject to controversy because interested observers may disagree about the assumptions made and the values assigned to costs and benefits. Economist Lester B. Lave noted that "there is no unique set of assumptions that everybody agrees are best."[20] Considering vinyl chloride regulation, Doniger wonders whether society should be willing to allow some workers to die "so that all can have see-through food packaging."[21] The Subcommittee on Oversight and Investigation of the House Interstate and Foreign Commerce Committee advised against the use of cost-benefit analysis for social issues. "The limitations on the usefulness of benefit/cost analysis in the context of health, safety, and environmental regulation decision-making are so severe that they militate against its use altogether."[22]

The second problem is that *cost-benefit analysis incurs its own costs*. Morrison comments acidly that the Reagan administration was negligent in its failure to conduct a cost-benefit analysis on the instrument of cost-benefit analysis itself.[23] Cost-benefit analyses consumed costs of up to $800,000 per analysis.[24]

The third problem is that, *when applied selectively, the analysis requirement is discriminatory*. Many social activists object that the cost-benefit analysis requirement has been used to target social regulations for oblivion, while other types of government spending are not subjected to equal scrutiny. Jonathan Lash, representing the Natural Resources Defense Council, said bitterly:

> It is curious that there is no proposal for economic analysis of new buildings. There is no proposal for economic analysis of the cruise missile. It might in

> fact be difficult to justify the cruise missile through a cost-benefit analysis. Many of the same problems that arise there suggest why there should not be a separate requirement for economic analysis of regulations.[25]

The paradox noted by Bryner is that regulatory analysis is conceived as a way of "limiting and directing administrative discretion and as a means of insulating administrative decision making from external pressures." In truth, however, cost-benefit analysis seems to be a handy method of erecting barriers against proposed regulations opposed by the president's constituency.[26]

Notwithstanding the criticisms against cost-benefit analysis, officials at the Office of Information and Regulatory Affairs (OIRA) during the Bush era, the self-proclaimed experts in the science of regulation, pushed the frontiers of the science further by embellishing cost-benefit analysis. The innovation was "risk-risk analysis," and was based on an article written by Ralph L. Kenney, a professor of management at the University of Southern California, and cited in a 1991 decision by the United States Court of Appeals in the District of Columbia Circuit. The theory is that costly regulations designed to save lives will paradoxically create the risky state of indigence for people whose wages are reduced or whose jobs are lost. Reduced salaries may deprive people of necessities of life such as medical care.[27] Based on that rationale, OIRA applied the additional criterion of risk-risk assessment to regulations submitted for its review.

The various assessments of the deficiencies of cost-benefit analysis are worth noting, because they properly warn that public policy can be distorted when analyses are misused. On the other hand, policy analysts persuasively argue that programs whose benefits are theoretical while their costs are very real may constitute a blatant disservice to the general public or to particular subsets of the public. If government officials wish to avoid cost-benefit analysis, there are several strategies that can be used as alternatives. Some methods can also be used in conjunction with cost-benefit analysis.

First, a *regulatory budget* may be established, in which each agency is allotted a limit on the compliance costs it can impose.[28]

Second, a *regulatory calendar* may be employed: This is a periodic listing of contemplated regulations that provides advance notice to other agencies and to interested parties about regulatory proposals under study. This device has been used in the Carter, Reagan, and Bush administrations.

Third, a *qualitative regulatory analysis* may be done: This method has been advocated by Eileen Siedman, who is critical of overreliance on quantitative measurement.[29]

Fourth, *a cost effectiveness approach* may be adopted. Some observers, while opposing the use of cost-benefit analysis to ascertain the preferred option, condone its use to eliminate options whose costs exceed benefits.[30] The cost effectiveness approach seeks to identify the policy that delivers the maximum output per unit of resource or that minimizes the expenditure for a certain level of output.[31]

Fifth, a *procompetitive standard* may be adopted as an alternative to cost-benefit analysis that perpetuates the deregulatory spirit. Such a standard requires that any proposed regulation be inspected to determine its effects on competition.

Sixth, *agency-by-agency reform* may be called for. This alternative stems from criticisms of across-the-board regulatory reform efforts, based on the insight that each agency develops unique problems, and that the array of problems experienced by various agencies cannot be solved by imposing uniform remedies on them. Calling for agency-by-agency reform in place of such across-the-board strategies, Senator Edward M. Kennedy (D-Mass.) said, "We have found that the most effective reform takes place on an agency-by-agency basis. First, we focused on the [Civil Aeronautics Board], now the [Food and Drug Administration]."[32] Instruments that treat agencies uniformly also tend to be interpreted as penalties by agencies that have already made efforts to reform, and may thus discourage future initiatives to innovate and to operate efficiently.

Finally, *changes in personnel* may be required. The discretionary character of regulation may create policies to which the president or Congress objects, but the disputes do not necessarily justify basic structural reforms. "If individuals or management is at fault," writes Barry Mitnick, "this should be changed, not the regulatory system."[33]

PERSONNEL SELECTION

A procession of presidents has expressed frustration with the inflexibility and insubordination of the bureaucracy.[34] Fully aware of this history, President Reagan and his top aides were determined to avoid whatever errors his predecessors had made that may have given rise to decisions being made against the president's will. In November 1979, Reagan adviser Edwin Meese III asked former White House official E. Pendleton James to devise a preliminary personnel plan in preparation for a possible Reagan victory. In April 1980, with the smell of Republican victory in the air, Meese signalled James to implement the personnel plan.[35] James, awarded the prestigious title of assistant to the president in the Reagan White House, was succeeded by John Herrington as personnel director for the White House. Their objectives were facilitated by a gift President Jimmy Carter left behind for Reagan—namely, the Civil Service Reform Act of 1978, which "substantially increased Reagan's ability to fill high-level executive policy-making positions with his own appointees rather than having to cope with the senior civil servants who had traditionally occupied many of these posts."[36] G. Calvin Mackenzie wrote that the Reagan team "undertook transition personnel selection with more forethought, with a larger commitment of resources, and with more systematic attention to detail than any administration in the post-war period, perhaps more than any administration ever."[37] Under director Donald Devine, the Office of Personnel Management was politicized, according to Rockman, and civil service appointments were "manipulated," a process facilitated by the Civil Service Reform Act.[38] Administration officials James C. Miller III and Murray L. Weidenbaum asserted that the political appointees in the executive agencies would have to be "the first line of defense against overregulation" and "the first line of *offense* in ferreting out ineffective and excessively burdensome regulations."[39] Benda and Levine report: "Even while the new President was publicly extolling the virtues of cabinet government, steps were being taken to ensure that ultimate control over subcabinet appointments—indeed, over *all* lower-level political appointments—would remain firmly in the hands of the White House."[40]

Observers agree that the Reagan White House considered ideological consistency the most important criterion for selecting appointees. In September 1980, Reagan said: "Crucial to my strategy of spending control will be the appointment to top government positions of men and women who share my economic philosophy. We will have an administration in which the word from the top isn't lost or hidden in the bureaucracy."[41] Mackenzie reported, "There was achieved in [Reagan's] appointments an uncommon degree of ideological consistency and intensity."[42] White House political affairs aide Lyn Nofziger disclosed the primary qualification for service in the Reagan administration when he declared, "As far as I'm concerned, anyone who supported Reagan is competent."[43] OIRA administrator Miller exulted, "All of our appointees have religion."[44]

Reagan's top aides sought to insulate department secretaries and assistant secretaries from career civil servants to avert the usual "cycle of accommodation" between political appointees and civil servants. Reagan's appointees were directed to avoid contact with their own agency staff during the transition period, and they were inundated with reports and briefings about agency policies, prepared by conservative think tanks like the Heritage Foundation. Rourke explains, "This strategy was designed to inoculate [the political appointees] with conservative antibodies that would provide protection [against] the liberal viruses to which the administration expected appointees to be exposed once they began to have close contact with civil servants."[45] For the same purpose, to avoid the "cycle of accommodation," presidential counsel Meese designed a system of cabinet councils, which was established in February 1981.[46] Hugh Heclo attributes success to the cabinet councils because they forced "department policy development into a system of strategic decision making closely held at the White House."[47] Meese himself said, "The difference is that Reagan has used his system so that cabinet members all feel closer to him than they do to their departments. And he gives them a lot of opportunity to remember that."[48]

Bureaucrats left over from the Carter administration feared for their careers as the Reagan era was beginning in early 1981, but the expected "bloodbath" never occurred. Reassignments, however, were used liberally in some agencies, which fueled bureaucrats' suspicions of the regulatory reform effort.[49] Overall, the size of the regulatory work force decreased sharply, sustaining a 16-percent drop from 1980 to 1984.[50] Over twelve thousand employees lost their jobs in reductions in force in fiscal years 1981 and 1982.[51] The administration showed a preference for discretionary, politically inspired appointments. Between 1980 and 1986, the number of career officials holding senior executive service positions declined as more noncareer officials occupied those influential posts. Discretionary Schedule C appointments increased 12.8 percent during the same period.[52]

A grim picture of the results of Reagan's ideologically oriented appointments[53] emerges. The EPA scandal of 1983, which resulted in Anne Gorsuch Burford's downfall, motivated the administration to decrease the amount of publicity it sought for the regulatory relief program. But Eads and Fix also concede that the appointment of ideologues commanded the attention of Congress, which acted hastily "to confirm these [deregulatory] actions legislatively, if only to limit the degree to which this discretion could be used."[54]

Because defiance from appointed officials and civil servants had become a focus of concern by incumbent presidents and a fearsome threat to the ideological designs of incoming presidents, the problem of disloyalty was a preoccupation of the Oval Office. Although it did not eliminate all problems, Reagan's effective use of the appointment power to send a message of "no business as usual" may prove to have been a new point of departure for his and George Bush's successors.[55] Some government officials interested in the cause of good executive branch management have warned that the ideologically pure patronage appointment process has implications for the efficiency of OMB's management planning component (the "M" side of OMB) and for other systematic pursuits of institutional reform. But such reforms tend to require the approval of Congress. Even if the votes could be obtained in the legislative branch, they might come only at the cost of a quid pro quo unwanted by the White House. The opportunity to imitate Reagan by achieving instant gratification by appointing loyal ideologues may prove irresistible to future presidents-elect.

ADMINISTRATIVE STRATEGY

By learning from the experience of three previous administrations, President Reagan and his aides were able to avoid the repetition of deficiencies in his predecessors' regulatory review programs. To the Reagan circle of advisers, regulatory policy was too important to let drift.[56]

Convinced that regulatory relief would never be as high on Congress's agenda as it was on the president's, the Reagan administration rolled out a program authorized by executive order rather than a legislative agenda, which might have led to permanent statutory authority.[57] OIRA's administrator, Christopher C. DeMuth, explained:

> The history of deregulation is that administrative reform is a necessary prerequisite to statutory reform. Before Congress itself will act, external changes are required to dislodge accumulated interests in the status quo and to assure the doubtful of the economy's ability to continue functioning in the absence of federal controls.... If we are to achieve major statutory reform in the last two years of President Reagan's first term, we must first build a solid foundation of administrative deregulation.[58]

Once Reagan abolished the Council on Wage and Price Stability (CWPS) and placed oversight authority in OIRA, he had, in fact, jettisoned the only statutory authority that preexisted his presidency. As shown in chapter 2, it was the prerogative of CWPS to intervene in regulatory proceedings by inserting comments into the public record that required an explicit response from the agency. Reagan's decision was a gamble with advantages and disadvantages. But the Reagan administration, which seems in many ways to have preferred short-term political benefits to long-term planning, succeeded in achieving a one-time, step-change deregulation that brought it satisfaction.

Administration officials often sought legislation after the fact to validate and institutionalize the regulation clearance operation. They supported S.1080, the proposed Laxalt-Leahy Regulatory Reform Act of 1982, which passed the Senate but not the House. But the partisan appearance of the OIRA review process created much distaste in Congress, and by 1986 influential members of Congress were seeking to defund OIRA. Furthermore, there was no momentum to confer statutory authority on OIRA's regulation clearance program. Therefore, a plea from OMB director Miller—"We have supported and continue to support legislation that would explicitly authori[ze] review of regulations by the Executive Office of the President"[59]—to a Senate subcommittee in 1986 came at a time when members of Congress were more interested in modulating OMB's influence than in enhancing its status.

The Reagan administration's program was distinguished from those of his predecessors by virtue of its ubiquitousness and depth. Whereas Richard M. Nixon's, Gerald R. Ford's, and Carter's oversight programs were selective and in some ways haphazard in their impact on contemporary regulatory proposals, in principle, the Reagan program clearly targeted every major regulation for scrutiny.[60] Accordingly, few designers of regulatory policies in the federal regulatory agencies failed to be cognizant of the inevitability of OIRA scrutiny, and proposals that *were* generated tended to be more sensitive to the Reagan ideology. This awareness was a key factor in getting regulatory policy to mirror Reagan's tastes to the extent that it did. Goodman and Wrightson report that their research confirms this proposition. "After six years in operation the Reagan regulatory reform program has clearly been *institutionalized.* The goals have filtered down through the bureaucracy and, to a remarkable extent, they have been accepted across regulatory agencies."[61]

Executive Order 12291 required agencies to proceed with rule-making efforts only when they could demonstrate that net benefits to society were being maximized while net costs were being minimized. Although this standard may have been difficult to achieve, it was easy to comprehend. HHS senior health policy specialist Jacquelyn Y. White found that the Reagan administration's regulatory program contrasted most sharply with the Carter program in its clarity of purpose. "The Carter Administration's objectives were not so clearly defined. You had to interpret them from speeches. . . . The Reagan Administration has a *process*. . . . A 'blueprint' has existed from the outset." She added that, by making good use of think tank recommendations, such as those provided by the Heritage Foundation, the administration "hit the ground running" and took advantage of the honeymoon period to launch the aggressive regulatory relief program.[62]

The Reagan administration's major schematic approach was to centralize power in the EOP. In contrast, the approach of previous administrations had been to operate programs as a check on otherwise autonomous agency rule making. This centralization facilitated Reagan's plan to force federal regulation into conformity with his policies.[63] However, Reagan neither eliminated the structures which, according to law, generate new regulations[64] nor did he succeed in institutionalizing his review program in statutory form. This raised concerns—or hopes, depending on one's perspective—that the Reagan format would not long outlive the Reagan administration.

RATIONALE FOR REGULATORY RELIEF

In defending the creation of a regulatory relief program and its location in OIRA, Reagan administration spokespersons, their supporters, and, occasionally, even a critic cited a number of rationales that do not bear the taint of partisanship.

Advocates insisted that OIRA was a strategic place for *coordinating* rule making across regulatory agencies and solving problems that could not be addressed by individual agencies. Former OIRA administrator Wendy L. Gramm said, "OIRA is like all other parts of OMB—partly umpire, partly coordinator." She added that OIRA, like OMB, contributed independent judgments and reevaluated judgments made elsewhere in the bureaucracy.[65]

Alan B. Morrison, a critic of the Reagan regulatory relief program, concedes that an oversight program in OMB could promote good regulation.

> I do not dispute that OMB can perform some useful functions in the rulemaking process. Its role in coordinating related proceedings between agencies and in assuring that relevant scientific information, cost data, and alternative approaches are shared between agencies, are entirely proper. And to the extent that OMB review can help ensure that agencies give careful consideration to the principal comments submitted in a rulemaking, that is also an appropriate goal. Similarly it is proper for OMB to insist that agencies take a hard look at the necessity for a rule, provided OMB does so in an even-handed manner.[66]

Advocates maintained that OIRA was more likely to inject considerations of *efficiency* into the regulatory process, which regulatory agencies might not do on their own initiative. Insofar as rule-making procedures are an "imperfect compromise between competing concerns and expectations of administrative discretion, expertise, political accountability, and due process,"[67] the OIRA review process was touted by Reagan administration partisans as mitigating that imperfection. The administration hoped that the commitment to economy and efficiency that OMB was expected to display in the budget process could be applied by analogy to regulatory review.

OIRA spokespersons credit OIRA with having the capacity to apply *special expertise* to the regulatory process without introducing the distortion of partisanship. OIRA desk officer Scott H. Jacobs said, "People at OIRA are professional career staff. We try to come up with as wide a range of situations as possible. Sometimes, we proposed tightening regulations." He explained that OIRA staff members did not perceive their roles as deregulatory. "I don't view my role as being ideologically biased," Jacobs said, insisting that OIRA staff members did not discuss their personal ideological viewpoints. "We are not Republican operatives out to destroy regulations. [The accusation] is not borne out by the evidence. There is no pattern of regulations being knocked down systematically." Jacobs cited the efforts of OIRA deputy administrator James B. MacRae Jr. "to insulate staff from political discussions."[68]

Former OIRA administrators DeMuth and Douglas H. Ginsburg wrote that OIRA analysts had an important advantage over their counterparts in the agencies. The responsibility to review and analyze regulatory proposals originating in all of the agencies gave OIRA a unique perspective. The two former administration officials recalled how OMB helped the Federal Aviation Administration to replace its traditional procedure for transferring airport landing slots (which required the unanimous consent of all competitors serving the airport) with a market format under which slots could be bought and sold. OMB devised the recommendation based on previously successful market-based reforms adopted by the EPA, the Department of Agriculture, the Department of the Interior, and the Federal Energy Regulatory Commission. "The OMB staff is more expert than the agencies in one field—the field of regulation itself," DeMuth and Ginsburg contended.[69]

Efforts of past administrations to improve the rule-making process so that its product met a higher standard of some kind all proved to have a common characteristic: These oversight programs attempted to intervene near the end of the life cycle of a regulatory proposal. Believing *earlier intervention* to be necessary, OIRA administrator Ginsburg said that under EO 12291 the review process "often comes too late." Agencies worked on the proposed regulation for a long time, and then "we get ourselves in a confrontation with the agency over the end product."[70] President Reagan agreed:

> Developing a government rule often involves years of studies, hearings, and intermediate decisions before even a proposed rule is issued for public com-

> ment. Frequently, senior agency officials are involved only after these earlier activities have greatly narrowed the options for final action and precluded effective Administration policy review.[71]

OIRA officials claimed the existence of an effective stratagem perpetrated for many years by low-level agency officials. When a regulatory proposal was considered in an agency, an agency official might float the trial balloon in a congressional hearing, and then hastily commit his or her agency to promulgate a rule implementing the proposal. OIRA intervention would come too late, because Congress would expect the agency to go forward without further analysis.[72] To rectify this problem, President Reagan issued Executive Order 12498, "Regulatory Planning Process," on January 4, 1985. The order required executive agencies to establish a regulatory agenda and to submit it to OMB. The agenda had to identify rule making "planned or underway," including the "development of documents that may influence, [may] anticipate, or could lead to the commencement of rulemaking proceedings at a later date." A key provision required agencies to "explain how [planned regulations] are consistent with the Administration's regulatory principles."

Morrison concedes that the theory underlying EO 12498 had value. "No sensible person can be opposed to planning or to allocating resources meaningfully in order to insure that the most serious problems receive attention first." If the order were designed to restrain agencies from developing remedies that they were incapable of carrying out—for financial, manpower, or legal reasons—it would be defensible.[73]

Reagan's advisers also looked to the regulatory relief strategy to contribute to the "New Federalism," by allowing some regulatory implementation to *devolve onto state and local governments*. The Council of Economic Advisers offered this rationale:

> Regulation should take place at the appropriate level of government.... National standards have been too severe in some regions, while being too lax in others. Federal regulation should be limited to situations where the actions in one State have substantial external effects in other States, constitutional rights are involved, or interstate commerce would be significantly disrupted by differences in local regulation.[74]

Like other facets of Reagan's "New Federalism," the regulatory relief approach was designed to fortify state governments with legal authority while relieving the national government of certain expenditures. (For example, the EPA announced in 1981 that it would "zero fund" regulatory efforts by state governments within four years, a plan that was never carried out.)[75] The state governments were left with the choice of raising additional revenues or underfunding the transferred authority. The effectiveness of regulation suffered insofar as new revenue sources were difficult to obtain. The fear by business leaders that fifty separate sources of state-level regulation would generate more compliance costs than one central source faded as underfunded state regulation proved to be toothless most of the time.

Reagan's aides promised an attractive array of benefits, such as better coordination, more efficient regulations, and the application of unique expertise in regulatory analysis. In many circles, the promise attracted early support for OIRA or at least a willingness to tolerate, observe, and evaluate the operation of regulatory review. Nevertheless, potential sympathizers with the review process were troubled by the persistent suspicion that the true purpose of the program was to engraft a monolithic, conservative, proindustry standard onto the entire regulatory system, notwithstanding the will of Congress and the public. By politicizing regulatory review, the administration sacrificed the nonpartisan legitimacy of regulatory reform and legitimated inevitable partisan challenges to the innovations. Ultimately, the regulatory review process served the cause of rational policy analysis less well than it had the potential to do. Its principal result was to enhance the incumbent president's influence.

LEADERSHIP AND ATTITUDE

OIRA's top officials displayed an arrogant attitude in the early days of the agency. Veiled threats that recalcitrant agency officials would pay a heavy price—presumably dismissal—and OIRA's self-declared status as "the toughest kid on the block" ingratiated OIRA with no one in the bureaucracy. Furthermore, OIRA seemed ubiquitous. "They were constantly meddling," one agency official recalled.[76]

Many veteran agency staff members were rankled by their newly acquired supervision by OIRA staff, whose credentials they found suspect. A Senate report quoted an OIRA desk officer who supervised EPA regulations.

> I didn't have the technical expertise to work on EPA issues. I would receive studies on both sides of [a toxic substance] issue and I just didn't know [how to evaluate the conflicting arguments]. I knew I would do well from my boss' perspective if I got rid of rules on [the toxic substance]. . . . A good desk officer does change a rule. To make your mark, you get changes made. I felt kind of funny handing [my supervisor] back a rule saying it was consis-

> tent [with EO 12291]. . . . It would have been very difficult to advocate EPA's position.[77]

An agency official said resentfully, "GS-12 and -13 budget analysts and GS-14 and -15 division directors are calling with orders to get rid of regulations or to make regulations written by OMB."[78] Another agency official complained about "a 22-year-old M.B.A." at OIRA who would call to speak directly to the agency administrator or assistant administrators.[79]

The reward system did not seem to exhibit much in the way of rationality. While OIRA desk officers were not favored with cash awards for cost-cutting recommendations, OIRA deputy administrator MacRae was collecting tens of thousands of dollars in awards for such recommendations.[80] For their trouble, many of the desk officers, whose workloads were enormous, got burned out,[81] although many OIRA administrators and desk officers found the experience useful as a stepping stone in their careers.[82]

The atmosphere at OIRA changed once the early zealotry wore off and political damage from the confrontational posture was assessed. S. Jay Plager, the last OIRA administrator of the Reagan era, was not reticent in admitting that OIRA had acquired an unflattering image. OIRA needed to "cast off the Darth Vader image as much as possible without sacrificing presidential prerogative." He attributed the "Darth Vader image" to two factors: First, OMB director David A. Stockman admitted that he manipulated budget figures. "I'm sorry that's the way he ran OMB," Plager said, but he insisted that OMB was not operating that way in the post-Stockman era. Second, Plager said there was a genuine, irreconcilable tension between OMB and OIRA's role as the representative of the president and the role of the agencies, which responded to other motivations. To tell an agency administrator, "You can't do that; it will embarrass the president," sometimes seemed to act as a provocation.

Plager pledged to run OIRA in an open, responsible manner so that its damaged reputation would be mended.[83] He left OIRA when President Bush appointed him to the Federal Circuit of the United States Court of Appeals. The position of OIRA administrator remained vacant for the remainder of the Bush era, with MacRae serving as acting administrator of the office.

4 Concerns About Implementation

APPEASEMENT OF BUSINESS

Reagan administration critics, especially social action interest groups, vehemently denounced the review process conducted by the Office of Information and Regulatory Affairs (OIRA) as representing the ultimate concession to the business community—i.e., the elimination of regulations that would otherwise constrain its operations. In 1981, George C. Eads wondered aloud whether the new administration would really "coordinate" rule making or would simply be a "sharpshooter, taking aim at this or that politically sensitive regulation." He predicted then that OIRA would opt for the sharpshooter approach.[1] By the next year, advocates of regulation concluded that Eads's prediction was all too accurate. Robert J. Pleasure, associate general counsel for the United Brotherhood of Carpenters and Joiners of America, testified angrily in 1982 concerning action taken by the Task Force on Regulatory Relief targeting a regulation that limited the depth to which commercial divers could be directed to dive.

> We heard the campaign rhetoric about split toilet seats, about the height of fire extinguishers in the hallway, about all the unnecessary regulations, and the carpenters union has worked with [the Occupational Safety and Health Administration, OSHA] to try to advise as to how those regulations can be made less burdensome. We never suspected that the standard that covered commercial diving would be the first item on the agenda when the thrust of the President's review was directed toward burdensome regulation, unnecessary regulations in low hazard industry.

> [Q. Rep. M. Caldwell Butler (R-Va.):] When you say first on the agenda you mean one among the first 30?
>
> [A.] No, Congressman Butler. I mean the only safety standard targeted by the task force.[2]

Eads compared the Carter and Reagan regulatory review programs and concluded that there was a major difference in the "burden of proof." Under the Carter program, the burden of proof lay with senior White House aides, who needed to prove—possibly to President Jimmy Carter himself—that a proposed regulation was not cost effective. Ronald Reagan's Executive Order 12291, in contrast, called on agencies to bear the burden of proof by demonstrating that proposed regulations satisfied a cost-benefit test. This shift, of course, placed regulatory proposals in a more tenuous position.[3] OIRA deputy administrator Jim J. Tozzi confirmed the inclination to reject regulations, confessing that the Office of Management and Budget (OMB) had a "loving bias against regulation . . . a rebuttable presumption against regulation." However, Tozzi attributed this bias to neutral competence, not to probusiness bias.[4] An OSHA staff member went further: "They'd like to have no regulation at all," he protested.[5]

The plethora of tools used by OMB to oversee regulation—including EO 12291 and the Paperwork Reduction Act—prompted Tozzi to describe OMB as "sort of a full-service bank" for agency rule making.[6] Thomas Rollins, staff director and chief counsel for the Senate Committee on Labor and Human Resources, complained, "Some of OMB's activities are fraudulent, like those conducted under the Paperwork Reduction Act. It's cost reduction for the administration's friends."[7] The analytical legitimacy of cost-benefit analysis appears to have been a charade; Tozzi acknowledged that costs and benefits were not actually compared: "Let's say you had a real bad environmental [regulation] that didn't cost much. Maybe we should—all that good stuff—but we didn't. The cost was the alarm bell." And he acknowledged, "Of course, this isn't benefit-cost. . . . We're just here to represent the President."[8] Michael D. Reagan makes the intriguing observation that when Vice President George Bush's office announced in 1983 that the operations of the Task Force on Regulatory Relief had been suspended, the "claims of success were based on money ostensibly saved for consumers and business firms, and not on an improvement in net benefit ratios resulting from hard-nosed" cost-benefit analysis.[9]

OIRA staff members defended the implementation of regulatory review as basically even-handed and neutral. One staff member recalled that OMB director David A. Stockman would occasionally request OIRA to make "an unjustifiable change" in a regulatory proposal. In contrast, as the Reagan administration progressed to its final year, the OIRA staff member estimated, "99.8 percent of what OIRA does is apolitical." The remaining 0.2 percent he conceded to the inevitably political nature of every process in government.[10]

Jefferson B. Hill, chief of OIRA's Commerce and Lands Branch, citing OIRA's "instinctive bias towards neutral competence," also denied that OIRA was acting out of probusiness bias. "In OIRA, all men are created equally," he asserted. "Where else does 'one man-one vote' apply?" He said it is illegal to inquire about the political affiliation of an applicant for work at OIRA. "If I'm going to be able to work for the next [president]," Hill said in the last year of the Reagan administration's existence, "I have to be neutral." He insisted that the best bet was still to entrust the Executive Office of the President with regulatory oversight in order to benefit from the president's national perspective. "The president is the only [official] who has everybody as a constituent."[11] James B. MacRae Jr., acting OIRA administrator, also claimed neutrality: "I am a career employee. I have been there a long time under different Presidents—Republicans and Democrats. I have never been given instructions of an ideological partisan nature. And if I were, I would quit."[12]

Of course, a civil servant can have nonpartisan, neutral intentions and still produce policies that strike observers as manifestly "political." In fact, that happens as a matter of course. President Reagan's Republican predecessor, Richard M. Nixon, was not unique in attributing partisanship to civil servants. Nixon loathed the "Democratic-infested" federal bureaucracy and sought to put Republican civil servants in the place of Democratic civil servants to reverse what he perceived as partisan-based recalcitrance.[13] Although civil servants may initially approach their jobs with no preconceived notions about policy, they are trained to learn and repeat "programmed behavior," which the manager's successor will find difficult to change.[14] Therefore, civil servants in OIRA could be taught by their managers to assume roles that had other than neutral impact on policy. Although President Bill Clinton may prefer policies that are diametrically opposed to those of Reagan and George Bush, and may order OIRA to reverse its course, the neutral civil servants might be hard pressed to adapt to the new arrangement. In short, the instruction, "Do it this way," is at least as effective as the partisan directive, "Act like a Republican." It seems clear that instructions from OMB director David A. Stockman, OIRA administrators James C. Miller III and Christopher C. DeMuth, and OIRA deputy administrator Tozzi to "do it this way" produced behaviors among OIRA's civil servants that had a distinct probusiness flavor.

SUPPRESSION OF SOCIAL REGULATION

"After Ford and Carter," OIRA official Hill said, "only social regulation was left."[15]

Eads and Fix describe the factions that contended for primacy among those who wanted to see a reduction in social regulation at the dawn of the Reagan era. The libertarian group called for eliminating all social regulation in favor of market devices and other instruments of nonregulatory control—for instance, civil litigation. A more pragmatic group, which included most business people, was offended more by the volume of social regulations than by the concept.

> They favored virtually any remedy that promised to reduce the burdens of regulation, including a stronger, more effective presidential oversight role; placing a cap on regulation's costs through a "regulatory budget"; mandatory cost-benefit standards for regulation; and changes in social regulatory statutes to eliminate what were considered to be some of their more unrealistic goals.[16]

Economists formed the core of a third group, which touted social regulation as a remedy for "market failure" and preferred incentive regulation to command-and-control regulation.[17]

The Reagan aides involved in the clearance process collided with a "motherhood-and-apple-pie" issue when, in the spring of 1985, they disapproved a Public Health Service (PHS) survey on the relationship between federal funding cuts and infant mortality rates. According to reports, OIRA used its authority under EO 12498 to kill the study. While no written record of the disapproval ever surfaced, the study was known to be a part of PHS's draft regulatory program. Plocher of OMB Watch reported, "Administration sources have acknowledged that OMB quashed the study."[18] At an August 8, 1985, news conference, OIRA administrator Douglas H. Ginsburg insisted that the PHS had withdrawn the proposal after OIRA identified some problems in it. But an OMB Watch document released in opposition to Ginsburg's ill-fated appointment to the Supreme Court noted, "A different impression about the demise of the proposal is found in a 3/21/85 PHS memo in which it was noted that OIRA had already said the proposal would not be approved."[19]

In this manner, and according to many other accounts, the social regulatory agencies absorbed the brunt of the Reagan administration's program to deregulate. The first Reagan budget slashed funding for major social regulatory agencies, in accordance with an OMB briefing document promising that "fewer regulators will necessarily result in fewer regulations and less harassment of the regulated."[20] The Center for the Study of American Business reported an 11.0-percent decrease in the number of permanent full-time positions for twenty-eight regulatory agencies from 1981 to 1983. Six consumer safety and health agencies sustained a decrease of 14.5 percent.[21] Indeed, several regulatory agencies became incapable of effective action once they had sustained deep budget cuts in the first two years of the Reagan administration. Agency staff became frustrated and demoralized, and reluctant to innovate regulatory designs that would be virtually doomed from the outset.

OIRA's Hill considered the outcry over the Reagan administration's treatment of social regulation predictable. Social regulation policies involve emotional issues with emotional symbols. Any paring back of social regulation can always be paired with some anecdote of how "somebody died" as a result. "Little Susie died from Cause X," some critic might say. "Let's make sure it doesn't happen again." The result was that "every time somebody dies, the agency [is] on the defensive." Thus, every time OIRA reduced regulatory costs, social action interest groups raised a hue and cry about the mean-spirited regulatory policy.[22]

Hill seems to be suggesting that any attempt to roll back social regulation will automatically be subject to such outcries. This is even more true because Congress was on record as supporting the continuation, not the suppression, of social regulations, and public opinion was in agreement. The argument over the review program's effect on social regulation had much to do with whether the Constitution's "take care" clause[23] required the president to facilitate the intent of a statute or to restrain agencies from implementing it pending exhaustive study within the executive branch. Representative Mike Synar (D-Okla.) likened the Reagan administration's restraint in executing social regulation statutes to President Nixon's provocative impoundments of appropriations.[24] Thus, the Reagan White House consciously placed itself on a collision course with the coalition that had accomplished the enactment of a plethora of social regulation statutes. Reagan's aides understood that political capital would be expended in this controversy and were prepared to bear the expense in exchange for the appreciation they expected from their industrial constituency.

THREATS, SECRECY, AND DENIAL OF DUE PROCESS

Complaints

The implementation of the Reagan administration's regulatory review program led to allegations and suspicions that regulatory agency officials were threatened into compliance with OIRA directives and that the process occurred in secrecy, imperiling rights to due process.

OMB threatened a number of agency officials with dismissal if they defied decisions disapproving proposed regulations. The classic account from former Environmental Protection Agency (EPA) administrator Anne Gorsuch Burford tells of such a threat, issued by OIRA deputy administrator Tozzi to EPA officials:

> About halfway through my time at EPA we found ourselves in a real crunch. We were under a court order to release some pollutant guidelines for pharmaceutical manufacturers. We had done our work, and then submitted the guidelines to OMB for their review as required. The manufacturers had put on a lot of pressure for certain changes, which we had resisted, but the court deadline was swiftly approaching, and there was still no word from OMB. Finally, they told us that [the proposed regulations] weren't approved, though OMB would not put it in writing, as required by the Executive Order, which might have allowed us to buy some time from the judge. This despite the fact that an Executive Order said that if OMB held anything past a certain length of time, they had to put their objections in writing.
>
> All Tozzi would tell us was, "They're not approved." That continued to be OMB's response right up to the last minute. It was the night before the deadline, my last day to obey the court order and sign and release the regs. It got so dark in my office that we could see the moon outside. Finally, John Daniel [EPA chief of staff] said, "Anne, I recommend you sign the regs without OMB's approval."
>
> We called OMB to tell them what we were going to do. I called Stockman, who had surprisingly little to say, and John called Tozzi. Tozzi didn't say anything for a few moments after he'd heard the news. Then he said in a quiet voice, "Daniel, I hope you people know that there's a price to pay for this, and you've only begun to pay."[25]

In various ways, OMB kept pressure on political appointees throughout the bureaucracy to toe the line on administrative policy. In 1986, a former high-ranking official of OMB said, "We didn't require everyone to submit speeches for approval, but one might argue that an administration official who spoke out in a way inconsistent with administration policy would sooner or later hear from OMB about it."[26]

This arrangement created concern in Congress, because it had deliberately vested discretionary rule-making power in agency heads rather than in its rival, the president. Senator Albert Gore Jr. (D-Tenn.) thundered: "The Director of the OMB's Office of Information and Regulatory Affairs cynically tells the public that agency heads will still be making the final decisions on regulations, when he really knows that people who defy his office will be fired."[27]

The undue pressure on officials was seen to have the potential to redefine the concept of delegating legislative power—without the consent of Congress.

Perhaps nothing has sullied OIRA's—and even OMB's—reputation as much as the plethora of eyewitness accounts and credible suspicions that OIRA's regulatory review process created preferential treatment regarding access for the president's constituency in the business community. Representative Gerry Sikorski (D-Minn.) described OMB as a "back-door conduit by which industry can lobby in secret to save its own selfish interests."[28]

The OIRA's supposed passion for secrecy is illustrated in the hearsay evidence that OIRA tried to keep its activities off the record. During OSHA rule making concerning maintenance of grain elevators to prevent grain dust explosions, OIRA officials reportedly insisted on minimal written communication between OIRA and OSHA and prohibited note taking at meetings. According to Deborah Berkowitz, an official of the AFL-CIO's Food and Allied Services Trades Department, OMB officials would communicate their positions to OSHA over the telephone in order to create no memoranda. "In fact," Berkowitz related, "in one instance, rather than present a 27-page written rebuttal from OSHA to OMB, OSHA itself [through Department of Labor deputy solicitor Francis Lilly] orally transmitted the information to OMB at OMB's insistence."[29] OMB director Miller denied the allegation.[30] Berkowitz also claimed that OIRA contacts deliberately took place off the record in a men's room.[31]

The allegation reminds us of Tozzi's notorious explanation that he "didn't want to leave fingerprints," to ensure that his activities could not be traced.[32] "Very little is placed in writing," a social regulation official confirmed. "When there *is* communication, it is hard to tell where it's coming from."[33]

An official at the Department of Health and Human Services observed the difficulty of determining the exact source of OMB decisions. Underlings at OMB always claimed that their superiors were making the decisions; superiors declined to admit they had made those decisions. However, the superiors also tended to make no denials of responsibility either. The result was a shell game of evasion of responsibility.[34]

Many observers felt that the OIRA regulatory review procedures would have a deleterious effect on the due process rights of affected groups and individuals. Representative Dennis E. Eckart (D-Ohio) decried the impact on HHS rule making: "Given its druthers, the Federal Department of Health and Human Services would just as soon make its regulations in a secretive, dimly-lit back room and spring them full-blown and relatively impregnable from public uproar."[35] Advocates of social regulation felt frozen out of a process that appeared to offer a welcome mat only to large business interests. Attorney William Warfield Ross advised: "Now more than ever . . . the race will be to the swift, to the enterprising and to those with access to the levers of power, not only in the Congress and the regulatory agencies, but also in the presidential office."[36]

When an OIRA official assured Representative Synar that anybody—even Synar's parents—had access to OIRA, the congressman read a list of business representatives who had visited OIRA on a certain issue and countered, "It does not look as if my mom and dad are getting in there."[37]

In the 1986 District Court case of *Environmental Defense Fund v. Thomas*,[38] concerning EPA regulations governing underground tanks, OMB made a concerted effort to prevent any discovery by attorneys from the Environmental Defense Fund (EDF). OMB's request for a court order prohibiting EDF discovery was rejected. Claiming executive privilege, OMB then refused to provide documents revealing its role in changing the proposed regulations. OMB issued a gag order to the former director of EPA's Office of Solid Waste. According to EDF senior attorney Robert V. Percival, OMB asked the court to order suppression of EDF's brief to avoid disclosure of OMB's actions. OMB placed its own brief on the public record. "OMB apparently wanted its version of the facts to be available to the public, but not EDF's."[39]

Some observers have questioned the completeness of the collection of documents in OIRA's public reading room. OMB promised that communications from outside entities would be available there for inspection by any citizen. Erik D. Olson visited the reading room, asking to see the "public docket." This was the result: "When the author [Olson] requested access to the docket, he first was told that no such docket existed." When Olson cited the testimony of OMB officials that there was a "public docket," "he was shown a thin set of seven folders containing comments on as many EPA rules. . . . Pursuant to the author's [Freedom of Information Act] request for any materials

OMB had received from outside parties regarding a number of EPA rules under review, the Office produced scores of documents, almost exclusively from industry representatives, none of which had been in the OMB 'docket.'"[40]

Another participant in the regulatory system, who requested anonymity, told of problems that he and others experienced in gaining access to the OIRA reading room. He claimed that once OIRA knew that one of its critics wanted access, it would make the interaction a procedural obstacle course. One ruse, this source said, involved the guarded entrance to the New Executive Office Building; the component of the Executive Office of the President granting access had to authorize the visitor's entry in advance. Reportedly, OIRA neglected on frequent occasions to place such authority in the security computer system, or entered an incorrect version of the visitor's name or social security number. The guards dutifully denied entrance until the visitor straightened out the problem over the telephone. All but the most determined individuals eventually threw in the towel.[41]

Houck quotes a "former high-ranking OMB official" as admitting in 1986: "Shredding testimony?—we did plenty of that."[42]

An ongoing complaint was that meetings held in OMB with favored interest groups were not announced, either before or after the fact. "The open door is meaningless unless you know a decision is being made," said Natural Resources Defense Council (NRDC) senior attorney Frances Dubrowski.[43] Gary D. Bass of OMB Watch reported that Scott H. Jacobs, OIRA desk officer for OSHA and the Mine Safety and Health Administration, routinely met with business representatives about proposed regulations he was reviewing.[44]

Documents exchanged between OIRA and EPA have shown that instructions for regulatory changes issued by OIRA bore a remarkable resemblance to demands being made by industry at the same time, according to a House subcommittee counsel, Patrick M. McLain. "OMB was just a conduit for industry," he claimed.[45] OMB Watch complained that OIRA desk officer Timothy Hunt, while reviewing a pesticide manufacturing census proposed by EPA in 1988, called a meeting for industry officials to provide him with input, while not inviting the NRDC, which had expressed interest.[46]

In summary, OMB's contribution to the rule-making process may have substantially influenced the results of a regulation proceeding. But, according to Viscusi,[47] OMB's hidden analysis may not have been carefully formulated and could thus have led to an inferior result. Also, this process—as an administrative and not a conspicuous legislative device—created potentially substantial changes in policy without the public airing of the matter through discussion and debate.[48] Finally, EO 12498 is arguably a political far more than an analytical tool in that it allows OMB to block an idea deemed inconsistent with the president's policy orientation. "Before any cost/benefit analysis, impact statements, or debate on the merits of a policy, OMB makes a political judgment call," said Gary Bass of OMB Watch.[49]

OMB Responses

For their part, OMB officials deny that there was a pattern of threats and reprisals, and have even seemed bemused by the suggestion. Called to a hearing of the Manpower and Housing Subcommittee of the House Government Operations Committee in 1982, OIRA administrator DeMuth insisted that agency heads were free to exercise their discretion regardless of OIRA's position.

> [Q. Rep. Cardiss Collins (D-Ill.):] When OMB disagrees with an agency and feels that a standard does not comply with the cost-benefit analysis, based on Executive orders, could that agency actually proceed to implement it, or target a standard anyway?
>
> [A. DeMuth:] Sure.
>
> [Q.:] It could. Do you know of any that have done that?
>
> [A.:] No.[50]

In similar testimony, Ginsburg made the same declaration of laissez-faire. "We can't make a decision for any agency. Indeed, the only thing that we can do, if we can't reach an agreement about the interpretation of evidence, is return the rule to the agency for reconsideration. We can't prevent them from going forward and promulgating a regulation."[51] Asked whether OIRA ordered an EPA official to change a regulatory proposal, OIRA deputy administrator Robert P. Bedell responded that the merit of the change itself had to be deemed the more important issue. "Who the hell cares how it occurred?"[52]

OMB has consistently denied the charges that its regulatory review procedures deprive any individuals of due process or create circumstances of secrecy that do not already have timeless precedent in bureaucratic culture. DeMuth insisted that the Reagan-era procedures differed from those of previous administrations in their unprecedented openness. During an interrogation by Representative Collins, DeMuth declared:

> I think that by any measure the approach of the Reagan administration to regulatory policies is far and away more open than that of any administration. First of all, all of the facts and analyses that go into any decision are on the record.

> When the White House, the Vice President, and members of the administration believe that there are problems with the regulation sufficient that it ought to be considered on the record, it is not just something that boom, suddenly appears out in an agency someday. We have a press release on the matter and give a brief description of why we think that the agency should reconsider it.
>
> I do not know that any other administration has ever done that.[53]

OMB director Stockman advised the executive agencies on June 11, 1981, that OMB would recommend to any groups or individuals interested in regulatory proceedings that they contact the agencies directly. OMB indicated that, in its opinion, the agencies were in charge of rule making.

A Senior Executive Service employee, Bedell had been OMB's deputy general counsel, supervising OIRA's legal affairs and defending the office against legal challenges to EO 12291. He became OIRA's deputy administrator in June 1983 and looked into the matter of unequal access. He recalls that he didn't know who, if anyone, was influencing OIRA's staff and that he tried to find out. No suspects were ever identified, but Bedell announced that all discussion of regulations with those outside the federal government would henceforth be prohibited for all OIRA employees subordinate to the administrator. Written documents would be made available to outside parties upon request. "We had no desire to keep them secret," Bedell noted.

But Bedell insisted that, as a courtesy, anyone contacting OIRA was allowed to speak to some representative of the office, and all written communications were received graciously. Otherwise, the situation would be dysfunctional, he said, insofar as citizens do not expect to be repelled from any government agency with which they choose to interact.

Bedell bristled good-naturedly at accusations that he and OIRA had close contact with lobbyists. The most frequent allegation identified B. J. Pigg of the Asbestos Information Association, who sought OMB support against asbestos regulations planned by EPA.[54] Bedell recalled that Pigg corresponded regularly with OIRA economists John F. Morrall III and Gail Coad, and these letters came to the attention of congressional committees, which interpreted the letters as proving an unholy alliance.

"Pigg's letters all came out of the OIRA file," Bedell said. He found it ironic that the evidence for supposed conduit communications was all compiled through the reading room process.

"What they [OIRA critics] don't believe is that we are telling the truth when I say *under oath* [—and here he reviews the penalties for perjury—] that we are *not* receiving telephone calls" from business lobbyists. Asked about claims by some lobbyists that they had influence with OIRA through telephone calls, he speculated that such individuals made such claims to appear influential so that they could sign up more clients in the business community. Thus, they could say, "We have access to OIRA." "But they're lying!" Bedell said emphatically.[55]

Continuing suspicion of OIRA collusion with business motivated OIRA to experiment with new procedures for reviewing EPA regulations, beginning in April 1985. The reform included the following provisions: (1) Copies of correspondence from outside interests sent to OIRA on the topic of EPA rule making would be sent to EPA, usually within five days of receipt; (2) whenever the administrator or deputy administrator of OIRA scheduled meetings with persons outside the federal government on matters of EPA regulation, OIRA would invite EPA officials to attend the meetings; (3) OMB interventions would become part of the formal rule-making record.[56]

By late 1985, congressional anger had been kindled to levels adequate to threaten OIRA's reauthorization. In hearings, members of Congress probed reports of OIRA collusion with the business community. Senator David F. Durenberger (R-Minn.) interrogated OMB director Miller about AFL-CIO official Deborah Berkowitz's accusation that the OMB conducted a secret meeting in a men's room to avoid discovery.

> [Q.] You do not have to go to the men's wash room? We had some testimony here and some evidence of some information that was passed in a men's washroom some place here in Washington.
>
> [A.] Probably this poor man was given wrong directions.
>
> [Q.] Do you mean that it should have been the women's restroom?
>
> [A.] No. We now have a public reading room at which the public can read the written information we receive from persons outside the Federal Government.
>
> We also limit who can talk to persons who are not employed by the Federal Government. In OIRA, only the Administrator or the Deputy Administrator or those explicitly authorized by them may meet with a person outside of the executive branch for the purpose of discussing a rule subject to Executive Order 12291.
>
> In opinions approving the relevant Executive order, the Department of Justice reviewed our procedures and concluded that they are, indeed, lawful. Not one rule, not one rule, in more than 12,000 that we have reviewed

has [ever] been overturned by a court because of our review procedure. Not one rule in over 12,000 has been successfully challenged in court because of our review procedures.

[Q.] You are trying to be forceful on that point?

[A.] Yes; I do realize that Executive orders and OIRA's role are before the courts in two cases—*Public Citizen v. Roland* [*sic*] and *EDF v. EPA and OMB.* I say this, and I emphasize it, Mr. Chairman, because in 1981, I heard allegations that all of this was [unconstitutional], was unlawful, et cetera, but there has not, 5 years later, been a single successful challenge to the lawfulness of the Executive order or our review procedures, despite our having conducted reviews of 12,000 rules.[57]

The experimental rules became permanent in 1986 when it became apparent that OIRA would be defunded if it resisted.[58]

PAPERWORK REDUCTION

The successor to OMB's Office of Regulatory and Information Policy, OIRA was assigned the role of reducing paperwork burdens under the Paperwork Reduction Act of 1980. OIRA's charter was quickly expanded to include execution of regulatory relief under Executive Order 12291. The paperwork reduction mission, as a statutory mandate, would ordinarily be deemed legally superior to the regulatory review process, which was founded on the vague inherent power of the presidency. However, critics charged that the Reagan administration was distorting the purpose of paperwork reduction. OMB Watch said: "Since enactment of the [Paperwork Reduction] Act in 1980, OIRA has been repeatedly criticized for using its paperwork powers primarily as a tool to reduce federal regulations."[59] Bass of OMB Watch complained that OIRA's use of its paperwork reduction authority revealed that the office had clearly taken aim against social regulation for policy, not paperwork, reasons.

> OIRA has used its paperwork powers in a disproportionate manner by targeting certain agencies for drastic paperwork reductions, while leaving other agencies practically to their own devices when it comes to imposing paperwork burden on the public.... Agencies with the least paperwork burden on the public—[Housing and Urban Development], EPA, and Labor (particularly OSHA and [the Mine Safety and Health Administration (MSHA)]—have the hardest time getting paperwork through OIRA. Yet those agencies imposing the greatest burden on the public—Treasury (which includes

> the [Internal Revenue Service]) and Defense (which includes procurement-related paperwork)—have little problem getting through the OIRA review process. Thus, OSHA/MSHA account for less than 7% of all paperwork imposed on the public, but have had 14% of their proposals rejected by OIRA. Treasury, on the other hand, accounts for nearly half of all government paperwork, but OIRA has disapproved less than 1% of its forms.[60]

Combining paperwork reduction and regulatory relief contradicted OMB's own regulations, which acknowledged that "OMB authority over paperwork should not be expanded to cover non-paperwork matters."[61] An official of the Department of the Treasury confirmed the overlap. "What OMB often does is to blend its 12291 authority with the Paperwork Reduction Act." The official also explained that regulations such as the Foreign Assets Control regulations were exempt from the Administrative Procedure Act and from EO 12291, given the universal acknowledgment of the president's dominant role in foreign affairs. But, he added, OMB was still securing a role in rule making in this area by using the Paperwork Reduction Act.[62]

Nevertheless, the two powers of authority seemed to overlap extensively in the case of OSHA's hazard communication standard,[63] a rule that requires employers to maintain detailed reports for inspection by their employees concerning hazardous materials present in the workplace. In 1985, the Court of Appeals in the Third Circuit ordered promulgation of a standard as the Occupational Safety and Health Act implicitly called for. The court also ordered the secretary of labor to consider the merits of extending the rule's application beyond the manufacturing sector.[64] On May 29, 1987, the same court, in *United Steelworkers of America v. Pendergrass* [I],[65] noticed a two-year delay and ordered the administrator of OIRA to issue regulations forthwith. The regulations appeared on August 24, 1987. But on October 28, 1987, OMB disapproved of several of the documentary requirements, using its powers under the Paperwork Reduction Act. OIRA administrator Wendy L. Gramm notified the Department of Labor's assistant secretary for administration and management, Thomas C. Komarek, of OIRA disapproval of the paperwork obligations that were to become effective May 23, 1988. OSHA's formaldehyde standard would provide information about the presence of formaldehyde to workers so that they could make an informed decision about whether to remain at the worksite. Again, OMB intervened in the execution of the standard, using the Paperwork Reduction Act. A United Auto Workers memorandum lashed out at the use of the Paperwork Reduction Act to undermine other Acts of Congress. "It would be the height of hypocrisy to advocate increased hazard communication to inform workers of hazards in the legislative arena, while at the same time chopping away at information available to workers in practice under the guise of [the] Paperwork Reduction Act."[66] The resulting 1988 lawsuits were *USWA v. John A. Pendergrass* [II] and *Public Citizen, Inc., et al. v. Pendergrass*.[67] The United Steelworkers and Public Citizen objected that the Paperwork Reduction Act covered paperwork submitted to government agencies, but did not apply to communication provided by one private party to another. The two groups asked the court to hold OMB director Miller and OSHA administrator Pendergrass in contempt for interfering with the execution of the court order. The court denounced OMB's involvement as inconsistent with the court's explicit directives to OSHA. Judge John J. Gibbons held no one in contempt, acidly explaining that his restraint with respect to Department of Labor officials stemmed from the fact that "the instant dispute arose as the result of *another* federal agency's attempt to exceed its statutory authority" (emphasis added; the other agency in question, of course, was OMB).

DELAY

From the time that the incoming Reagan administration declared a freeze on the Carter administration's "midnight regulations," advocates of social regulation have been agitated by the imposition of delays in promulgating regulations. Many advocates say that the impact of OIRA disapprovals of regulations may actually pale in comparison to the impact of delays that cause a multitude of regulations to emerge months or years after they otherwise would have. In the period of delay, all the evils the regulations were designed to remedy are perpetuated, and the evolution of regulations is retarded. Morrison says, "Contrary to the ostensible aim of the original Executive Order [12291], the system of OMB control imposes costly delays that are paid for through the decreased health and safety of the American public."[68]

An OSHA manager described how the combination of review procedures and the complicated interaction between OSHA and OIRA devoured staff time and delayed promulgation. Paperwork reduction reports and extensive regulatory analyses represented unprecedented demands on the staff that prolonged the gestation period for regulations. Then, once the review process had begun, a flurry of letters was exchanged and a series of meetings arose, as the regulatory staff was diverted from its regular duties. In some instances, OIRA sent proposed regulations back for revision after lengthy delay, and when the revised proposal went back, another period of delay ensued. "OMB claims that it reviews regulations within fifty days," the OSHA manager observed skeptically, "but I've had some stuff there for six months."[69]

Another OSHA manager cited OIRA's review of a proposed regulation that would require some industrial machinery to be equipped with locks designed to prevent unintended access to the machinery when it had been taken out of service for repair. Numerous accidents occurred after "out of order" signs taped to such machines unaccountably disappeared. When the interview with this OSHA manager took place, the "lock out-tag out" proposal was being held up in OIRA. The OSHA official complained that the regulation was a sure way to save 100 to 150 lives annually. Thus, the delay in the review process was inevitably creating a body count of fatally injured workers. The official explained his perspective. "I like a system that moves slowly. The power to regulate is the power to put people out of business. But OMB is too stringent on their oversight in health and safety areas. They don't take them seriously enough."[70] An OSHA official indicated that the traditional rule-making process, which was designed to admit members of the public as partners in the regulatory system, was being undermined. "In OSHA, there are public hearings." And, he added, it was inappropriate for an OIRA desk officer to hold up regulations for up to six years.[71]

Similarly, it seems clear that EPA regulations were targeted for especially lengthy reviews at OIRA. In May 1983, OMB extended review of 73 rules proposed by EPA and 85 EPA final rules. In 1984 and the first nine months of 1985, OMB extended its review of 196 EPA regulations. For the period 1981 to 1989, EPA "major" rules underwent an average of sixty-four days of OIRA review, 60 percent longer than the forty-day average for all agencies and second only to Labor (home of OSHA), whose rules spent an average of one hundred fourteen days at OIRA. For "non-major" rules, EPA's twenty-six-day average exceeded the average for all agencies by 19 percent.[72] In 1986, Senators Durenberger and Max Baucus (D-Mont.) found that major rules were meeting with a delay of four months or more and some rules were being delayed for over a year.[73] In 1985, EPA acting administrator Charles Elkins wrote to Bedell objecting to OMB's practice of "grossly" delaying reviews of eleven out of twelve Clean Air Act regulations—even beyond OIRA's own review deadlines, in some cases by over four months. "In short, we have a management problem which is getting out of hand," Elkins wrote.[74] OMB signed off on the regulations within days after receiving the communication from Elkins.[75]

Responses by the judicial and legislative branches motivated OIRA to act with more dispatch in processing proposed regulations. The 1986 case of *Environmental Defense Fund v. Thomas*,[76] which provided a stinging rebuke to

OIRA's occasional overriding of court-ordered deadlines, discouraged OIRA from flouting judicially established schedules. EPA's Odelia C. Funke also described the "deadline hammers" that Congress placed in some legislation as an answer to OIRA's delay behavior.[77] For example, the Hazardous and Solid Waste Amendments of 1984,[78] amending the Resource Conservation Recovery Act, provided that a land ban would be set at a tough default level if no rule were promulgated by the deadline. Thus, OIRA's incentive to hold up regulatory proposals was replaced in certain instances by a new incentive to facilitate their promulgation.

An OIRA staff member voiced his opinion that the criticism of OIRA delays and the pressure to speed the review process caused reviews to be expedited in the later years of the Reagan era—but at a price. From the outset, the quality of OIRA reviews was largely a function of the capability of the desk officer, with top desk officers producing excellent reviews. A good review would tend to be backed up by OMB, which was an incentive to write good review evaluations. However, as the process and the Reagan administration "aged," a routine set in, and quality reviews were less likely to make an impact. "The incentive to do 'good work' now is less," the staff member said in a 1988 interview. "The incentive now is to 'get the stuff out.' "

Criticism of alleged delays is always constructed to illuminate "worst case" situations. For example, as the OIRA staff member explained, an agency might submit a large stack of proposed regulations to its OIRA desk officer. The desk officer would process the first regulation and return it to the agency, getting no credit for his promptness. Then the desk officer would process the second, third, and fourth regulation in turn, again receiving no praise. But when the desk officer processed the *last* regulation in the pile, agency personnel might denounce the desk officer for the lengthy delay.

The OIRA staff member said that 80 to 85 percent of 1988 reviews were completed in ten to twelve days, but OIRA was not averse to recognizing agency priorities when necessary. He said that desk officers "expedite [regulatory reviews] all the time" upon request.[79]

5 The Executive Agencies

BARGAINING AND CONFLICT AMONG PARTICIPANTS

The ingenuity of the framers of the Constitution is reflected in the competition for power institutionalized in the separation of powers and the system of checks and balances. But unlike combatants in a war, who may be motivated to inflict severe damage on each other, or the competitors in the business world, who might obtain economic benefits from driving others out of business, the officials of the United States political system rarely have any incentive to inflict lasting damage on other centers of influence in the same system. If Congress were to inflict heavy damage on the executive branch (say, by defunding it), it would cripple the institutions that are empowered to carry out the statutes enacted by Congress itself. Accordingly, each center of influence tends to protect its own power and to seek to enhance it without damaging other centers of influence in the same system.

The History of Regulatory Relationships

Prior to the Reagan era, the regulatory establishment enjoyed substantial autonomy in relation to Congress, the president, and the top echelon of political appointees. Most dramatic was the autonomy of the independent regulatory commissions (IRCs), which are situated outside the executive branch. Challenged by President Franklin D. Roosevelt, this autonomy of the commissions was defended by the Supreme Court, which overturned Roosevelt's dismissal of a Federal Trade Commission (FTC) member on the grounds that the commission exercised quasi-judicial authority.[1] At Roosevelt's behest, the Brownlow Committee subsequently condemned the IRCs as a "headless 'fourth branch' of the Government."[2] The president's authority over the independent commissions was largely confined to his power to appoint their members, who would then be beyond the reach of his dismissal power in most circumstances. In any event, even the agencies located firmly within the executive branch and hierarchically accountable to the president displayed a low level of attentiveness to presidential policy preferences. More attention was paid to congressional committees, clientele groups, and agency personnel than to the president's directives.[3]

The literature identifies five behaviors characteristic of the pre-1981 autonomy of IRCs from presidential control. First, *technically oriented personnel in the regulatory agencies have always displayed resentment toward any review and revision* of their work by nontechnical analysts and managers. Scientific and technical employees (such as scientists, physicians, and engineers) formed professional organizations, and, through them, fended off review of their work by insisting that laypeople lacked the necessary expertise to evaluate it.[4]

Second, *agency officials made binding commitments to issue rules* during testimony at congressional hearings or while issuing consent decrees. Such rules were usually based on an idea for a regulation that germinated within the agency. By the time top political appointees discovered the binding commitment, it was irreversible.[5]

Third, *rules were often promulgated without involvement from top political appointees.* President Jimmy Carter's Executive Order 12044 was an effort to involve senior-level officials in the rule-making process, but the effort was not systematic. Carter instructed each cabinet member to read every new regulation made within his or her department, but the volume of regulations precluded any such complete review.[6]

Fourth, *agency officials were attuned to the interests and demands of clientele groups and members of Congress.* Interaction between regulatory agencies and their respective interest groups, and interaction between regulatory agencies and congressional committees, occurred systematically, as the subgovernment model of the "iron triangle" illustrates. Interaction between regulatory agencies and the White House was less frequent; the White House conducted no regular oversight of rule making.

Fifth, *agency officials were oblivious to compliance costs.* Officials in the social regulatory agencies appeared to make regulations without regard to the costs that the regulations would impose on private enterprise. Peter J. Petkas, a former director of the Regulatory Council, testified in April 1981 that agencies rarely attempted to estimate such compliance costs. "Fairly complete cost and benefit information is available only on 20 percent of the regulations we reviewed. No cost and benefit information was prepared by these agencies for 34 percent of the regulations in the calendar."[7] J. Richard Crout, director of the Bureau of Drugs of the Food and Drug Administration (FDA), admitted, "We do not pay any attention to the economic consequences of our decisions."[8] The determination to avoid enumerating costs was common throughout the regulatory establishment.

Regulatory Relationships in Transition

Two types of behavior arose during the period when Reagan's Executive Office of the President (EOP) put Executive Order 12291 into effect. The first type involved attempts to secure an exemption from the regulatory review process. In the case of the IRCs, the Reagan administration conceded that they could not be compelled legally to obey EO 12291, but Office of Management and Budget (OMB) officials recruited the commissions to participate voluntarily. Seven volunteered: the Civil Aeronautics Board, Federal Energy Management Agency, Federal Energy Regulatory Commission, Federal Home Loan Bank Board, Federal Mine Safety and Health Review Commission, Interstate Commerce Commission (ICC), and Securities and Exchange Commission.[9] However, the commitment made by the seven commissions proved to be an insufficient guarantee of follow-through. The first administrator of the Office of Information and Regulatory Affairs (OIRA), James C. Miller III, who later served as chairman of the FTC and then as director of OMB, provided this recollection of the aloofness shown by the commission.

> We could [apply EO 12291 to the independent agencies]; the Justice Department concluded we could. But the Vice President [George Bush] concluded this would be unwise. Instead, he sent a letter asking the independent agencies to make their rulemakings in accord with the requirements of the executive order [12291]. Most said they'd take the issue under advisement or something like that, but none chose not to comply with the requirements of the executive order. And none to my knowledge, including the FTC even when it had a Reagan majority, took the initiative to comply with the order. Probably I [as FTC chairman] should have tried such a thing; it would have been very controversial, I'm sure.[10]

The Internal Revenue Service (IRS) acted quickly to avoid regulatory review. Commissioner Roscoe Egger testified in 1981:

> [H.R. 746 should not apply to IRS because], with very few exceptions, all of the regulations which we write are merely interpretative of the Internal Revenue Code itself. The Internal Revenue Code is perhaps the most comprehensive legislation in the entire Federal Code and, therefore, when we're issuing interpretative regulations, we have little or no room to make decisions on our own.
>
> As you know, Executive Order 12291, has many of the same features as the proposed legislation. We sat down with OMB and worked out very carefully an arrangement whereby most Internal Revenue regulations and rulings are exempt from the Executive order.[11]

Accordingly, the Department of the Treasury—the umbrella organization that includes IRS—and OMB struck a bargain, memorialized in a "Memorandum of Understanding," providing that OMB authority would be limited with regard to tax regulations.

The Department of the Treasury seems to have succeeded in escaping from nearly all review under EO 12291. Asserting that it is a law enforcement and revenue collection agency and not a regulatory instrument, the department denied having much discretion that could productively be reviewed by OMB.[12] Dramatically, the department succeeded in avoiding the burden of advance notification to OMB of regulatory proposals, as required by President Ronald Reagan's Executive Order 12498, issued on January 4, 1985. Treasury attributed this exemption to the technical nature of its work, but rumors suggested a different explanation.

> Sources say Treasury obtained the secret MOU [Memorandum of Understanding] through "sheer bravado" when former Treasury Secretary Donald Regan ... refused to give his assent to the executive order as chairman of the Cabinet Council on Economic Affairs unless its application to Treasury was narrowed considerably. Sources say OMB had to offer Regan and his powerful successor James Baker a special arrangement to get both Treasury and the White House to "sign off" on the directive late last year [1984]. Sources say several other Cabinet heads—most notably Transportation Secretary Elizabeth Dole—also fought the OMB directive in Cabinet Council debate last year, with most Cabinet members "wondering why OMB has to get its hands in the cookie jar all the time." But apparently only Baker and Regan were able to "pull rank" and successfully resisted OMB's "grab for regulatory power."
>
> The new OMB-Treasury agreement builds on and greatly expands an

> existing MOU between Treasury and OMB under E.O. 12291, which limits OMB authority only over tax regulations. The new agreement, sources say, covers all potential Treasury regulations, from Comptroller of the Currency banking regulations, to Bureau of Alcohol, Tobacco [and] Firearms wine labeling rules, to Customs Service regulations and Internal Revenue Service tax rules.[13]

A second, related form of behavior involved protests against the review program and efforts to abolish it. The personnel of the regulatory agencies had reservations about the review process from the outset. This is an account reported in the *Washington Post* describing the agencies' first exposure to EO 12291.

> It was February 17 [1981], less than a month after the Reagan Administration took office, when the Office of Management and Budget called in the top attorneys of the executive branch regulatory agencies to have a look at the President's new executive order on regulatory policy, an order that had been in preparation for weeks.
>
> Seated around a table in a second-floor office in the Executive Office building next door to the White House, the attorneys began to read, several taking out pens to note changes they wanted to make or parts they found objectionable. Not until the last page—when they saw President Reagan's signature—did they realize this was not the draft of a proposed order. It was the last word.[14]

Former OMB director David A. Stockman has described the animosity of cabinet members when he unveiled the regulatory review process at a meeting shortly after Reagan's first inauguration. "What kind of bureaucracy are you building up over at OMB?" demanded Secretary of Transportation Drew Lewis.[15]

Reportedly, the issuance of EO 12498 also evoked criticism from the agencies for the increasingly elaborate and time-consuming review procedures. The Department of Commerce was driven to "file objections" over the level of "specificity" required by the "new format" demanded by OMB. A department official fumed that OMB was "darn lucky to get what it already has."[16]

Resulting Regulatory Relationships

As centralized regulatory review became the routine, the relationship among participants in the regulatory process changed and needed redefinition.

The executive agencies and the IRCs exhibited *reluctance to issue new regulations,* perceiving that few initiatives would pass through the OMB gate. Said one OSHA official, "It's no use regulating now [on certain issues]. Reagan's OMB would never allow it."[17] While 7,745 documents were published in the Rules Section of the *Federal Register* in 1980, only 6,481 appeared in 1981 and 4,697 in 1988.[18]

The behavior of some agencies appears to have resulted from their speculation about what would please OMB, and their desire to accommodate OMB's expected preferences. Olson reports:

> A more subtle and consequential [Environmental Protection Agency, EPA] development induced by OMB review is a "guessing game" in which EPA attempts to draft rules it believes will clear OMB. As one EPA official put it, "we are practicing the art of the possible": the agency staff starts with reduced expectations, and drafts initially a proposal that will clear both the EPA hierarchy and OMB.[19]

Similar behavior by the Department of Labor and its constituent agency, the Occupational Safety and Health Administration (OSHA),[20] has also been reported.

In a 1985 article, Gerd Winter identified a form of regulatory behavior called "bartering rationality." The concept provides that the agency's "basic bargaining chip" is "its ability, either in law or in practice, to refrain from exercising its full authority." The agency's restraint would come at the cost of a quid pro quo, which would require its bargaining partner to deliver something desired by the agency.[21] Winter's description of bartering rationality shows how a regulatory agency transacts business with an entity it regulates. However, there is a substantial amount of evidence that agencies attempted to draw OMB into a similar bargaining relationship. For example, the secretary of health and human services is reported to have agreed to suppress certain proposed regulations in exchange for clearance of legislative proposals. Similarly, one OSHA manager reported that OSHA officials who entered meetings with OIRA desk officers would be in possession of two lists—one list of proposed regulations that were negotiable in return for undetermined considerations and a second list of proposals that were sacrosanct.[22]

Alan B. Morrison cites a series of recent court decisions overturning agency decisions, claiming they provide evidence that agency actions became arbitrary, capricious, and irrational, reflecting a willingness to bend over backwards to please OMB.[23] For example, the Supreme Court reversed the attempt of the National Highway Traffic Safety Administration (NHTSA) to repeal the passive restraint rule for automobiles, because NHTSA was arbitrary when it ignored mandatory air bags as a possible cost-effective alternative.[24] The Court of Appeals in Washington, D.C., criticized the NHTSA's elimination of the treadwear portion of the tire grading system, calling it a "silly" decision.[25] Judge Antonin Scalia, speaking for the same court, said that the reasons cited by the Nuclear Regulatory Commission (NRC) for a decision made "no sense" and lacked a "rational connection between the facts found and the choices made."[26] The Court of Appeals in the Third Circuit voted that three aspects of an OSHA standard on hazard communication were arbitrary and capricious.[27]

In addition to their reluctance to issue regulations, agencies also *designed additional layers of internal review.* Sociologist Georg Simmel observes that organizations tend to acquire the characteristics of the institutions with which they are in conflict.[28] Consistent with this principle, the agencies reacted to the perceived growing complexity of the OMB apparatus with more complex structures of their own. Offices of policy analysis and similarly named offices specializing in regulatory analysis proliferated in the federal bureaucracy.

Whereas the commissioner of the FDA theretofore might have been able to issue rules on his own authority at one time, no FDA rule thereafter would see the light of day until it had been approved by the assistant secretary for health and the secretary of health and human services. EPA's Office of Policy, Planning and Evaluation acquired an Office of Policy Analysis (EPA employees sometimes referred to it as the "mini-OMB," to the consternation of the policy analysis staff). Each "media" office (i.e., a program office specializing in one medium that carries pollution, such as water) acquired its own policy group and economic analysis group; for example, the Office of Air and Radiation developed its own Office of Policy Analysis and Review.[29]

Each of the Department of Commerce's eleven agencies established an office to analyze the impact of the agency's regulations and of other agencies' regulations on its own agency. There is no central policy review group in Commerce. An elaborate process in OSHA requires that draft proposals circulate among numerous offices, including the Department of Labor's Policy Review Board and the department's Office of the Solicitor.[30] "There are a lot of fairy godfathers," an OSHA official said. "Rulemaking takes so much longer now because everyone and his brother wants to get into the act."[31]

The Department of the Interior's policy analysis capability expanded when a high-level policy analysis group that reports to an assistant secretary was established. Interior's Office of Program Analysis initiated a "hierarchical screening process" through which it would screen all major rules before submitting them to OMB. The office would also "keep its ear to the ground" to identify regulatory proposals undergoing development that should be reviewed in the early stages to avoid possible policy problems later. Quantitative reviews would be done if circumstances warranted, but most of the reviews conducted by this office were qualitative.[32] Each program office would perform regulatory analysis of major rules.

The Department of Education's Division of Regulations Management in the Office of the General Counsel would conduct administrative management of the department's regulatory process. Each program performed its own qualitative regulatory analysis. Most of the division's analyses were qualitative in character as well. The department's planning and budget office no longer employs an economist to do cost-benefit analyses as it once did, apparently because few of the department's regulations qualify for major status (that is, they do not require $100 million or more in compliance costs by regulated parties).[33]

At the Department of Agriculture (USDA), each agency prepared a Regulatory Impact Assessment (RIA) for every major rule, and each RIA needed four approvals—from the administrator of the agency, the assistant secretary who supervised the agency, the assistant secretary for economics (who is the department's chief economist), and the director of the Office of Budget and Program Analysis. That office is the only one to report to the deputy secretary of agriculture.[34]

In terms of procedures, the agencies have added another layer in the rulemaking process—they proceeded to provide advanced notice of proposed rule making, soliciting "comments on a general problem but propos[ing] no solution."[35] This is an example of a desperate attempt by the agencies to leave no stone unturned in averting criticism from OMB.

Another accommodation that many agencies developed was an *early warning system* by which agency staff members alerted OIRA desk officers about proposed regulations still on the drawing board, so that they would not catch OIRA by surprise. Agency employees found this contact helpful, in that problems could be identified and remedied before formal submittal to OIRA, thus speeding the review process in some cases. Said one department official who requested anonymity: "When regulations go to OMB, a lot of them are not surprises to OMB. They know a regulation on that topic is coming over, though they may not be aware of the details. Program people [at the agency] talk to OIRA desk officers." This may happen most often when time is of the essence or when problems are anticipated.

While that official observed that the pre-submittal contacts had been "going on for years"—that is, since the early years of the Reagan administration—an official in another agency said that such contacts were "more prevalent now"—that is, during the Bush administration. He said that agency staff people preferred that OIRA desk officers be given advance notice so that "regulations don't hit them cold."

An official at a third agency said that advance briefings were "common throughout" (i.e., since the Reagan era) and were "more likely to happen for controversial rules."

While agency structures may have been elaborated to accommodate the regulatory analysis process, *enforcement procedures were eviscerated.* Social regulatory agencies, believing that the EOP had targeted an existing rule for revision or repeal, abandoned the enforcement of the threatened rule. McGarity notes that this practice subjected agencies to accusations that they had prejudged the outcomes of future regulatory proceedings. Agencies would also declare an interest in resolving disputes with industries through discussion and conciliation, which generated complaints that the agencies were "coddling" industries engaged in offensive practices.[36]

The characteristics of enforcement in the Reagan administration included smaller civil penalties, narrower criteria for identifying violators, less discretion for field enforcement staff, devolution of enforcement functions onto state and local governments, more flexibility toward regulated parties, and concentration on violators of regulatory statutes where there was apparent criminal liability. From 1980 to 1982, citations by OSHA declined by 27 percent, while penalties assessed decreased by 78 percent. Cases filed by EPA under the Resources Conservation and Recovery Act fell from forty-three in fiscal year 1980 to three in 1982. While in 1980, the last year of the Carter administration, EPA referred two hundred fifty-two cases to the Justice Department for investigation, in 1981 EPA referred only seventy-eight cases. In 1980, EPA's regional offices forwarded three hundred thirteen cases for enforcement action to EPA's central office; in 1981 there were sixty-six cases forwarded. At a 1981 meeting of officials from EPA's ten regional offices, EPA enforcement counsel William Sullivan declared, "Every case you do refer [to EPA's enforcement office] will be a black mark against you."[37] EPA administrator Anne Gorsuch Burford abolished the Office of Enforcement (it reappeared later in the EPA's legal office), in an effort to reduce the incidence of enforcement of environmental regulations.[38]

A similar pattern took shape at OSHA. A report issued by Essential Information, a group affiliated with Ralph Nader, stated that, between 1977 and 1990, the agency imposed penalties for only 32 percent of the citations issued against the nation's fifty largest corporations.[39]

Agencies exercising their prosecutorial discretion in this restrained manner found public support more difficult to obtain, because the enforcement process lost its appearance of purpose and its credibility. Eads and Fix note that even the regulated industries, which usually respected (even if they did not willingly accept) enforcement that appeared consistent and even-handed, grew restless with the haphazard enforcement pattern. "Enforcement is the area in which the Reagan administration's regulatory relief effort has come most conspicuously to grief."[40]

Another behavior exhibited by agencies in the aftermath of the Reagan reform was *sensitivity to compliance costs*. Frederic A. Eidsness Jr., EPA's assistant administrator for water, expressed a commitment to cost-benefit analysis and an exasperation with the policy of "throw[ing] money at non-problems." "I came to Washington to help put a stop to such waste," Eidsness declared.[41] The FDA's Bureau of Foods designed a cost-benefit analysis to predict costs to baby food manufacturers resulting from FDA seizure of their product due to a certain level of contamination.[42] And in recent years, the Consumer Product Safety Commission (CPSC) has developed its analytical capabilities, drawing praise from former Council of Economic Advisers chairman Murray L. Weidenbaum as "the only regulatory body I know that is really weighing costs imposed against benefits that might be gained—and trying to behave rationally."[43]

Not all resulting agency behaviors reflected concessions to OMB's agenda. Disgruntled employees carried out *acts of sabotage* and attempted to circumvent the review process. When OMB intervened in OSHA efforts to regulate exposure of hospital workers to ethylene oxide during sterilization of medical equipment, an angry OSHA manager tipped off the Public Citizen Litigation Group that OMB's "fingerprints" could be found on the official copy of the regulations. As Public Citizen lawyers inspected the official copy at the Office of the Federal Register, they saw the crossed-out words and revisions that clearly indicated OMB's input, despite the absence of any record to indicate the process through which the agency had opted for the changes.[44]

I referred in chapter 4 to the discovery that OMB had disapproved a Public Health Service (PHS) study of the relationship between federal funding cuts and infant mortality rates. The mere design of such a study indicates an attempt by PHS staff to subject the Reagan administration's cutbacks in social programming to public ridicule. The late James J. Delaney, a former executive secretary of health and human services who once had some supervisory contact with the PHS, denounced the proposed study in a 1988 interview as "impolitic," in that it was designed to embarrass the administration.[45] Rogowsky reveals the existence of "underground control" of regulatory affairs that exerts "the bulk of economic control. . . . The Reagan administration's attempt to control regulations through [OMB] left the underground regulatory structure largely untouched."[46] The hidden regulatory establishment was made manifest in OSHA project officer James Scully's proposal for a regulation that would reduce the risk to workers who repair and service dangerous industrial machines. Although Scully was instructed to drop the proposal when Reagan took office, he patiently nurtured the embryonic rule, kept a daily log of every order he received, and kept Senator Edward M. Kennedy's Labor Committee posted. "I was letting them [Scully's superiors] know that I was documenting every damn thing they were doing," he said. OMB released the rule just before Kennedy convened hearings about OMB's delaying of safety regulations. Then, satisfied with his accomplishment, Scully retired. Waldman comments:

> Persistent civil servants, frisky congressional committees, aggressive interest groups—these and other forces have combined to accelerate the pace of federal regulation in the Reagan administration's final year. . . . Real spending by regulatory agencies last year exceeded the pre-Reagan level for the first time. Fred Smith of the conservative Competitive Enterprise Institute calls it "the empire strikes back" phenomenon—the victory of the permanent bureaucracy over political ideology.[47]

COMPARISON OF AGENCIES SUBJECT TO AND NOT SUBJECT TO EO 12291

The hypothesis that President Reagan's imposition of the regulation clearance process created changes in agency behavior implies that agencies would not exhibit such changes if they were not subject to the process. We can therefore test the credibility of the hypothesis by comparing the behavior of covered agencies to that of exempt agencies.

The issuance of EO 12498 was followed by a flurry of decisions about which agencies would be covered. Within the executive branch, the Departments of Agriculture, Commerce, Education, Energy, Health and Human Services, Housing and Urban Development, Interior, Labor, and Transportation were all covered. Also covered were EPA, the Equal Employment Opportunity Commission, the General Services Administration, the Office of Personnel Management, the Small Business Administration, and the Veterans Administration.

The Department of Justice, which would ordinarily have been subject to EO 12498, was specifically exempted.[48] The Department of the Treasury secured an exemption through the force of its influence in the administration. Agencies exempt from EO 12498 were the Department of Defense, the Department of State, and OMB. All the independent regulatory commissions were exempt.[49]

As a pure matter of law, the Reagan administration quickly conceded that the IRCs could not be compelled to comply with the regimen established under EO 12291. The independence of the commissions notwithstanding, the president possessed a fair amount of control over them, in the form of appointment power, budget review in OMB, the prerogative of clearing legislative proposals by the commissions, and the reliance by the commissions on the Department of Justice to supply counsel for judicial proceedings. A 1950 reform proposed by the Hoover Commission and approved by Congress gave the president authority to appoint and remove commission chairmen. It also gave commission chairmen authority over the appointment of staff, the distribution of work, and the allocation of resources.[50] But when the regulation clearance process became compulsory for almost all agencies except the IRCs, the principle of independence went beyond the limits of prudence. The vice president's general counsel, C. Boyden Gray, however, preferred to explain the exemption of IRCs as a practical policy because "we had our plate more than full with the Executive Branch agencies."[51] Nevertheless, OIRA administrator Miller ventured out on behalf of Vice President George Bush to recruit the commissions to participate voluntarily. Seven commissions volunteered, but none proved to be motivated to participate fully in the process.

In addition, by arrangement with OIRA, certain categories of regulations developed by covered agencies were left out of the review process. For example, EPA and OMB agreed that OMB would not review approvals of state implementation plans under the Clean Air Act (although conditional approvals and disapprovals were reviewed).[52]

While the agencies covered by EO 12291 tended to acquiesce to OMB's regulation analyses, with the apparent exception of Anne Gorsuch Burford's EPA,[53] the *exempt* agencies exhibited a *continuing aversion to cost-benefit analysis and other forms of regulatory analysis.* Robert E. Lee, acting chairman of the Federal Communications Commission (FCC), testified against cost-benefit analysis in a 1981 hearing, warning against arbitrary and subjective analyses that would result in interminable delays.[54] As the Reagan era was concluding, it appears that FCC regulation writers continued to forgo the opportunity to subject their own work to cost-benefit analysis, preferring to rely on staff of other offices in the FCC to carry out the analysis[55] or—more likely—simply letting their initiatives stand "on their own merits." Terry D. Johnson, chief of the FCC's Information Resources Branch, observed in 1988 that the FCC's staff was finally developing the habit of factoring OIRA's perspective into their initiatives. "It makes my job easier," he added.[56] However, the FCC's decision to repeal the Fairness Doctrine despite a vote in Congress of 301 to 100 in favor of its continuation indicated to Representative Edward J. Markey (D-Mass.) that the pro–New Right politicization of the commission was proceeding apace.[57]

The Department of the Treasury exhibited a similar aversion to regulatory analysis. In order to avoid analysis requirements, officials of the Department of the Treasury—whether in the IRS or in other parts of the department—uniformly denied that much quasi-legislative activity was occurring there. Rather, they claimed, the department executes statutes and issues perfunctory interpretation of laws. On the whole, the Department of the Treasury denied it was a conglomeration of regulatory agencies. "We're only regulating the banks," a Treasury official said, further explaining that the Department of Treasury's supervision of the banking industry existed in tandem with supervision exercised by other federal agencies. All together, he added, the IRS, Customs Service, and Bureau of Alcohol, Tobacco, and Firearms accounted for 75 percent of the departmental activity that could be remotely considered regulatory. OMB waived review of about 90 percent of the regulations issued by these agencies. OMB exercised more regular review of the Treasury's Office of the Comptroller of the Currency. But the department insisted it had no day-to-day influence over the course of the economy, and that it was solely an agency of law enforcement and revenue collection. Those regulations that reached OIRA met with good fortune. In six or seven years, said associate general counsel Richard S. Carro, OMB disapproved few if any Treasury regulations.[58]

Subsequently, the Department of the Treasury secured an exemption from the requirements of EO 12498. Critics maintained that the exemption was not related to any nonregulatory nature of the department, but rather to the political influence of the outgoing and incoming secretaries—Donald Regan and James Baker. A source in Treasury seemed to confirm the speculation. "We're different because we're the Department of the Treasury," he reflected. "The department carries a lot of weight."[59]

A second difference in behavior between covered and exempt agencies lies in the *degree of accommodation to the president's constituency*. The agencies subject to the regulatory review program exhibited a somewhat more pronounced sensitivity to the preferences of the political constituency most closely associated with President Reagan. While exempt agencies may have moderated their approach toward the regulation of business interests, the covered agencies acted with more resolve to circumscribe the limits of their regulatory activity in its impact on business. For example, EPA, OSHA, FDA, and the Department of the Interior announced in the early days of the Reagan presidency that many of the most "burdensome" proposed regulations would be delayed, suspended, or eliminated.[60] This interruption in the momentum of regulation was credited with, or blamed for, a permanent loss of several years of regulatory progress, which would have occurred in the absence of the Reagan administration's regulation restraint policy.

It is also apparent that covered agencies reflected a *marked sensitivity to compliance costs*. Bryner described the FDA's unusual rejection of a consumer group's petition calling for ten food dyes, identified as carcinogens in laboratory animals, to be banned under the Delaney Amendment.[61] The agency branded the threat from the food dyes "*de minimis*."[62] The FDA conducted a cost-benefit analysis to weigh the need to order a baby food recall against the economic impact on baby food manufacturers.[63] A regulation management official in EPA observed, "The public record, background technical documents, and preamble for EPA regulations would probably show sensitivity to costs imposed on industry."[64] An official at PHS reported that agencies "have become sensitive to OIRA policy" preferences.[65] After Reagan's inauguration, EPA, FDA, OSHA, and the Department of Interior sent word to the corporate sector that many regulations most resented by industry would be delayed, suspended, or eliminated.[66]

As an exempt agency, the CPSC's commitment to deregulation was rather unusual. It can be explained at least in part by a 1981 statute requiring the commission to do cost-benefit analysis. The statute essentially overrode a 1978 judicial decision permitting the CPSC to forgo an "elaborate" analysis as long as "relevant factors" and "evidence" were presented for justification.[67] The appointment of Nancy Steorts, a loyal Reagan appointee, limited the regulatory output of the agency.[68]

With the exception of the CPSC's acquiescence, the commitment of exempt agencies to reducing compliance costs was mild. Many IRCs were reluctant to volunteer to produce cost-benefit analyses; even the volunteers exhibited only a halfhearted commitment to regulatory analysis. An example that illustrates the less than extensive devotion of exempt agencies to compliance cost reduction is the ICC's listless implementation of the Railroad Deregulation Act.[69] But some evidence of cost reduction efforts does exist, such as the FCC's elimination of the Fairness Doctrine, the FCC's virtual abandonment of antitrust policy,[70] and the NRC's poorly justified decision to eliminate the Atomic Energy Act requirement that an electric utility seeking a license to operate a generating facility establish its financial qualification.[71] A number of commissions established or embellished offices of policy analysis. In short, there was a limited but measurable commitment to compliance cost reduction.

For agencies *exempt* from the provisions of EO 12291, the *paperwork review process loomed larger* in importance. Evidence indicates that the OIRA made up for the inapplicability of EO 12291 by more extensive application of the Paperwork Reduction Act. Agency personnel reported that OIRA looked at paperwork requirements from the point of view of a substantive policy. Asked to describe the policy guidelines that OIRA was applying, an FCC official responded, "That's a good question. Sometimes we're surprised by their interpretation."[72]

At the outset of the paperwork reduction program, the FCC estimated that it was imposing a paperwork burden of 50 million labor hours of work annually on the communications industry. (Estimates are rough, because OMB prohibited surveys being taken to confirm the data.) Under statutory and OMB pressure to reduce the burden, the FCC jettisoned the bulk of its paperwork demands. With this alleviation of paperwork requirements, the FCC estimated near the end of Reagan's second term that the industry had to devote 10 million labor hours annually to the commission's forms. Despite the impressive magnitude of this 80-percent reduction, which left the FCC with what it deemed a minimal flow of information, the OIRA continued to demand further reductions of 5 percent per year.

The significance of paperwork review is expanded by the OIRA's habit of stretching it beyond its intended purpose, even where agencies covered by EO 12291 were concerned. The hazardous communication rule discussed in chapter 4 was an instance where, through the use of its authority to reduce paperwork, OMB acted to prevent a rule from going into effect that would have required employers to make disclosures to their employees. Incredulous attorneys at the steelworkers' union and the Public Citizen advocacy organization sued, protesting that the Paperwork Reduction Act was not designed to limit required disclosures on the part of employers but was rather intended to monitor the volume of forms filed with government agencies. The court agreed, denouncing OMB for nullifying a court order by substituting its own discretion.[73]

Finally, agencies *exempt* from EO 12291 *experienced unprecedented levels of ad hoc political pressure* emanating from the White House. From the days when the Reagan transition team recommended its first nominees to the

Table 5.1
Behavior of Agencies Covered by and Exempt from Executive Order 12291

Covered Agencies	Exempt Agencies
Acceptance of regulatory analysis	Aversion to regulatory analysis (dissipating)
Extensive accommodation of president's constituency	Moderate accommodation of president's constituency
Extreme sensitivity to compliance costs	Moderate sensitivity to compliance costs
Some paperwork-reduction concern	Extensive paperwork-reduction concern

new president, appointments to all slots in the Reagan administration were awarded to loyalists, who could be counted on to help carry out the Reagan Revolution even if the president did not have the means to penalize recalcitrants. Accordingly, many commissions were being run by individuals who did not need to be shown statutes or executive orders to carry out the will of their commander in chief.[74]

One commission official explained that the Paperwork Reduction Act allowed his commission to override an adverse OMB decision by a majority vote, at which point OMB had to defer to the commission and approve the specific paperwork requirement. But the official said, "We don't do that too often." When the commissioners had occasion to override OMB, the chairman would receive an invitation from OMB director Miller to join him for dinner, where he would be reminded of who appointed him to the chairman's office.[75]

When political pressure was applied, exempt agencies tended finally to exhibit the same behavior as covered agencies—i.e., compliance. In a 1982–83 proceeding, the FCC, the Departments of Justice and Commerce, and OIRA agreed on the desirability of repealing the Financial Interest and Syndication Rules.[76] But after a private meeting in which actor Charlton Heston expressed to President Reagan his opposition to the repeal, the Department of Commerce suddenly reversed its position. The FCC dropped the docket soon after.[77]

Wood and Waterman noticed the same relationship described here concerning the distinctive effects on exempt and covered agencies caused by the Reagan administration's regulatory reform program. They noted:

Table 5.2
Application of Executive Orders to Various Agencies and Departments

Subject to EO 12291	Not Subject, but Volunteered to Participate	Not Subject, Did Not Volunteer	Exempt from EO 12291	Exempt from EO 12498
Agriculture	CAB	All other IRCs	Treasury (*including IRS*)	Justice
Commerce	FEMA			State
Education	FERC			Defense
FERC	Federal Home Loan Bank Board			OMB
Energy	Federal Mine Safety and Health Review Commission			
HHS (*including FDA*)	ICC			
HUD	SEC			
Interior				
Labor (*including OSHA*)				
Transportation				
EPA				
EEOC				
GSA				
OPM				
SBA				
VA				

The agencies most responsive to executive influence . . . were those situated in the executive departments. The FDA . . . , the [National Highway Traffic Safety Administration] . . . , and the [Office of Surface Mining] . . . had outputs that remained lower than their preintervention levels for the duration of their series. These agencies also implemented programs lower in issue salience, weaker in constituency, and further from congressional attention.

On the other hand, the agencies with the most stable outputs were the independent regulatory commissions. The NRC reflects the extreme position since its outputs moved only briefly away from an equilibrium to return quickly without external intervention. The [Equal Employment Opportunity Commission] Office of General Counsel responded for a time to executive influence, but outputs rebounded when Congress and aroused constituencies intervened. The FTC was the single exception to this rule, since its outputs remained depressed throughout the Reagan administration. However, the FTC was also exceptional in that both the president and Congress agreed that decreased FTC activity was desirable.[78]

MECHANICS OF AGENCY-OIRA INTERACTION

The procedures of EO 12291 generated interesting patterns of interaction.

A surprising level of comity developed between politically appointed agency heads and OIRA, which disturbed those who championed vigorous regulation in the name of the public interest. As Bryner describes the arrangement:

> There have been few disagreements between agency heads and officials of the regulatory review bureau in the Office of Management and Budget; the few times that the head of OSHA or EPA [has] tangled with OMB reviewers are rare, attention to ideology in appointments having assured general agreement in executive agencies over policy concerns and priorities.[79]

James Fite, executive director of the White Lung Association, was bitter in describing EPA's and OSHA's cooperation with OMB. He quoted EPA officials as telling him: "We can't do that, Jim. Are you kidding, we can't get that by OMB. Don't you understand how things are done these days?"[80]

On the other hand, there were also reports of resistance to OMB. A number of appointees at the Department of Health and Human Services (HHS) described how they had resisted OMB initiatives to control departmental policy. A counselor to the secretary and undersecretary of HHS, Lawrence J. DeNardis, said that OMB extended its prerogative over regulations "to an extraordinary and unprecedented degree" until its involvement could be classified as "tyranny." DeNardis speculated in a 1986 interview, however, that OMB "heavy-handed tactics" had already reached their "high-water mark."[81]

A former associate commissioner, Jo Anne B. Barnhart, who operated the Aid to Families with Dependent Children program in HHS, recalled that a "GS-15" employee in OMB directed her to promulgate a quality control regulation drafted in OMB. The OMB employee threatened to embargo AFDC funds if the regulation were not issued. She objected to the appearance of "extortion," and recalled, "They were constantly meddling" in HHS policy making.[82]

In speculating why some political appointees would accept the review process in principle while others deemed it objectionable, we may consider numerous variables—degree of "loyalty," the likelihood that the agency's regulations were to be on the "hit list," and so forth. However, the most important variable seems to be the appointee's demonstrated ability to pull the strings of the bureaucracy successfully. The late James J. Delaney was executive secretary of HHS when that department was having some of its first experiences with regulatory review. During a 1988 interview, he recalled that, in his two years in that position, he never "got into a squabble" with OMB. He said that he would arrange for a policy coordinator or a deputy executive secretary to go to OMB and discuss differences in opinion, and, as a result, he would rarely get involved personally. On rare occasions, he would work the problem out with the associate director of OMB. Many of the staff members at HHS would be chomping at the bit to get into a "dogfight" with OMB. "It's difficult to maintain a good relationship [with OMB] when you have 30,000 people under you who want to get emotional," he said. But, he continued, "As a political appointee, I wouldn't allow a cat-and-dog fight." He reflected, "Why get into a fight when you're working for the same guy?" Delaney attributed much of the conflict between OMB and various agency officials to their inexperience. "There's no room for emotional responses at that level."[83]

Walton and Langenfeld echo Delaney's opinion. They compare the successful implementation of Reagan's reforms at FTC and OSHA with the debacle at EPA under Anne Gorsuch Burford. Burford's "top staff... lacked experience in management and environmental programs and possessed a deep distrust of the bureaucracy."[84] HHS official Jacquelyn Y. White, expressing sympathy for an OIRA subjected to the criticism that it failed to pay due respect to the staff at the regulatory agency for its expertise, contended that "[the] process breaks down when you have mediocre people, or those who don't do their homework."[85]

To the permanent staff of the agencies, whose loyalties may have lain closer to the missions of their agencies than to the partisan agendas and political fortunes of the president, intervention by the EOP was an entirely unwelcome feature of the times. Symptomatically, the emergence of this relationship between the agencies and EOP resulted in a *Washington Post* headline on February 23, 1979 (p. A14): "If you don't like it, get out, White House tells EPA staff." This prescription survived the Carter era and remained in effect during the Reagan and Bush administrations. An OIRA desk officer was moved to express some sympathy for the civil service staff. "The staff in the agency is caught in the middle between Congress and OIRA."[86]

Even if EPA's political appointees in the post-Burford era—for example, William Ruckelshaus, whom President Reagan appointed to a second tour of duty as EPA administrator—tried to be more accommodating toward OMB, the staff showed less inclination in that direction. As a result, EPA's political appointees and its staff frequently reflected opposite points of view. On issues of asbestos regulation, "EPA expertise is on our side, and the shell of the Agency is on the other," testified Dan Guttman, speaking for the Service Employees International Union.[87] Representative James J. Florio (D-N.J.) had much the same analysis.

> At first the career staff at EPA mobilized to protest the OMB assault [on asbestos regulation proposals]. These voices in favor of objective, dispassionate, and factual decisionmaking have slowly but surely been stifled. Today the OMB machinery is close to its ultimate goal of throwing the awesome responsibility of dealing with a virtual public health emergency into the laps of confused and poorly prepared State and local officials.[88]

OMB sources reported that most of the complaints about its requirements arose "from the staff level," attributing them to "growing pains." Indeed, civil service employees in the various departments and commissions appeared to be decidedly aloof toward the regulatory review process, ignoring the specter of inevitable OMB review when they drafted proposed regulations. Hugh Conway, OSHA's director of regulatory analysis, reported that the safety and health staff members in OSHA almost always opened the process by writing a proposed rule that would be most protective of workers. He explained that the staff members were usually not economists, and thus not oriented toward costs.

Even at EPA, the anti-OMB tide turned. Dr. Odelia C. Funke, chief of the Regulation Management Branch in EPA's Office of Policy, Planning, and Evaluation, said that eight years of experience under EO 12291 resulted in growing acceptance of the prevailing circumstances. Attrition may have accounted for much of the difference. "New people are quickly enculturated," she explained. "We try to get their attention right away." For the veterans—like EPA staff at the stationary air program in Raleigh, N.C., a program that has been beleaguered by constant OMB oversight—the strong negative perceptions were more durable.

Sundquist found that the attitude of agency staff toward OIRA may have been a function, to some extent, of the personality of the desk officer with whom the agency dealt. If agency representatives dealt with a desk officer who they felt was mature and reasonable, they had a more positive opinion of OIRA than if they dealt with a desk officer they found petty.[89]

The trend was toward slow, grudging acceptance. As Richard A. Eisenger, deputy chief of the Human Resources and Housing Branch in OIRA, stated in a 1987 interview: "The shock has worn off after six years."[90]

As a day-to-day routine emerged in the relationship between the agencies and OIRA, the agencies came to accept the concept that their regulatory proposals were subject to revision by the OIRA staff. Whereas the agencies had traditionally enjoyed the autonomy to promulgate their own innovations without involvement by the president or his advisers, such innovations in the Reagan era represented a gambit, a point of departure for negotiations with OIRA.

OIRA desk officer Scott H. Jacobs explained that he had been able to exercise a measure of influence in his dealings with employees of the agencies whose rules he reviewed. "I have a lot of informal authority," he asserted. This informal authority was of two kinds: one was "persuasion," he said, estimating that 90 percent of issues were resolved through jawboning. "The most powerful tool is the power of persuasion. The advantage of having a small staff at OIRA is that we can bring a sense of perspective to the table."[91] The second kind of informal authority, which helped resolve the remaining 10 percent of issues, stemmed from OIRA's relatively flat hierarchy. In a period of a few hours, Jacobs calculated, he could contact the administrator of OIRA, and within a few hours more, he could get the ear of the director of OMB. Within a few hours after that, he could be speaking with a cabinet-level official. "The agency staff can't do it that fast—[the staff] can't get [the issue] to the secretary nearly that quickly." To Jacobs, this difference was a pivotal advantage. "The agency staff doesn't want [issues] to be escalated." But in cases where agency staff members did want to escalate issues, barriers stood in the way. "Agencies waste a lot of time trying to get the attention of superiors." On the other hand, "OMB is lean and efficient. We don't waste time on memos that go up 40 layers."[92]

Whenever the Department of Health and Human Services sent a proposed regulation to OIRA, a desk officer marked it up and sent it back to the department. The Executive Secretariat in HHS circulated OIRA's comments to the affected agencies for their reaction. Then, negotiations sometimes took place. HHS found OMB's interest to be rooted in several disparate categories, such as budgetary considerations (OMB wanting to deregulate to save money) and policy issues (based primarily on cost-benefit analysis).

Disputes were handled initially by HHS policy coordinators and OIRA desk officers. If necessary, a deputy executive secretary became involved. Less frequently, the executive secretary intervened. If the secretary of HHS felt that the department's mission or integrity was threatened, he might raise the stakes by confronting OMB himself. Involvement in negotiations in health matters by the Office of the Assistant Secretary for Health or by FDA was often prohibited by the secretary's office, which preferred to conduct many negotiations itself.[93]

OSHA officials described the feedback they received when they presented their regulatory proposals to OIRA. In many cases, the OIRA desk officers offered "very good suggestions," said an OSHA official. The desk officer may have identified internal inconsistencies in the regulation, or inconsistencies with other OSHA regulations. Some suggested changes were simply grammatical (e.g., a disagreement in number between subject and verb). In other cases, OSHA officials perceived an attempt to weaken the regulation's impact, and often resisted the effort to reverse the results of months or years of developmental work.[94]

In adapting to the new regimen, agency officials settled on coping strategies. The reaction of HHS to OMB input depended on the issue, and on the department's assessment of the merits of OMB's intervention: An HHS official observed that some OMB input was acknowledged to represent a genuine improvement, some wasn't worth fighting against, and some was deemed ridiculous and rejected.

The secretary of HHS needed to decide how to respond when attempts to resolve conflicts at lower levels failed. The secretary may have occasionally decided he would need OMB director Miller later, said the HHS official. The secretary may have been able to "horse-trade" regulations in exchange for such considerations as a favorable OMB decision or an HHS request for legislative clearance. Or, as a last resort, "The secretary may tell OMB to take a flying leap."[95]

In the spring of 1985, EPA administrator Lee M. Thomas confronted OMB officials with the objection that the secretive nature of contacts between EPA and OMB was damaging to the agency's reputation and its compliance with the Administrative Procedure Act. Thomas succeeded in extracting OMB's agreement to include in the public record any involvement in environmental rule making. "It took a lot of negotiation, believe me," said Thomas of his successful campaign.[96]

Barry J. White, OSHA's director of safety standards, said that the meetings between OSHA and OIRA officials were reminiscent of "Japanese theater." OSHA's representatives entered these meetings with items to concede and others that were not considered negotiable. "We've learned what to give and what to fight for," White said.[97]

In some cases, OSHA's top official—Assistant Labor Secretary John A. Pendergrass—vowed to approve a regulation, whether OMB authorized it or not. He communicated this message to OMB in the case of the hazard communication rule, in which a judicial deadline was in effect. OMB withdrew its objections.

An FCC official reported that the commission attempted to accommodate OIRA within reasonable guidelines. But, he observed, his office bristled when an OIRA desk officer seemed to be challenging a proposed regulation because of an apparent personal interest; serving EOP employees' personal biases was never intended to be a purpose of the Paperwork Reduction Act. The FCC would sometimes write a diplomatic letter intimating that the matter was none of his business. In cases of persistent conflict, the issue would move up the hierarchy of the FCC and the OIRA.[98]

In March 1985, EPA and OMB were at an impasse over regulations to reduce emissions from trucks and buses. OMB director David A. Stockman reportedly visited EPA administrator Thomas's office to object to the demanding nature of the proposed standards. After the meeting ended, Thomas issued the order as planned. An editorial in the *Los Angeles Times* stated that the "logical conclusion seems to be that Thomas stared Stockman in the eye and told him there would be no compromising the nation's health and environment."[99]

These accounts support what we intuitively suspected. The agencies and commissions were willing to concede items to OIRA in marginal cases where their mission was not threatened. But for the sake of institutional survival, the agency heads would draw the line and decline to surrender their last vestiges of influence and discretionary authority. Exchange theory suggests that working relationships endure only when each party is cooperative and delivers some benefit to the other. It also indicates that either party will attempt to terminate the transaction if no incentive for remaining in the system remains. Some of the benefits and sacrifices may be traded across a bargaining table by the two parties engaged directly in the exchange, but—in a setting such as government where other parties have a stake in the process—relationships with the other parties may be affected for better or worse. David Houston, administrator of the USDA's Food Safety and Inspection Service, indicated that the regulation analysis requirement imposed on the agencies by the EOP may have enhanced agency accountability to the public by improving information to affected citizens and may have encouraged effective citizen participation.[100] McGarity said that the regulation analysis requirement enhanced agency accountability to Congress. He observed: "While a regulatory analysis document may not satisfy the losers of the regulatory battle, it can reassure remote decision makers in the White House, Congress, and reviewing courts that the decision was reached in a consistent and nonpartisan fashion."[101] Accordingly, it can be argued that an agency, by complying with the

Table 5.3
The OMB-Agency Exchange Relationship: Theoretical Components

OMB	Agency
Receives	*Gives up*
Policies that please president's coalition (political)	Policies that please advocacy groups
Policies that establish and solidify presidential influence (constitutional)	Policies that please Congress
Influence over technical decisions	Political independence
	Professional independence, resulting in appearance of partisanship
	Freedom from concern about compliance costs
	Ability to schedule work
Gives up	*Receives*
Blamelessness for regulatory policies	Democratic legitimacy
Freedom from negotiation over budget considerations and legislative proposals	Economic and managerial legitimacy
	Favor from new constituency
	Chance to barter for budget considerations
	Chance to barter for legislative clearance

regulatory review process, can benefit from a more favorable appearance of accountability and legitimacy.[102]

Within OIRA's frame of reference, EO 12291 was a long needed tool to restore order to the hierarchy. "Among the people whose behavior we're trying to influence," OIRA administrator Miller said, "are the GS-13s and -14s who draft the rules."[103]

OIRA officials have repeated the concerns of President Jimmy Carter's Council on Wage and Price Stability (CWPS) and of the Regulatory Analysis Review Group (RARG) that OSHA compels industry to conform to requirements based on "design standards over performance standards, engineering standards over personal protective devices, and industry-wide exposure levels over levels that vary among industrial segments according to varying risks of exposure and costs of control."[104] Given this set of predilections, OSHA would be inclined to insist that industry cleanse workplaces of certain particulates rather than outfit employees with oxygen masks. Miller and Christopher C.

Table 5.4
Agency Behavior Before and After Executive Orders 12291 and 12498

Before	After
Technical employees resist review by political officials	Technical employees resent review, but cede in most cases (except in cases of sabotage)
Low-level officials make binding commitments to promulgate regulations	Binding commitments are not made (violation of EO 12291 and 12498)
Low-level officials make rules without involving department heads	Upper-level officials are more involved; there are more levels of review
Agency officials are attuned to the interests and demands of clientele groups and Congress	Agencies attempt to please and defer to OMB, even acting in an arbitrary and capricious manner when OMB-prescribed action conflicts with agency mission
Agency officials are oblivious to compliance costs	Agency officials are sensitive to compliance costs
Agencies regulate with enthusiasm	Agencies are reluctant to regulate
Agencies act autonomously, make non-negotiable demands	Agencies negotiate with regulated parties and barter with OMB
Zealotry is common	Morale is low

DeMuth thus attempted to carry out the recommendations of CWPS and RARG through Reagan's OMB, insisting that OSHA's selection of cost-ineffective methods of protecting workers was a heavy burden on the economy.

To justify its imposition of order on the agencies and its disapproval of numerous regulatory proposals, the OIRA found it necessary to challenge (and, occasionally, ridicule) the competence of agencies to make rational regulations. OMB's *Regulatory Program of the United States Government* for 1987–88 questioned OSHA's capability for formulating a fair estimate of risk. The document accused OSHA of basing the regulatory impact assessment of the ethylene oxide rule on "worst-case estimates" of carcinogenicity, by using the assumption that workers are exposed to the chemical continuously rather than intermittently, which is closer to the reality.[105]

To OIRA desk officer Jacobs, a proposed regulation should not be mistaken for a Decalogue carved in stone. "Eventually, you begin to see that regulations are very ephemeral documents. They reflect a current state of flux of pressures, forces, and opinions. They reflect what is going on up to the minute that the last period is written on it."

Because a proposal is a "living document in a state of transition," Jacobs approached each one with some skepticism about its claims made concerning rationale and expected benefits. He said that the purpose of many proposals could be identified readily through an understanding of the private and public parties that contributed to the development of the proposed regulation.

Jacobs cited OSHA's regulations on hazardous waste sites as a case study of regulatory proposals that solve a nonexistent problem. "Congress declared there was a risk, so OSHA assumed there would be benefits to taking action."[106] OIRA officials cite agency sensitivity to congressional demands as the key to the agencies' inability to implement cost-benefit tests themselves. Thus, the regulation analysis process could not be conducted independently by the agency, said OIRA senior desk officer Samuel W. Fairchild.[107] But, by the same token, observed OIRA administrator S. Jay Plager, the interests of the OIRA and the agencies are "irreconcilable." This is because the agencies have Congress and interest groups as constituents, while OIRA's only constituency is the president.[108]

NEW BEHAVIOR, NEW RESULTS

More Accommodation of Presidential Preferences

Whereas previous presidents and their advisers experienced frustration in their attempts to exact compliance from the bureaucracy, President Reagan and his OMB directors extracted an unprecedented degree of accommodation from the regulatory agencies. Veteran observers described a federal regulatory establishment in retreat, obeying orders from OMB to suppress the fruits of years of regulation proposal development—a once unthinkable occurrence.

The case studies demonstrate that agencies were willing to make remarkable reversals in their policies when prodded to do so by OMB. When EPA sought to regulate asbestos, shortly after the enactment of the Toxic Substances Control Act of 1976, OMB ordered EPA to defer to OSHA and the CPSC. OMB contended that "CPSC has authority to order disposal of consumer products even after installation in the home and has issued rules banning the household use of some consumer products (patching compounds containing asbestos)."[109] On February 1, 1985, EPA's acting deputy administrator, A. James Barnes, announced that EPA was discontinuing its efforts to regulate asbestos and deferring further regulatory initiatives to OSHA and CPSC. EPA's staff was enraged by the concession.

Although the case studies most likely to emerge in the literature are the most egregious instances of OMB interference, day-to-day experience reflects a noteworthy degree of comity as agency officials—even some agency staff—attempted to avoid conflict with OMB by conceding minor issues. Staff members of the Department of the Treasury frequently made "courtesy calls" to OIRA desk officers to apprise them of emerging regulations. Therefore, said the Department of Treasury's Carro, "We all have good relationships with our desk officers at OIRA."[110] An HHS manager explained that the relevant statute was used as a starting point for writing regulations—but then the proposal would be "tempered" in deference to the slant of anticipated OIRA preferences.

"Get in below the bow line" is an old OMB saying. OMB officials sought to get involved in rule making before the rules took shape. EO 12498 was designed for this purpose. The frequently cited data about the proportion of proposed regulations that were approved or disapproved by OIRA may understate OIRA's impact. "While, as of 1982, eighty-six percent of all draft rules sent by agencies to OMB had been 'cleared without change,' it is likely that OMB had some impact on their substance. Often the Office is in close contact with the agency staff drafting the rules, and sometimes helps to fashion the proposal before it is 'logged' for review."[111] OMB was involved in EPA rule making for over a year under the National Ambient Air Quality Standard for particulate matter before any proposal was made public. Even if OMB did not exercise prior clearance, Olson revealed, the EPA played a "guessing game" in attempting to draft rules it believed would clear OMB.[112] EPA's regulation management branch chief Odelia C. Funke observed that there was a "very high awareness of OMB" among agency staff as they developed regulatory proposals.[113]

As noted in chapter 3, Goodman and Wrightson have concluded that their research confirmed the speculation of earlier researchers. The Reagan regulatory reform program was "institutionalized," they determined, insofar as the agencies acquiesced to White House demands for compliance.[114] OMB director Miller noticed the difference, too:

> I'd call up an agency [in 1976 when he was involved with CWPS and RARG] and say, "We just saw this morning in the *Federal Register* a regulation you published. We think it is a major rule which requires an IIS [inflation impact statement]." They'd say no and that was the end of the conversation. Today they say, "Oh yes, we're very sorry, we weren't sure but if you think so, we'll prepare an RIA [regulatory impact assessment]."[115]

Under the supervision of a probusiness president and an efficiency-oriented OMB, the regulatory agencies of the 1980s developed a new level of sensitivity concerning compliance costs borne by businesses, and a greater receptivity toward the opinions and needs of the business community. The assistant secretary for policy evaluation in the Department of HHS closely examined the relationship between costs and benefits in regulatory proposals arising in HHS constituent agencies. The assistant secretary's office would attempt to identify cost-cutting opportunities. By 1985, the FDA's autonomy in making regulations had been almost entirely eliminated by the Office of the Secretary of HHS. In recent years, the FDA has been far more agreeable to the accelerated approval of new drugs.[116]

The CPSC also became more sensitive to compliance costs. Although this sensitivity can legitimately be traced back to judicial decisions of the late 1970s, an additional impetus was provided by some statutory amendments in 1981, in which Congress required CPSC to provide flexible regulatory analyses. The commission now relies more on voluntary than mandatory compliance methods.[117]

EPA's emerging efforts to show more accommodation toward business were reflected most dramatically in its Regulatory Negotiation Project, designed in 1983 and first utilized in 1984. As of March 1988, EPA had arranged seven negotiated rule-making episodes, most conducted by the Regulatory Negotiation Project in EPA's Office of Policy, Planning, and Evaluation. In one "reg-neg" activity, a dispute between the Natural Resources Defense Council and the state of New York on the issue of residential woodstoves was resolved. The result was a set of EPA regulations governing new source performance standards for woodstoves to deal with their emissions of particulate matter and carbon monoxide.[118] While negotiations designed to determine the kind of regulations that industry would find palatable would have once been unthinkable, agencies encountered incentives to minimize the incidence of provocations against business.

OSHA provided another demonstration of its growing accommodation in the context of an OSHA rule on lead exposure standards that required manufacturers to provide respirators to exposed workers. The 3M Corporation, which manufactured a disposable respirator that did not appear to satisfy the OSHA standards, filed suit to invalidate the test procedures in the standard. 3M lost in district court and was expected to lose on appeal. Nevertheless, OSHA officials met in 1981 with representatives of 3M and agreed to change the standard. Other interested parties were not invited to comment. A proposed regulation was published by OSHA to carry out its pledge to 3M.[119] Bryner concluded:

> OSHA has moved from being one of the most often criticized regulatory agencies by regulated industries to one of the most popular ones. One official of the U.S. Chamber of Commerce explained the reversal of perceptions: "I don't think there's a regulatory agency in Washington that has delivered more on candidate Reagan's promises on regulatory reform—OSHA's way out in front in that respect.... OSHA, really for the first time, has widespread acceptance in the business community."[120]

Better Management

While critics of the Reagan administration denounce many of the actions of OMB mentioned above as constituting a pattern of deprivation of due process, an assault on the Administrative Procedure Act, and an erosion of access to the quasi-legislative process, the case studies may also be construed as caricatures that reveal "growing pains" in a bold, innovative program. Given the impatience of the American public with the erratic regulatory system that had emerged in the decades preceding the Reagan era, few Americans would opt to return to the regulatory world of 1980.

What has been gained? First, it is more difficult for various agencies to trap a regulated entity in a maze of inconsistent regulations that deprive the hapless party of its "right to comply."[121] The regulatory policy areas in which OIRA coordinated the regulatory actions of various agencies include (1) the 1981 hydrogen sulfide issues, involving a toxic, carcinogenic gas that emerges with crude petroleum during oil drilling (involving EPA, OSHA, and Commerce's National Oceanic and Atmospheric Administration); (2) the animal welfare statutes relating to treatment of laboratory animals (involving HHS's Public Health Service and USDA's Animal and Plant Health Inspection Service); (3) the production of nuclear waste at the various National Laboratories (involving Energy, EPA, and NRC); and (4) the 1991 controversy over definition of wetlands (involving the Army Corps of Engineers, EPA, USDA, and Interior). In these and other cases, OIRA brought representatives of agencies together to avoid overlap and contradictions in regulations.

When OIRA reviewed a proposed regulation and had reason to believe that there was an overlap of jurisdiction with other agencies, the reviewer would often inquire of the proposing agency whether it had coordinated with other agencies. Even if the agency claimed to have consulted with other agencies, the OIRA reviewer might call the other agencies to confirm that no jurisdiction problem persisted. If the consultation with the other agencies led the reviewer to believe that there was the potential of an interagency dispute or that overlapping and conflicting regulations might be produced, then the reviewer might recommend that the proposed regulation be disapproved.[122] Even Reagan critics often concede the need for the EOP to act as a "traffic cop" to avoid the collision of conflicting regulations.

Second, the regulatory review process induced nearly every agency and commission to establish offices of regulatory analysis staffed by economists and other analysts who took one last, hard look at proposed regulations to ensure some semblance of economic rationality and defensibility, before the proposals left the agency. The spectacle of "nonsense regulations," which imposed substantial costs while providing minimal benefits,[123] nearly disappeared under the rigors of careful review. The comforting aspect of the existence of offices of regulatory analysis to avoid inefficient regulations had to be weighed against the concern that regulatory analysis could be used as a smoke screen behind which politically motivated decisions could masquerade as impartial economic decisions.[124] But, today, it is inconceivable that major regulations will ever be issued without a regulatory analysis, and this is a contribution of the Reagan Revolution.

Third, the involvement of the partisan Executive Office of the President—which may have compromised the aura of pure "neutral competence" in the quasi-legislative process—may have contributed some democratic legitimacy to a government activity that had fallen into disrepute because it was being carried out by unelected but autonomous (and often low-level) bureaucrats. The president ascends to his position by obtaining votes. His involvement may lend credibility to what had become a largely discredited instrumentality.[125]

Some evidence suggests that the regulatory agencies are doing their jobs better. Cabinet-level department heads and agency heads are more involved in rule making. OIRA's Eisenger considers EO 12291 and 12498 to be instruments that enable agency administrators to manage and control their agencies more effectively. The entire hierarchy is activated in the rule-making process because of the clearance process. The opportunity for an obscure corner of the bureaucracy to generate costly, nonsensical regulations seems to have been delimited substantially by the Reagan regulatory reform program.

6 Congress's Involvement in Regulation and Reform

CONGRESSIONAL CONTROL OF REGULATION

Congress's Historical Involvement

President Ronald Reagan's regulatory review process tested prevalent understandings of the relationship between the legislative and executive branches. The commonplaces of bureaucracy portray a president who exercises unity-of-command authority over the bureaucracy; the legislative branch's control over agency charters and authority and appropriations within agencies suggests that Congress exercises control over an agency's life and death. The growth of congressional oversight over the years prompted scholars to place Congress in the lead in the competition for control over the bureaucracy.[1] However, Congress had also sown the seeds for a rising presidential role. As Rourke observes:

> In placing broad discretionary powers in the hands of administrative agencies, Congress produced one result that it almost certainly did not intend. The legislature made it much easier for a new president to shift the direction of policy when he takes office without having to ask Congress to amend the law before doing so.... [This] may... enable a president to turn public policy in directions that Congress does not want to take.[2]

The Reagan administration's determination to shift the balance in its favor compelled Congress to evaluate several options for conflict, compromise, or concession.

In this chapter, I shall examine Congress's reaction to the regulatory review process. Exchange theory can help to explain why Congress, in the aggregate, chose to be more cautious than confrontational in its reaction to presidential initiative. Congress recognized that its own mechanisms for overseeing regulatory agencies were creating gaps of coordination and realized that a moderate level of presidential leadership was preferable to a vacuum of leadership. Members of Congress also sought innovative ways to make presidential regulatory review contribute toward their own political objectives.

Congress has exercised control over the bureaucracy through various mechanisms. According to Harris, these include drafting detailed statutes, prescribing internal organization and procedures for departments, making appropriations, overseeing agencies, and conducting investigations.[3] Michael W. Kirst describes how appropriations committees can apply relatively informal pressure on agency heads. This induces the agency heads to comply with demands of committee members without the committee being obliged to enact statutes.[4] Many of Congress's devices to control administration are dysfunctional. As Harris writes:

> Legislative controls which are unduly detailed stifle initiative; make for inflexibility and inefficiency in the conduct of government programs; sometimes result in imposing the will of individual legislators, or small groups, in matters in which they do not speak for the entire legislature and which are best left to executive officials; and end in frustrating the basic will of the legislative body.[5]

One of Congress's dramatic initiatives for controlling the actions of regulatory agencies was the legislative veto. Although some of the early provisions regarding the legislative veto were favored by Presidents Herbert Hoover and Franklin D. Roosevelt, such provisions have attracted the ire of eleven presidents, from Woodrow Wilson to Ronald Reagan, who regarded the device as an unconstitutional violation of the separation of powers.[6] Candidate Reagan expressed sympathy for the concept of a legislative veto in the 1980 campaign, but in April 1981 his attorney general, William French Smith, pledged that the Department of Justice would systematically challenge provisions for such a veto in the courts on constitutional grounds.[7]

As Congress grew more attached to the legislative veto, observers such as Assistant Attorney General Theodore B. Olson noticed that, by the early 1980s, congressional micromanagement of the executive branch was on the rise.[8] Then came the 1983 decision in *Immigration and Naturalization Service v. Chadha et al.*,[9] which nullified all provisions for a legislative veto. The

Supreme Court, according to West and Cooper,[10] sought to explain away the quasi-legislative power of executive agencies by denying it was really legislative. The court observed:

> Executive action under legislatively delegated authority that might resemble "legislative" action in some respects is not subject to the approval of both Houses of Congress and the President for the reason that the Constitution does not so require. That kind of Executive action is always subject to check by the terms of the legislation that authorized it.[11]

Construed in that way, the legislative veto had to be considered an encroachment on executive power.

But to David Plocher, staff attorney of OMB Watch, Congress was already extremely limited in its practical options for molding policy. "*Chadha* took the crutch away from somebody already on the floor."[12]

The *Chadha* decision does not seem to have eliminated the legislative veto entirely. Louis Fisher noted that Congress enacted fifty-three legislative vetoes between the *Chadha* decision and the adjournment of the Ninety-eighth Congress. Although he noticed that the character of legislative vetoes had evolved—they focused primarily on appropriations and transfers of funds between programs (reprogramming)—he predicted that the court's activist opinion would not be the last word: "The court painted with too broad a brush and offered a simplistic solution that is unacceptable to the political branches. Its decision will be eroded by open defiance and subtle evasion."[13]

If anything, *Chadha* emboldened Congress to press its claim that it should be permitted to second-guess the regulatory agencies. Said Secretary of Transportation James A. Burnley IV, "We have to recognize that Congress, one way or another, is going to assert certain prerogatives." Burnley saw a deteriorating relationship between the executive and legislative branches after *Chadha*. Norman Ornstein of the American Enterprise Institute reported "a sharp and continuing erosion of trust" between the branches. With the legislative veto curtailed, Congress was searching for other alternatives, with more "micromanagement" the likely result.[14] Crovitz and Rabkin warned: "Laws that limit executive discretion reduce the protections of individual liberty and equally cripple the efficient pursuit of national goals. Good government requires a vibrant executive branch free of improper constraints."[15] Congress's plan to control the agencies through prescription and proscription would have solidified the president's outsider status. Had the other branches allowed the format to continue, the president would have had difficulty attracting any notice from his subordinates. Congress's fateful decision to delegate regulatory power necessitated more trust than the legislative veto could express.

Congressional Capacity to Control Regulation

Speaker of the House Sam Rayburn (D-Tex.) explained the creation of regulatory agencies this way: "We created the regulatory agencies to do what we don't have time to do."[16] This rationale, while defending one congressional invention, ironically tends to discredit Congress's inclination to second-guess the agencies on a daily basis (this was the purpose, for example, of its invention of the legislative veto).[17]

Office of Information and Regulatory Affairs (OIRA) administrator S. Jay Plager indicated that the very nature of a legislative body makes it impossible for Congress to control regulation: "There are over 100 agencies. The independent regulatory commissions [IRCs] think that they are independent of everybody. The president ought to exercise overall coordinating and policy formulating. Congress can't do it. Congress comprises 535 individual fiefdoms."[18] House Majority Leader Richard Gephardt (D-Mo.) has conceded the point: "We're usually a reactive institution. It's very hard to lead."[19]

Observers have noted that Congress's input into regulatory policy is limited by the legislature's focus on *process* rather than actual policy design and impact. Foreman writes that politicians rarely concentrate on policy goals: "Oversight is, at bottom, a shortsighted, *means-focused* political enterprise, little concerned with or able directly to promote distant protective ends."[20]

In 1981, Gilmour found Congress's incapacity to control regulation effectively to be predictable, since it was intrinsic to Congress's structure. This leadership crisis created a "stunning loss of governmental accountability." Congressional oversight was "fragmented into more committee and subcommittee units than ever before." The winners of a struggle for bureaucratic control between the president and Congress were "the agencies themselves, their clientele groups, and uncoordinated committees and individual members of Congress," as well as the congressional staff.[21] Sundquist categorized Congress's institutional incapacity in 1977 with the terms "parochialism," "irresponsibility," "sluggishness," and "amateurism."[22]

Having proclaimed through its own leadership that it lacked the time to perform detailed regulation of the economy, Congress delegated the rule-making power to executive officials, maintaining control through oversight.

This oversight has tended to overinvolve the agencies in dysfunctional arrangements involving demands by congressional committee members for counterproductive policies,[23] for appointments of friends of members of Congress to positions in agencies,[24] and for other actions that do not promote the public interest. Congress has shown no incentive to improve regulation by taking more effective responsibility for developing viable rules, except when it has been accused of "micromanagement," which has been denounced by various observers. Congress appears to be uninterested generally in taking responsibility and "heat" for the impact of specific regulatory policies it might develop. Part of its exchange relationship with the executive agencies calls for the agencies to remain on the firing line. Members of Congress can then point an accusing finger at them when it is politically convenient to do so.

CONGRESSIONAL REACTION TO PRESIDENTIAL CONTROL OF REGULATION

The presidency and Congress each claims the authority and duty to control the bureaucracy's implementation, to the exclusion of the other branch. Although the competing claims are contradictory, the constitutional system of coequal branches makes the duality of command unavoidable. Christopher H. Pyle and Richard M. Pious explain the collision of interests this way:

> Presidents assume that any powers or responsibilities that Congress by law assigns to department officers become part of the president's authority, subsumed under his duty to execute the laws faithfully. Congress assumes, when it delegates authority by law directly to an agency official, that the president is to be excluded from the business.[25]

Louis Fisher has noted that presidents misunderstand Congress's motivation: "Presidents and their supporters face continued frustration because they ignore, or try to overlook, the legitimate stake and interest of Congress in administrative matters."[26]

Congress has greeted rising presidential involvement in regulatory control with considerable skepticism. Senator Thomas F. Eagleton (D-Mo.) expressed this skepticism in an exchange with the chairman of President Jimmy Carter's Council of Economic Advisers, Charles L. Schultze.

> [Q. Eagleton:] ... I think it is very conceivable that this Congress will give to the President of the United States the authority to overrule [EPA administrator] Costle ... or overrule any ... regulatory agency.

> [A. Schultze:] With all due respect to Mr. Costle, my strong belief, in fact, conviction, is that the President already has that authority.
>
> [Q.:] Well, there is some doubt about it.[27]

Congress seems to have been caught by surprise by the extensiveness of President Reagan's influence in regulation. Patrick M. McLain, counsel for the Subcommittee on Oversight and Investigations of the House Committee on Energy and Commerce, recalled that the committee first examined the OMB's involvement in regulation in June 1981. "The record of that hearing is amazing," said McLain. "It was impossible to get anyone interested in this." Representative John D. Dingell (D-Mich.) and Senator Albert Gore Jr. (D-Tenn.) understood the problem, but could not generate interest among other legislators. "There was no 'OMB Watch,' other congressmen weren't interested, and the press wasn't interested either."[28]

Several members of the House of Representatives were promptly agitated by the Reagan initiative and its appearance of secrecy. The expressions of anger arising from the lower house seemed to generate curiosity in the Senate, which increased its oversight activities. In 1985, the Senate's Environment and Public Works Committee began its series of frequent subcommittee hearings on delays in environmental regulation.[29]

While the champions of regulation in Congress had sought to ward off deregulatory innovations during the Carter era, the Reagan administration's initiatives created alarm as some members of Congress noticed the step change in the president's influence on the regulatory establishment. Curiously, Congress's reflexive reaction was "to confirm these actions legislatively, if only to limit the degree to which this discretion could be used," as Eads and Fix wrote. They explained this outcome by the fact that economic regulation had been discredited by 1981,[30] so that few politicians were willing to expend political capital to protect economic regulation. However, no majority in Congress had written off social regulation or was willing to give the president carte blanche to undermine the objectives of social regulation.

The classic, and most effective, medium for the expression of congressional will is still the statute. The ultimate victory for Reagan and for advocates of presidential review of regulation would have been the enactment of a law permitting it, while the ultimate victory for opponents would have been an enactment (over certain presidential veto) prohibiting the process. Dingell reflected: "Now, I observe that almost every Congress since I have come here has had regulatory reform legislation submitted to it. As a matter of fact, there have been several submissions of regulatory reform legislation giving

OMB this kind of regulatory power over the other regulatory agencies." But advocates have not made much headway:

> The Congress has consistently rejected those kinds of offerings from the administration. That tends to indicate to me that the administration neither thinks it has the authority nor does the administration, in fact, have the authority. As a matter of fact, the administration wishes to set forth in statutory language the power for the Office of Management and Budget to commence functioning as essentially a review body, judicial, quasi-judicial or administrative.[31]

In the other house, Senator Charles Percy (R-Ill.) emphasized that the Republican-controlled Senate was not responsible for Congress's refusal to enact a regulatory reform law, citing the Senate's unanimous approval of the proposed Laxalt-Leahy Regulatory Reform Act of 1981. The preliminary draft of the bill, S.1080, included provisions to permit application of cost-benefit analysis to regulatory decisions and to make the IRCs subject to regulatory review. OMB would be given statutory authority to conduct the review process. With some revisions, the bill was reported by the Senate Judiciary Committee on July 14, 1981. The companion measure in the House of Representatives was H.R.746. The House Judiciary Committee reported H.R.746 out in early December 1981. The Senate approved S.1080 unanimously in March 1982. But the House Rules Committee under chairman Richard Bolling (D-Mo.) did not report H.R.746 with a rule by the time the second session of the Ninety-seventh Congress ended, and thus the attempt to legislate regulatory relief stalled.[32] Percy pinned the responsibility for continuing uncertainty about the legal status of regulatory review on the House of Representatives. "I might note, for the record, [that a regulatory reform bill] has passed in the Senate in the last two sessions of Congress. We've just simply been blocked in the House. We're hoping now with [House Minority Leader] Bob Michel's help we can carry it through the House."[33] A number of specific incidents during which regulatory policies dictated by OMB conflicted with the preferences of members of Congress have provoked congressional ire. Representative Mike Synar (D-Okla.) offered this account of the frustration:

> I am reminded of one of Mr. Reagan's predecessors, Richard Nixon—when he did not like the purposes for which Congress had appropriated money, he impounded the funds.
>
> Now we have another President who, when he does not like the purposes for which Congress has created executive and independent agencies, seeks to impound the intent of Congress.[34]

One such incident inciting congressional anger involved plans by the Occupational Safety and Health Administration (OSHA) to regulate ethylene oxide (C_2H_4O), a carcinogen to which hospital workers are often exposed. The Senate Committee on Labor and Human Resources agitated for years for a short-term exposure limit (STEL) concerning ethylene oxide. Finally, under threat of a contempt citation, a rule—still bearing obvious OIRA editorial revisions—was submitted to the *Federal Register* office.[35] In June 1985, the chairmen of five congressional committees—Dingell, William Ford (D-Mich.), Augustus Hawkins (D-Calif.), Peter Rodino (D-N.J.), and Jack Brooks (D-Tex.)—joined with the Public Citizen Health Research Group and other groups to sue OSHA.[36]

The ethylene oxide incident served as a prelude to another incident a year later, which would restore the balance between the presidency and Congress. In 1986, OIRA ordered the Environmental Protection Agency (EPA) to defer asbestos regulation to OSHA and the Consumer Product Safety Commission. To labor union officials, the OIRA demand amounted to a sellout of worker interests to the asbestos industry. But, as OMB Watch staff attorney Plocher said, "Dingell caught them red-handed on worker exposure."[37] In exasperation, Dingell enlisted support from other committee chairmen to defund OIRA pending reauthorization of the Paperwork Reduction Act. Joining with him were Brooks, chairman of the Government Operations Committee; Dan Glickman (D-Kans.), chairman of the Subcommittee on Administrative Law and Government Relations; and Appropriations Committee Chairman Jamie L. Whitten (D-Miss.).[38] Senator Gore, one of the most outspoken legislators on health and safety issues, denounced presidential regulatory review as a violation of the Constitution.[39] In 1986, Senator Levin and several other members of the Senate Governmental Affairs Committee introduced the proposed Rule Making Information Act, S.2023, designed to force OMB to open its regulatory review process to public inspection and to complete any regulatory reviews within sixty days. In June 1986, Dingell set in motion actions designed to terminate OIRA appropriations once the scheduled expiration date of the Paperwork Reduction Act arrived, soliciting and obtaining Brooks's support to defund OIRA.[40] On August 6, 1986, the House passed a defunding provision as an amendment to the Treasury, Postal Service, and General Government Appropriations Bills. The amendment read: "None of the funds made available by this act shall be available to fund activities of the Office of Information and Regulatory Affairs."[41]

The proposed defunding of OIRA was designed to terminate the regulatory review program, but it had severe implications for OIRA's other projects. These included paperwork reduction and the development of government information technology. President Reagan's Grace Commission had recommended improvements in data processing in the federal government, and Senate Governmental Affairs Committee chairman William V. Roth Jr. (R-Del.) wanted to implement the recommendations. The Senate committee had formulated fifty to sixty recommendations reflecting the Grace Commission's administrative management recommendations (including some concerning information management involving data processing) as part of S.2230, the proposed Federal Management Reorganization and Cost Control Act of 1986. Another senator, Lawton Chiles (D-Fla.), was interested in the OIRA funding issue because of his sponsorship of the Paperwork Reduction Act of 1980, which earned him the label "father of paperwork reduction."[42]

Thus, a constituency for some of OIRA's programs had a foothold in the Senate. OMB enlisted its support. Through contact initiated by OIRA deputy administrator Robert P. Bedell and directed to Margaret T. Wrightson, staff director of the Subcommittee on Intergovernmental Relations of the Senate Governmental Affairs Committee, Senator David F. Durenberger (R-Minn.), the subcommittee's chairman, was asked to broker a deal.[43] Durenberger, a moderate Republican, had reservations about the effects of the regulatory review process because of explosions in grain elevators in his state and OIRA's opposition to regulations to require safety measures to avoid such accidents.[44] An OMB Watch report explained:

> Durenberger, although frustrated with OMB, does not question the basic framework of OMB regulatory review and wants to maintain a working relationship with [OMB]. Accordingly, he was willing to make a deal that would get OMB to provide more public disclosure of OIRA's regulatory review process in exchange for his Subcommittee reporting out a Paperwork Reduction reauthorization bill.[45]

Durenberger, Wrightson, OMB director James C. Miller III, and OIRA administrator Wendy L. Gramm hammered out an agreement under which OIRA would establish expanded disclosure in exchange for Durenberger's facilitation of OIRA authorization.

Roth's committee staff hoped to combine the data processing provisions (some of which were opposed by OMB) with the OIRA reauthorization, in order to get the data processing rules approved. Alarmed that paperwork reduction might fall in the linkage, Chiles demanded that Title 6 be separated from the rest of the bill. These diverse interests complicated efforts to reach a reconciliation. Just before the August 1986 recess, various congressional staff members sought to arrange for the bill to be passed by unanimous consent. The dealing was unsuccessful, and Senators Roth, Chiles, Durenberger, Levin, and Warren Rudman (R-N.H.) cosponsored a revised bill, S.2887, the proposed Paperwork Reduction Act Amendments of 1986, *inter alia* requiring Senate confirmation of future OIRA administrators.[46]

The eventual support of OIRA funding by Brooks, Chiles, Durenberger, Levin, and Roth (each for his own reasons) brought about negotiations between Congress and OMB on reform of the regulatory review process. Several members of the Governmental Affairs Committee had introduced S.2023, a bill designed to force OMB to provide more disclosure of its regulatory review operation and to limit OIRA review to sixty days. In January 1986, OMB director Miller asserted to a Senate committee that S.2023 would interfere with the president's prerogative to execute the laws. Soliciting support for OIRA reauthorization, OMB officials approached Durenberger and Levin. In the ensuing horse trading, the senators extracted a promise of increased disclosure in exchange for their promise to support a Governmental Affairs Committee vote to reauthorize the Paperwork Reduction Act. On June 25, the committee did, indeed, approve a reauthorization of OIRA in S.2230. Roth's attempt to pass the bill through unanimous consent was thwarted when Senator Gary Hart (D-Colo.), acting at Dingell's behest, placed a hold on it.[47]

In accordance with an agreement with Levin and Durenberger, OIRA administrator Gramm wrote a memorandum on June 13, 1986, to executive agencies implementing new disclosure procedures. OIRA would thereafter provide upon request copies of preliminary proposed rules and final proposed rules that had been submitted for review under Executive Order 12291. OIRA would then provide upon request copies of correspondence between OIRA and agency heads relating to such proposals and review of them. OIRA would then disclose to EPA and to any other agency that desired it the same information on written and oral communications from individuals not employed by the federal government on the topic of the agency's proposed rules. OIRA would also invite an agency representative to attend meetings between OIRA and individuals not employed by the federal government concerning the agency's proposed rules, and would disclose the list of such meetings whether or not agency representatives had attended. OIRA would also provide an accounting of all review activities conducted pursuant to Executive Order 12291 and would keep on file for public inspection any proposed rules that were submitted under Executive Order 12498 after publication of the *Regulatory Program of the United States Government*, OIRA's compilation of the regulatory calendars of contemplated regulations drafted by the agencies.[48]

One additional price that the administration had to pay was acceptance of the checks and balances of Senate confirmation of future appointments of OIRA administrators.[49]

OMB Watch reported that OMB evaded a number of concessions demanded by critics of the regulatory review program, refusing to concede on four important issues. It refused to publicly disclose communications with agency personnel during reviews of proposed regulations. It refused to disclose the current status of OMB reviews. It maintained its position that judicial review of OMB activity was unwarranted because the activity purportedly had no substantive impact on regulations. It refused to admit that it lacked statutory authority to operate the regulatory review process.[50]

Gramm held the line on the underlying concept of regulatory review in OMB.

> These new procedures and OIRA's existing procedures are intended only to improve the internal management of the Federal Government, and are not intended to create any right or benefit, substantive or procedural, enforceable at law or in equity by a party against the United States, its agencies, its officers or any person.[51]

OMB Watch noted with some displeasure that OIRA agreed to disclose contacts with outsiders only *at the request of an agency*, impeding efforts by public interest groups to discover presidential involvement in rule making. The organization complained: "What this 'deal' means to the public is that OIRA can continue to remain largely unaccountable, operating behind the scenes with powers to shape agency policies and procedures."[52]

Negotiations between OMB representatives and members of the Senate ensued.[53] OMB director Miller withdrew opposition to S.2230 and Roth acquiesced to separating OIRA reauthorization from the computer provisions he had sought. With the deadlock broken, the Senate Appropriations Committee on August 14 approved an OIRA appropriation of $9 million for fiscal year 1987, $5.4 million of which was designated for paperwork reduction. The House had deleted funding for OIRA in passing H.R.5297, an appropriations bill for fiscal year 1987, but in subsequent negotiations, OIRA funding was saved. The eventual omnibus continuing resolution reauthorized OIRA for three years.[54] Goodman and Wrightson conclude:

> A line-item OIRA account was put into the continuing resolution and OIRA was precluded from using any of these funds to review rules, unless such rules were contained in or related to an information collection request. It

> is doubtful that this kind of congressional warning will have a significant impact on OIRA activities.[55]

Looking back, former OIRA administrator Gramm was at peace with the concessions she and Miller made. "A lot of the procedures already in place were formalized," she recalled. "It helped to let people know what the procedures are." She described the 1986 agreements as having been of no serious concern to her although "they did constrain me" to some degree. "Limiting the flow of information [circulating within the executive branch] is quite a problem." But, in recognizing that the dispute reflected tension between the legislative and executive branches, she may have preserved OIRA by being willing to negotiate.[56]

"Deadline hammers" were inserted into legislation, reflecting Congress's impatience with delay caused by the regulatory review process. These deadline hammers were tough default provisions that would kick in automatically if Reagan's executive agencies hesitated beyond a pre-set deadline to promulgate a rule. They were designed to reverse any incentive of the Reagan administration to delay regulations. The Hazardous and Solid Waste Amendments of 1984[57] contained such hammers; if EPA did not regulate by a certain date, disposal of specified categories of hazardous waste would automatically be substantially limited.[58]

The One Hundredth Congress, the last of the Reagan era, continued to show interest in regulatory reform legislation. The Committee on Labor and Human Resources, chaired by Senator Edward M. Kennedy (D-Mass.), met in July 1988 to discuss possible legislative responses through appropriations amendments.[59] Noll reports that most of the legislation proposed in the One Hundredth Congress was designed to reverse previous deregulation efforts. "Among these were bills that would reregulate the airlines, tighten the regulation of railroads and trucks, and declare a moratorium on further deregulation in telecommunications." Noll concluded that the Reagan reform was not likely to be reversed in the next few years, but denied that "recent reforms are safe from reversal."[60]

Throughout the Reagan era, the growing influence of OIRA and—by extension—of OMB and the president captured Congress's attention. Symptomatically, Senators Durenberger and Max Baucus (D-Mont.) complained:

> A combination of powers created through law and Executive Order has lodged in [OMB] the power to run virtually the entire regulatory program of the Federal government. Decisions made by and at OMB are not subject

> to either public scrutiny or effective Congressional oversight because none of the many laws created to assure fairness and openness apply.[61]

An angry Congress pigeonholed OMB as a politicized agent of the president with an obvious ax to grind. Gilmour and Sperry explain:

> Paradoxically, OMB's recent effectiveness in advancing the President's political agenda through the budget process may have diminished its influence on final budgetary outcomes. Congress has come to understand OMB as the agent of a point of view, not as a source of "neutral competence." Accordingly, in congressional offices, the President's budgets of the past two years have been widely termed, "dead on arrival"—even before they were presented. Increasing credibility—and deference—has been given the Congressional Budget Office as having "the best numbers in town."[62]

Congress has never fully mobilized to terminate the regulatory review program. One explanation is the threat of a presidential veto or the companion threat that the president will evade congressional action to terminate the program.[63] But this sort of threat does not explain the remarkable ambivalence of Congress toward a process that challenged its supremacy relative to the executive agencies. Many members of Congress have sought to use the OIRA review mechanism to affect the outcome of rule making through contacts with OIRA and the director of OMB,[64] thereby providing a tacit endorsement of the process.

As the three-year reauthorization of OIRA, approved by Congress in 1986, was expiring, some predicted controversy within Congress that would lead to another reauthorization. Senate Governmental Affairs Committee hearings in February 1990, one year into President George Bush's term of office, demonstrated that the regulatory review process had taken root. The hearings were scheduled to consider S.1742, the proposed Federal Information Resources Management Act of 1989, sponsored by Senators Jeff Bingaman (D-N.M.) and Joseph I. Lieberman (D-Conn.). Among other provisions, the bill offered a two-year authorization of OIRA. But it would have required OMB to provide detailed written justification of its disapprovals and would have required OIRA to report oral communications and to allow the public to review its records. Lieberman, a progressive Democrat, observed that "S.1742... recognizes the president's authority to review proposed regulations, but it also imposes reasonable procedural restrictions." He continued: "This legislation clearly recognizes the Executive's authority to enforce the law, but accepts the reality that Congress can set up statutes and procedures for guiding the

Executive in doing so."[65] In a prepared statement accompanying his oral testimony to the Governmental Affairs Committee, Lieberman wrote:

> Past abuses are not a reason for eliminating a centralized review of agency action by OMB, and I am confident that the Bush Administration will be more sensitive to congressional mandated action in general and to the need for safety and environmental regulations in particular. Nevertheless, the historical record does provide a basis for reasonable restrictions on the regulatory review process.[66]

In an exchange with Public Citizen Congress Watch senior attorney David Vladeck, committee chairman John Glenn (D-Ohio) indicated clearly that OMB's involvement in regulatory review would not disappear.

> [Q.] You would prefer to have OMB completely out of the loop?
>
> [A.] Right. But we recognize that that is not likely to happen.
>
> [Q.] I think you're correct. [Laughter.]

OMB director Richard Darman threatened a presidential veto, objecting to violations of the separation of powers and to time limits that could have encouraged agencies to wait to submit proposed regulations to OIRA until the office had no time to carry out its review. Representatives John Conyers (D-Mich.) and Frank Horton (R-N.Y.) sought a compromise in which OMB would agree to fundamental changes in regulatory review procedures at OMB. It appeared that certain members of Congress had reached a deal with the administration. However, White House Chief of Staff John Sununu expressed reservations about the agreement and, along with presidential counsel C. Boyden Gray, canceled it. To add insult to injury, on June 6, 1990, OMB released Draft Circular A-134 weakening some of the 1986 disclosure agreements to which it had agreed in a deal with members of the Senate. Members of the Senate Governmental Affairs Committee marked up S. 1742 on June 7, 1990.[67] It was reported to the Senate on October 2, 1990, "with an amendment in the nature of a substitute and placed on the Senate calendar."[68] It never came up for a vote.

Despite Congress's apparent acceptance of the concept of centralized review, OIRA was not reauthorized by Congress in 1989 or 1990. S.1742 was never acted upon by the full Senate. The Treasury and Postal Service Appropriations Bill was passed by Congress in the fall of 1990; it included funding for OMB and OIRA. Two bills that would have reauthorized OIRA—S.1139 from Senator Sam Nunn (D-Ga.) and S.1044 (the proposed Federal Resources

Management Act) from Senator Glenn—had been introduced. Neither bill was reported out by the Committee on Governmental Affairs. The bill that seemed to wind its way farthest through the process was Glenn's S.1942, the proposed Regulatory Review Sunshine Act. S.1942 would have established accountability to the public, while exempting oral communications of the president, the vice president, heads of Cabinet-level departments, the director of OMB, and the administrator of EPA from disclosure requirements.[69] The bill was a compromise that would not have authorized regulatory review in OMB (thus keeping its status inferior to that of statutory requirements) but would have refrained from tampering with the continued operation of the review process.

The Senate Governmental Affairs Committee voted eight to three on November 22, 1991, to report S.1942 to the Senate. Senator Glenn prepared this description of S.1942 for a speech on the floor of the Senate:

> Agencies would be required to publish in the Federal register a list of rules being reviewed by the Administration, as well as explain how such review has affected their rulemaking decisions. The Council [on Competitiveness, successor to Reagan's Task Force on Regulatory Relief] and OMB would have to disclose to the public and the rulemaking agency a record of all documents pertaining to review of an agency's rules, including communications with organizations outside of the government. They would also have to comply with reasonable time limits on regulatory review.

The bill was placed on the Senate Legislative Calendar on February 25, 1992, but it languished thereafter. Other bills proposed in the 102d Congress include the proposed Paperwork Reduction Act of 1991, a bipartisan effort headed by Senator Bob Kasten (R-Wis.), designed to reinvigorate OIRA,[70] and a bill introduced by Representative Thomas W. Ewing (R-Ill.) to institutionalize Bush's moratorium order in legislation."[71] Neither of these bills was enacted. The White House had little to say about legislation, perpetuating the Reagan-Bush practice of passively awaiting legislation that might place regulatory review in the statutes. Instead, the administration defiantly insisted that it would continue to carry out regulatory review under EO 12291. "We are the ones who are going to run this operation—and it's not going to be Congress," Vice President Dan Quayle vowed."[72]

Morrison noted that Congress was ambivalent toward regulatory review and predicted that Congress would exercise restraint. He observed that the OMB-operated review process permitted Congress to pass popular legislation while counting on OMB to defuse otherwise destructive confrontations with industry.[73]

Verkuil pointed out the paradox that congressional displays of legislative force, designed to restrain the president, can unintentionally restrict Congress's own power. He writes:

> Congress must recognize that regulation of direct presidential contacts is as much a restraint upon its own control over executive agency policymaking as it is upon the President's control. Unnecessary formalities will frustrate presidential accountability efforts, thereby depriving Congress of a ready ally in the fight against an increasingly unaccountable bureaucracy.[74]

Members of Congress share a fundamental characteristic with the president: they are elected, and the electorate depends on them to establish broad, responsive public policy. The unelected bureaucracy can bear neither the burden of establishing legitimate policy nor the responsibility of mediating disputes between the legislature and the White House. Instead, the elected officials must restrain their desire to vanquish other government institutions: Such restraint is behavior that, as we will show in chapter 11, exchange theory suggests is necessary. In an exchange relationship of mutual interdependence, an attempt by one party to handicap the other does palpable damage to both.

A plea for more accommodation came from O'Reilly and Brown, who warned OMB and the executive agencies that they "cannot afford to antagonize the congressional committees" as they did in the Reagan era. In a 1987 article, O'Reilly and Brown added that Reagan's successor would be well served by adhering to the 1986 agreements and ensuring that OIRA spell out criteria for regulatory clearance. They advised that the White House make an effort to reform Administrative Procedure Act rule making through statute, and they called for a political division of labor in the Executive Office of the President (EOP), where OIRA would focus on "policy rationality" while the White House domestic policy staff would concern itself with "policy outcomes."[75]

Unless Congress, the president, and the bureaucracy agree to this specialization, their disputes will steal attention from substantive issues. Congress's willingness to reconcile itself with the principle of shared oversight is constructive, holding the potential of infusing into the regulatory system the democratic legitimacy of representative governance, the managerial rationality advocated by public administration scholars, and the economic efficiency proposed by economists and policy analysts.

7 Judicial Reaction to Presidential Control

The federal judiciary received cases pertaining to presidential intervention in the rule-making process in the late 1970s and in the 1980s, on the heels of a series of judicial decisions that emphatically called for considerations of due process, openness, and equity for all interested parties.[1] Public interest groups turned reflexively to the judiciary, which had delivered impressive victories to advocacy groups in the past, confident that the judicial branch would rebuff the Reagan administration's unprecedented level of intrusion into the rule-making process. But the Supreme Court had already shown signs that it was displeased with the extent to which the Courts of Appeals—especially the District of Columbia Circuit Court (the "Supreme Court for Regulation")—had maintained an intricate involvement in the elaboration of regulatory rule making and adjudicatory procedures.[2] While an increased level of presidential control over the executive agencies could be interpreted as a threat to the level of influence of the judiciary, the Supreme Court opted to sustain a loss of control over the executive branch in the interest of exercising restraint. The notion that the Supreme Court would exercise restraint in this context conforms to the literature of public law, which confirms that the court must and does systematically pass up opportunities to frustrate the will of the other branches.[3] This notion also conforms to exchange theory by illustrating the court's recognition that to undermine the other branches would violate the "bargain" among the partners in the constitutional system, and thus would undermine the court's own authority. These historical and theoretical patterns combined to catch detractors of Reagan's regulatory policy by surprise and to leave them with virtually none of the judicial support they anticipated.

HISTORICAL RELATIONSHIP

Notwithstanding the court's 1892 ruling in *Field v. Clark*[4] that "Congress cannot delegate legislative power," the Supreme Court has actually looked kindly on delegations of legislative power, regarding them as invitations to the president and other officials to "fill in the details" of the statutes.

In 1825, Chief Justice John Marshall wrote: "The line has not been exactly drawn which separates those important subjects, which must be entirely regulated by the legislature itself, from those of less interest, in which a general provision may be made, and power given to those who are to act under such general provision, to fill up the details."[5] With the innovation of the independent regulatory commission form with the creation of the Interstate Commerce Commission (ICC), the Supreme Court proceeded to confer legitimacy on the ICC's decisions. In the 1914 case of *Houston, East and West Ry. v. United States*,[6] also known as the Shreveport Case, the court upheld an order of the ICC: "Having this power [to regulate interstate commerce], Congress could provide for its execution through the aid of a subordinate body; and we conclude that the order of the [Interstate Commerce] Commission now in question cannot be held invalid upon the ground that it exceeded the authority which Congress could lawfully confer."

The Supreme Court dutifully conferred legitimacy on the instruments of business regulation enacted by Congress during the four decades that followed the creation of the ICC. Then, the Republican-dominated Supreme Court, which sought to defy Franklin D. Roosevelt's New Deal agenda, took aim at delegation. In the 1935 case of *A. L. A. Schechter Poultry Corp. v. United States*,[7] the court declared that delegating authority was unconstitutional because its standards were unacceptably ambiguous. The court's opinion, written by Chief Justice Charles E. Hughes, objected that the "discretion of the President, in approving or prescribing codes, and thus enacting laws for the government or trade and industry throughout the United States, is virtually unfettered." Roosevelt's threat to pack the court weakened the court's defiance, and the delegation approach found renewed approval. In the 1941 case of *Gray v. Powell*,[8] the court said: "Where, as here, a determination has been left to an administrative body, this delegation will be respected and the administrative conclusion left untouched."

In the 1971 District Court case of *Amalgamated Meat Cutters & Butcher Workmen of North America v. Connally*,[9] Judge Harold Leventhal stated that the Constitution does not prohibit legislative power from being delegated to the president. Fleishman and Aufses commented disapprovingly on Leventhal's opinion, objecting that it legitimated presidential encroachments into the legislative policy-making power and invited Congress to abdicate its responsibility.[10]

A number of scholars have expressed deep concern over Congress's willingness to parcel out broad grants of legislative power to the executive branch and the courts' almost uninterrupted practice of condoning it. Theodore J. Lowi, for example, calls for a retreat to the rule in the abandoned *Schechter* decision, demanding that Congress specify exact standards under which the administrative entity may carry out its delegated authority.[11] Kenneth Culp Davis, while not agreeing with Lowi's insistence that Congress specify details when it delegates authority, still insists that the public is entitled to the assurance that *somebody* is establishing and publicizing standards. As Davis describes his "reconstituted nondelegation doctrine," such standards would be set in statute or in administrative rules and administrative standards, thus providing guideposts for the public and for reviewing courts.[12]

While court decisions have not reversed the endorsement of administrative discretion and the extensive tolerance of relatively unrestrained delegation, the courts have held the power of judicial review over the agencies like a sword of Damocles. On occasion, judicial pronouncements have raised the specter of *Schechter*.[13]

The "iron triangle" literature and the initiatives of recent presidents to secure the right to impose centralized regulatory review demonstrate that it is a mistake to equate the presidency and the bureaucracy. Therefore, it is appropriate to evaluate the president's relationship with the Supreme Court separately from the bureaucracy's relationship with the Supreme Court. And, in this context, it is useful to take note of a pattern of judicial decisions over the past forty years that have tended to be deferential toward *presidential* power. Theodore L. Becker observes that the struggle between the presidents and the court (*à la* Andrew Jackson's "John Marshall has made his decision, now let him enforce it") "may have run its course." Becker writes:

> Since [the *Youngstown Sheet & Tube Co. v. Sawyer* decision] there has not been even the faintest hint of a skirmish between the court and the three succeeding Presidents—even when sizable portions of the American population have been outraged by some Court decision or decisions. We may be entering an era of unprecedented good will between these two centers of political power.[14]

Congress has not fared as well at the bar. The Supreme Court's decision in the 1983 case of *Immigration and Naturalization Service v. Chadha*[15] prohibiting the legislative veto was one in a string of judicial decisions creating a standoff between the two branches of government and causing Congress to write more detailed statutes in defense. Observers tend to believe, however, that the courts have no taste for adjudicating cases clearly involving separation of powers.[16] In such cases,[17] where the constitutional confrontation is obvious, the court seems dedicated to suppressing congressional aggrandizement of power as a way of protecting the executive branch. But, says Rosenberg, other cases involving agencies to which power is delegated[18] result in a "more far-reaching" analysis that inspects the interrelationships among agencies and other holders of power and evaluates their effects on the balance of power. "In other words," Rosenberg concludes, "more lenient review is accorded in agency specific situations." Thus, he explains, cases of direct confrontation involve a zero-sum game, but cases involving agency power prompt the court merely to assure itself that the lines of authority are in place.[19]

While agencies may have reason to be grateful to the judicial branch for protecting their turf, they do not obtain analytical support, says Bryner. The courts do not know how to do better regulatory analysis, so they merely ensure that some analysis is done.[20] It is debatable whether the courts would be quite so tolerant of *de minimis* processes carried out by other government entities that might have similarly extensive effects on members of the public. Clearly, in the minds of federal judges, the agencies are entitled to leeway in their regulation of commerce and industry.

LITIGATION: CHALLENGING CENTRALIZED REVIEW

The pattern of judicial decisions that imposed a "partnership" with the courts upon the executive agencies indicated a firm judicial commitment to due process.[21] As increasing presidential intervention in regulation in the 1970s and 1980s impinged on the carefully protected position of parties in rule-making proceedings, the public interest groups predictably turned to the judiciary. No doubt, they expected vindication of their interests against the coalition involving the president and the business community, for whom "rational" regulation would mean lower compliance costs. In the judicial arena, an unwelcome surprise awaited the public interest groups.

The courts—notably the Supreme Court—have been most tolerant of recent process initiatives that allow contacts within the executive branch to be concealed from parties in rule-making proceedings. The 1981 Court of Appeals case of *Sierra Club v. Costle*[22] set the tone by permitting the president and his agents to comment behind the scenes on emerging regulations. Judge Patricia M. Wald wrote:

> The court recognizes the basic need of the President and his White House staff to monitor the consistency of executive agency regulations with Administration policy. He and his White House advisors surely must be briefed fully and frequently about rules in the making, and their contributions to policymaking considered. The executive power, after all, is not shared—it rests exclusively with the President.... Regulations such as those involved here demand a careful weighing of cost, environmental, and energy considerations. They also have broad implications for national economic policy. Our form of government simply could not function effectively or rationally if key executive policymakers were isolated from each other and from the Chief Executive.

With this ruling as a backdrop, public interest groups have found it difficult to get the courts to pay attention to their anguished complaints that the deck has been stacked against them because it is difficult to fight off presidential contacts that the public cannot see.

Much of the controversy about presidential involvement in regulatory rule making, which has been litigated in the federal courts, centers on the question of whether the president is "just like everyone else" and thus entitled to no more access to the rule-making process than any other citizen, or is rather entitled to exert extensive influence. Even if one is determined conscientiously to resolve the issue on the basis of what is "fair," the ambiguity of "fairness" creates complexity: Shall the system be "fair" to the electoral majority that elected the president, or "fair" to minority groups, or to parties whose prosperity may be affected, or—in a situation where Congress has often been controlled by the party in opposition to the president—"fair" to the electorate that supported the party of the congressional majority? If, as Rosenberg demands, the president is frozen out of rule making, then his appointees must be trusted to deliver one or more of these forms of fairness. As indicated in chapter 1, political scientists and economists have uncovered a pattern of preferential treatment toward the interests of regulated industries, in the case of agencies for economic regulation, and toward the interests of social advocacy groups, in the case of social regulatory agencies. This pattern was institutionalized as officials of an organization interacting with a particular environment came to identify with the interests of that environment.[23]

Presidential intervention arose in response to the irrational, detrimental policies that emerged; this intervention has portrayed itself as economically rational to justify its existence. Thus, the "just-like-everyone-else" approach, advocated by Morrison, has yielded unsatisfactory results. Morrison disapproves of another approach to presidential intervention, which he has given the unattractive label "anything goes." This approach would allow the president to "direct the outcome of specific proceedings without any procedural inhibitions." The phrase "without any procedural inhibitions" establishes a straw man in a society founded on the premise that voters cannot make informed electoral decisions and regulated parties cannot protect themselves from conspiratorial, adverse actions if the process by which governmental decisions are made operates behind a wall of secrecy. Perhaps Morrison offers this option for the sake of its shock value, so that his readers might develop an aversion to *any* exercise of executive power.

A third option identified (but rejected) by Morrison is "procedural intervention," under which a regulation approved by an agency would constitute a recommendation to the president whose review would be subject to an elaborate set of procedures. Hence, the president's action would be conspicuous and he would be politically responsible for the political consequences.[24] Presumably, the president would not want to expend the enormous political capital associated with an exhaustive review of every regulation. Congress could, by law, exchange its statutory stamp of approval on a formal review process—giving the White House the statutorily institutionalized role it has sought—for a limitation of the number of rules that the president could disapprove. Combined with his existing appointment power, this review process would probably be adequate to allow the president to exert necessary, selective, and judicious influence on rule making while requiring him to act openly. In that way, regulated parties could call the White House to account in court if they wished and the electorate could call the president and his party to account at the polls if it so desired. This procedure would probably be at least as palatable to the Supreme Court as is the nonstatutory review process under Executive Order 12291.

Perhaps the only category of recent regulatory reforms from the executive branch that has provoked the courts to hear the pleas of public interest groups is delay in promulgating regulations. Such groups have successfully gone to court demanding that agencies complete rule-making proceedings prescribed by statute. However, the Supreme Court has shown distaste even for this category, with Chief Justice William H. Rehnquist arguing that Congress—not the courts—should prod agencies to issue rules required by statute.[25]

Activists are understandably frustrated by the court's indifference to their demands. "It's very difficult to get the courts to address the issue" of centralized review, says Plocher of OMB Watch. "Skelly Wright or David Bazelon might have reached the issue. The times are keeping the judges out of these issues. Ten years ago, they were more inclined to get involved." Now, he says, courts are more in tune with conservatism, knowing that to act otherwise brings the risk of reversal by the Supreme Court.[26] Moreover, the likes of Wright and Bazelon have been succeeded by conservative Reagan appointees.

A significant event in the recent history of judicial uncertainty about presidential control of regulation is the issuance of Executive Order 12291. The order contains a provision designed to insulate the order from judicial reversal: The provision declares that the order has no effect that would violate any laws. Presumably, then, an administrative action taken by an agency in the name of EO 12291 that violates the laws must be a violation of the order as well. Thus, the order itself cannot be illegal; only an action purportedly taken pursuant to it can be illegal. Carrying this logic to its inexorable conclusion, complainants must go to court each time an administrative action that they dislike occurs. Public interest groups would prefer to go to court to challenge the executive order itself; the Reagan and Bush administrations preferred to force litigants into exhausting, expensive case-by-case litigation. Speculation arose as to whether the federal courts would see the situation from the administration's viewpoint and take complaints about EO 12291 case by case, or would nullify the order as a violation of the Administrative Procedure Act and other standards of due process.

For various reasons, no one case has succeeded in consolidating the issues. "There's been no administrative-law decision (like *Sierra Club v. Costle*) which has brought the whole issue squarely before the bar," says Plocher.[27] Thus, by default, the case-by-case model forced observers to glean unsatisfying principles from specific decisions, leaving the legal system of presidential control over regulations unclear.

LEGAL LEGITIMACY OF CENTRALIZED REGULATORY REVIEW

Congress created the ICC in 1887 as a component of the Department of the Interior, and lifted it out of the executive branch in 1889 in order to insulate it from presidential authority.[28] Subsequently, Congress delegated authority to executive branch officials, believing that such officials could be expected to act with discretion free from presidential influence.[29] The delegation of legislative authority was invented and has been perpetuated without constitutional basis. The expectation that executive officials would respond to congressional directive but not to presidential directive conflicts directly with Article 2, §3, which vests in the president the responsibility to "take Care that the Laws be faithfully executed." Presumably, presidents agreed to live with delegations of quasi-legislative power because such delegations transferred power from the legislative branch to the executive branch, where the president's influence is more commonly recognized. Still, the general agreement that the president should defer to the discretion of his appointees created an uncoordinated response to national problems. Presidents since Richard M. Nixon have sought systematic input into rule making and have looked to the courts to allow such input. The Supreme Court's more generous consideration of presidential prerogatives, typical of the past forty years, was demonstrated again when the court recognized that the president is entitled to direct the executive branch by guiding the making of regulations by those officials whom he appointed to his administration.[30]

An effort to chase President Jimmy Carter out of the rule-making arena resulted in the *Sierra Club v. Costle* case. The Court of Appeals in Washington, D.C., refused to prohibit intrabranch exchanges of views between the White House and regulatory agencies after the comment period of a rule-making proceeding, unless that judicial review had been prevented, an unsupportable decision had been issued, or a law had been violated. This procedural victory for the presidency comports with the identified trend of increasing harmony between the judicial and executive branches.

The Supreme Court provided a clear indication of its willingness to permit presidential contacts. In the 1984 case of *Chevron, U.S.A., Inc., v. Natural Resources Defense Council, Inc.*,[31] the court stated: "An agency to which Congress has delegated policy-making responsibilities may, *within the limits of that delegation*, properly rely upon the incumbent administration's views of wise policy to inform its judgments" (emphasis added). The court could be even more deferential to the president were it to permit agencies to indulge in activity ultra vires, but it has shown no inclination to do so. Within reason, however, the court has given the president a substantial amount of latitude. D.C. Circuit Chief Judge Wald said that her court and other federal courts read the election returns in 1980, just exactly as Mr. Dooley said they do. "President Reagan's election closed the era of aggressive regulation, and ushered in an era of unabashed *de*regulation."[32] In the 1983 Court of Appeals case of *International Ladies' Garment Workers Union v. Donovan*,[33] Judge Harry T. Edwards wrote: "We recognize that a new administration may try to effectuate new philosophies that have been implicitly endorsed by the democratic process."

Although the court has been generous to the president in approving his involvement in rule making, it has understandably drawn the line to proscribe abuses of procedural and substantive due process. In chapter 4, we saw that the Office of Management and Budget (OMB) and the Office of Information and Regulatory Affairs were prone to indefensible behavior in the early years; to be sure, the court has shown no tendency to condone blatant mischief. Also, it has formulated a basic canon to guide its decisions: An agency's actions and decisions must comport with the law.

That standard can be illustrated by a case involving an episode during the Carter era (though the case was decided in the first year of the Reagan administration). This is the 1981 case of *American Textile Manufacturers Institute v. Donovan, Secretary of Labor*,[34] the "cotton dust" case. Called on by the textile industry to invalidate an Occupational Safety and Health Administration (OSHA) regulation designed to reduce worker exposure to cotton dust, the federal courts, including the Supreme Court, refused to impose any cost-benefit standard on OSHA because the Occupational Safety and Health Act required only a *feasibility* test. Justice William J. Brennan defined "feasibility" as that which is "capable of being done," a far cry from cost-benefit analysis. Based on the cotton dust case, Ball drew the conclusion that OSHA had to be exempt from cost-benefit analysis required by EO 12291.[35] Robert V. Zener interpreted the decision as "a caution light more than a red light."[36]

The courts made their devotion to statutory conduct known in the 1980 case of *Lead Industries Ass'n. v. Environmental Protection Agency*.[37] The Court of Appeals for the District of Columbia prohibited Environmental Protection Agency (EPA) consideration of the economic or technical feasibility of policies designed to achieve certain air pollution standards.

> When Congress directs an agency to consider only certain factors in reaching an administrative decision, the agency is not free to trespass beyond the bounds of statutory authority by taking other factors into account.... A policy choice such as this is one which only Congress, not the courts and not EPA, can make.

Court decisions contain adamant declarations regarding the unacceptability of any OMB regulatory review that delays mandated regulations beyond statutory deadlines. Although Executive Order 12291 bars actions that are illegal, OMB has still held proposed regulations beyond legislated deadlines. Frustrated OMB staff members complain that executive agencies have deliberately held proposed regulations until just before the statutory deadline, and then released the proposals to OMB with but a few days to spare. OMB staff members respond that the agencies are to blame and should not have the prerogative to deprive OMB of its sixty-day review time. Courts have shown more inclination to defend the deadlines than to defend OMB's interest in having its full review opportunity.[38]

The judicial branch continues to be judicious in drawing boundaries for regulatory review. The surprising restraint that the Supreme Court exhibited throughout the Reagan era, to the consternation of progressives, who were initially confident that the courts would come to their aid, continued in the Bush era. (The 1984 *Chevron* decision provides an illustration of that restraint.) The Supreme Court deferred to executive agencies in the interpretation of ambiguous statutes delegating rule-making authority, provided the agency's interpretation was reasonable.

The District Court in the District of Columbia delivered a procedural setback to the Bush administration on September 30, 1991, when Judge Joyce Hens Green ruled that the Reagan-era task force was a covered "agency" under the Freedom of Information Act. The decision in *Meyer v. Bush*[39] compromised the freedom of similar entities, such as the Council on Competitiveness, a regulatory review group located in the office of Vice President Dan Quayle, to operate in their preferred secretive manner. The Department of Justice promptly appealed.

Other decisions have made life increasingly difficult for executive agencies. The Court of Appeals in the District of Columbia repudiated fuel economy standards for automobiles set by the National Highway Traffic Safety Administration because they failed to acknowledge the superior safety record of large cars.[40] The Court of Appeals in the Eleventh Circuit sitting in Atlanta disallowed OSHA regulations limiting air contaminants in the workplace. The court ruled that OSHA provided inadequate proof of both the risks of exposure to certain substances and the efficacy of the new standards. The decision eliminated the three-year-old standards, leaving only twenty-year-old standards in effect and throwing OSHA into "turmoil."[41]

These decisions indicate that the judicial branch has reasserted limited power over rule making, which might reassure conservatives provided the federal judiciary continues to be dominated by judges who share their political persuasion.

The occasional (and inevitable) judicial decision limiting OMB's power has struck OMB as a nuisance. Rosemary O'Leary writes:

> OMB staff who overview the EPA budget do not like court decisions for three main reasons. First, they are "sometimes impossible to implement." Next, a court decision limits the flexibility of OMB as far as what it can and cannot

> cut from EPA's budget. Last, court decisions "reflect badly on the Administration," although one OMB staff member admitted that "you may see a smile on my face when certain EPA regulations are overturned."[42]

OMB's reported dislike for judicial decisions may reflect the mind-set of an administration willing to condone no barrier that would impede the progression of the Reagan Revolution. By most accounts, the judiciary has been quite deferential to the presidency of late. But the Reagan administration had little use or patience for *any* institution that did not invariably ratify its processes, and may thus have been ungrateful for the court's rather generous willingness to award to the chief executive considerably more opportunities to control regulation than may have been contemplated by the framers of the Administrative Procedure Act.

CHECKS AND BALANCES: A SUMMARY

In this and the preceding chapter, we have examined the responses of the legislative and judicial branches to aggressive presidential initiatives in the regulatory arena. Although these two branches have shown some predictable wariness and have taken certain actions to protect their turf, we cannot help but notice that the responses fall far short of the capacity of the two branches to undermine or even terminate the regulatory review program. Partisans of Congress and public interest advocates, among others, joined in the call to Congress to shut down the Executive Order 12291 review program,[43] and yet Congress restrained itself and learned to live with the new development. The judiciary, which could have scuttled the review program by denouncing it as a violation of the Constitution or the Administrative Procedure Act or both, chose instead to draw lines that allowed presidential initiatives that did not neutralize specific statutory prescriptions. It would be far-fetched to attribute judicial restraint to a failure of will; the *Chadha* decision reflects a very willful court.[44]

The exchange theory model is a useful explanation for the willingness of the legislative and judicial branches to learn to live with a more prominent presidential role. We might speculate that each of these two branches expected to gain more than it would lose by permitting the process to survive. Some members of Congress may have perceived a need for control to be exercised over the regulatory agencies and may have preferred that the control be imposed by a different authority; forms of control other than the moribund legislative veto would have created a heavy workload on the beleaguered legislature. Having a White House-based regulation control program that members of Congress could blame when things went wrong might have been perceived in some quarters as rather handy politically. Similarly, the judiciary—directed by the Supreme Court—has been attempting to extricate itself from the exhausting "partnership" that generated such a heavy load of dockets; transferring some oversight responsibility to the president to eliminate problems of overlapping and inconsistent regulations might have been a welcome innovation in the eyes of judges trying, in the long run, to escape blame for irrational and expensive regulations. Beginning with the era of Franklin D. Roosevelt, great concern has been expressed concerning regulatory activity conducted without presidential supervision;[45] the other two branches may have been willing to concede that the presidency would have been so greatly weakened by continued exclusion from administrative rule making that the institution would have become an ineffective source of such benefits as coordination and rationality. Legislation such as the Employment Act of 1946 called upon the president to provide his unique coordinating capacity to economic problems.[46] The inaction on Executive Order 12291 likely represented grudging willingness by Congress and the courts to defer to him much the same function in the regulatory arena.

8 Three Case Studies

In this chapter, we will profile three rule-making efforts as a way of considering three possible fates that await the ideas of federal regulators. Each case illustrates a different category of intervention by the Office of Information and Regulatory Affairs (OIRA). First, we will consider a case study of a regulatory design that was reviewed by the OIRA and was eventually promulgated without OIRA-inspired substantive change. Second, we will study a regulatory design that was reviewed by OIRA and was promulgated with relatively minor OIRA-inspired substantive change. And third, we will consider a case study of a regulatory design that was reviewed by OIRA and eventually abandoned by the agency as a result of the review process.

In trying to identify suitable cases, I was surprised at the difficulty of identifying rule-making efforts that sustained major or even minor substantive OIRA-inspired revisions affecting the final rule. Some of the most notorious instances of OIRA involvement—ethylene oxide, hazard communication, and grain dust, to name a few—incited congressional activity (such as acrimonious hearings) and judicial review that shone a spotlight on the OIRA role and reversed OIRA's ambitions. In such instances, the eventual result of OIRA's involvement was merely delay. Delay has been a primary result of OIRA review, and federal regulators have been exasperated by the notion that their regulatory proposals, which could have saved lives *now*, were delayed for months or years. Nevertheless, delay does not constitute a substantive change in the text of a regulation. To find examples of amended regulatory designs, I often looked in vain through the literature, for it contained primarily examples of disputes in which OIRA involvement came to light, and was challenged, as executive interference in quasi-legislative activity. The literature is less apt to spotlight cases in which OIRA helped resolve a regulatory duplication or helped find a more efficient way to accomplish the same objective. Interest groups rarely had the motivation to lift the veil off noncontroversial OIRA suggestions, and thus such cases did not tend to come to the attention of scholars. OIRA's penchant for unobtrusiveness not only helped it avoid blame; it also placed restraint on its development of beneficial public relations. The literature also misses cases in which an agency sacrificed one regulatory design opposed by OIRA in negotiations, in order to save a second OIRA-targeted regulation more dear to the agency. Part of the "bargain" in such cases may have been concealment of its terms.

As a result of inquiries to many bureaucrats and interest group officials, I selected the following rule-making efforts as my three case studies: the grain dust regulation of the Occupational Safety and Health Administration (OSHA) (as an example of no substantive change), the proposed revision by the Environmental Protection Agency (EPA) of the Hazard Ranking System (minor substantive change), and EPA's proposed revision of the New Source Performance Standard for stationary-source nitrogen oxide emissions (a regulatory proposal that was undermined). These cases may be helpful in illuminating some of the combinations of forces that awaited any given rule-making effort during the Reagan era.

REGULATION SUSTAINING NO CHANGE: OSHA'S GRAIN DUST RULE MAKING

The first category—regulatory concepts that were subjected to the OIRA clearance process and eventually emerged intact—includes the substantial majority of rule making. Most proposals were routinely processed by OIRA without change. Sometimes, OIRA pointed out some helpful change in language or strategy that would help avoid a regulatory duplication or overlap. Because such instances lack the element of intrigue, I deliberately passed up those cases in favor of OSHA's grain dust standard, a case in which OIRA efforts to impede OSHA's rule-making process were overcome by the system of checks and balances.

The history of explosions in grain-handling facilities spans a period of well over a hundred years.[1] A 1978 Department of Agriculture report complained that the industry "has possessed the necessary knowledge and many of the prevention techniques to prevent grain dust explosions for at least 60 years . . . but they have not been adequately implemented."[2]

OSHA had an idea on the drawing board in 1980 for a regulation that would establish new requirements to prevent explosions in grain elevators. Meanwhile, incoming Reagan administration officials weighed in. In a December 1980 article, OMB director-designate David A. Stockman identified proposed regulations he would try to obstruct, including a grain dust regulation. As OSHA's rule making proceeded, OMB sought to influence the outcome, seeking certain provisions and exceptions. Labor unions and public interest groups accused OMB of acting at the behest of industry to try to undermine any serious OSHA effort to frame a meaningful regulation.[3]

Based on 1982 studies from the National Academy of Sciences (NAS) and on comments received in the ten-month period following publication of the notice of proposed rule making (NPRM), a notice containing two hundred questions, OSHA wrote a draft of a regulation. In May 1983, OSHA transmitted the draft to OMB, proposing that grain elevator operators be required to prevent the accumulation of one-eighth of an inch of grain dust, as recommended by NAS. OSHA officials reportedly opted for the one-eighth-inch standard, based on the Factory Mutual Engineering Corporation and Canadian association studies, instead of a one-sixty-fourth-inch standard demanded by labor unions. OMB Watch offered another explanation: "More cynical observers said OSHA had simply settled for a standard the agency thought it could get past OMB."[4]

OMB took eight months to review this draft, objecting to the costs of compliance and questioning its cost effectiveness. OSHA reviewed the issue and, in 1984, published a second notice of proposed rule making, soliciting at OMB's behest comments about three potential alternatives:[5] (1) sweeping would be done once per shift, regardless of dust accumulation level, as an indication of good faith; (2) pneumatic dust control equipment would be installed; or (3) the one-eighth-inch standard would still be used as a maximum, averaged over a two-hundred-square-foot area.

A proposed regulation was delivered by OSHA to OMB for review in accordance with Executive Order 12291. At OMB, review of the proposal was entrusted to economist John F. Morrall III, who was on record as opposing OSHA efforts to promulgate safety standards.[6] OMB met with or otherwise communicated with the American Feed Manufacturers Association, the National Grain and Feed Association (NGFA), and the Millers' National Federation. The NGFA confirmed that there was a meeting in the spring of 1983 attended by its own representatives and those of OMB.[7]

OMB dismissed the studies calling for a limit of one-sixty-fourth inch or even one-eighth inch in grain dust accumulation, leading one OSHA official to complain that "OMB demands reports, and then it doesn't believe the reports, casting them aside and asking for further studies." OMB cited the admission by one OSHA-commissioned study that even the one-eighth-inch standard was arbitrary. OMB also warned that the compliance costs to the industry for such a standard would be so high as to exceed the average pretax profits of ten thousand small grain elevator operators. Thus, OMB vowed to oppose the requirement for manual sweeping, concluding that OSHA's analysis exaggerated the benefits of sweeping and that the proposed rule was inappropriate in general for smaller facilities (such as feed mills). "To date," OMB stated, "no careful assessment of OSHA safety programs has found effectiveness rates even one tenth as high as ADL [consulting firm A.D. Little] and OSHA have assumed for the grain handling standards."[8] OMB also disputed the content of the OSHA studies that sets the value of a life saved at $800,000 or $3.5 million. It cited Viscusi's study, which theorizes that workers who accept risky occupations must inevitably value their lives less highly than other workers who opt for safer forms of employment.[9] "That may sound good over a cup of coffee in the new executive building," muttered an angry millers' union official, "but it won't play in the real world."[10]

The "sixty-day review" actually consumed eight months and, to the consternation of advocates of the OSHA initiative, was conducted in secret. AFL-CIO official Deborah Berkowitz objected that some OMB meetings involved industry officials whose opinions already appeared on OSHA's rule-making record. She also noted:

> At the insistence of OMB, the OMB review of the grain handling safety standard was conducted in a secretive fashion. OMB insisted that a bare minimum of documents be exchanged between it and OSHA and that no notes be kept of meetings. At various stages OMB officials would telephone their positions on the proposal to OSHA. Notes of these conversations were then shown to select OSHA officials for analysis. The resulting OSHA staff written response—or actually OSHA's rebuttal of OMB's comments—was then presented to the Department of Labor deputy solicitor Francis Lilly. In one instance, rather than present a 27 page written rebuttal from OSHA to OMB, Mr. Lilly orally transmitted the information to OMB at OMB's insistence.[11]

OMB called on OSHA to abandon its proposal and to pursue instead regulations involving the three alternatives previously enumerated (once-per-shift sweeping, control of grain dust accumulations in specified hazard areas, or pneumatic controls of dust). The unkindest cut of all was OMB's denunciation of OSHA's track record. In a thirty-nine-page comment for the rule-making record, OMB proclaimed: "Any projection of the effectiveness of a new OSHA safety standard must begin with the realization that OSHA's existing safety rules (aimed presumably at the most serious safety problems) have had very little and perhaps no effect on occupational accident rates."[12] In defense of OMB's opposition to OSHA's 1983 proposed regulation, one sympathetic bureaucrat echoed OIRA desk officer Scott H. Jacobs's observation about the "snapshot" effect: A regulatory agency makes a rule based on the record available to it when the draft is written, and rarely adapts to the advances in knowledge and technology that arise after the rule-making record is closed. "OSHA started with 1980 technology," the bureaucrat said.

> The draft came out in 1983. That's where [OSHA's assumptions] froze. Today we know more. Then, static electricity was considered a risk; now it's thought that static electricity won't create enough of a charge. Then, humidity was considered a factor; now, it isn't. Metal sparks were considered a threat; now, it looks like metal sparks won't start an explosion.

"I think OMB has an honest interest in improving grain-elevator safety," the regulatory official maintained.

The Senate Governmental Affairs Committee's Subcommittee on Intergovernmental Relations received numerous complaints about OMB's interference in OSHA's grain dust rule making. On January 28, 1986, the subcommittee convened a hearing to discuss grain elevator explosions. Labor unions were well represented at the hearing, and denounced OMB's involvement in the rule making. A highlight of the hearing was the animated interrogation by Senator Albert Gore Jr. (D-Tenn.) of OMB director James C. Miller III. Gore shouted at Miller, demanding to know whether the "risk" to the grain elevator workers who died in a Knoxville elevator was really "overstated," while Miller admonished the senator that he did not want to be shouted at (see chapter 3). One of the subcommittee staff members who had organized the hearing later apologized to a witness—a scholar in public administration who had been called on to deliver a general discussion of presidential clearance of regulation—for the hysterical tone of the hearing. In any event, the damage was done—or, depending on one's perspective, the benefit was achieved. A compelling chronicle of OMB's opposition to the grain dust standard and its contacts with industry was created. Laborers and their sympathizers, who by 1986 were on the alert to the Reagan administration's efforts to deregulate, found that the revelations of the OMB role were apparently fueling the campaign to overcome OMB's resistance and to advance the OSHA grain dust rule making.

Based on public comments and its own analyses, OSHA prepared a new standard defying OMB's recommendations for once-per-shift sweeping. OSHA had proposed a one-eighth-inch dust accumulation limit on average in any two-hundred-square-foot priority area; instead, in order to have a more readily enforceable standard, it prohibited a one-eighth-inch accumulation at any point within fifty feet of any priority area. OSHA also required facilitywide housekeeping.

The standard also mandated an emergency action procedure (alarm and evacuation); training; control over heat-emitting work, including relocation where possible; restrictions on entry into bins, silos, and tanks; involvement of outside contractors in the safety program; installation of filter collectors; preventative maintenance to avoid defective equipment; grain stream processing equipment; and emergency escapes.[13] The final rule was issued on December 31, 1987.[14]

When the rule was "posted" at the Office of the Federal Register the day before publication, the NGFA filed suit in the Court of Appeals for the Fifth Circuit in New Orleans, objecting to the rule's provisions, which were more stringent than industry wanted. The labor unions filed suit in the Court of Appeals for the District of Columbia Circuit, objecting to the absence of a one-sixty-fourth-inch limit on grain dust accumulation at any point anywhere in the facility. The NGFA asked that the two cases be consolidated in the more conservative Fifth Circuit, and the motion was granted. The Department of Justice exercised its prerogative to represent the federal government in place of OSHA's own counsel in the case of *National Grain and Feed Association v. Occupational Safety and Health Administration*.[15]

Industry contended that OSHA's commissioned studies were flawed, and that the one-eighth-inch standard was random. NGFA's brief criticized OSHA for using reports that dust accumulations of as little as one-hundredth inch could fuel an explosion as a basis for imposing the one-eighth-inch standard. NGFA portrayed OSHA's selection of the one-eighth-inch standard as an action that defied evidence and reason. Organized labor, however, countered that grain dust's capability to fuel an explosion merited all efforts toward frequent, repeated sweeping away of accumulations and an absolute accumulation limit of one-sixty-fourth inch. Union officials wanted grain dust classified as a "physical agent" which, according to statute, required the "most protective" rule and precluded reliance on cost-benefit analysis.

The court told OSHA it had to show a reasonable relationship of costs and benefits in its standard for sweeping. The court found that OSHA's analysis of the rate at which grain dust could be swept away and OSHA's program to protect grain elevator employees were both suspect. The court stayed execution of the sweeping rate and the dust accumulation limit, and speculated that a facilitywide standard might have more justification.[16] But Secretary of Labor Ann D. McLaughlin challenged the court's construction of the Occupational Safety and Health Act and petitioned for recognition of her discretionary authority. The court reversed its stay in the 1989 phase of *NGFA* v. *OSHA*, but still called for additional analysis relating to the appropriateness of a facilitywide standard.[17]

OSHA was slow to respond to the court's call for a revised analysis, according to the AFL-CIO's Keith Mestrich, who criticized the agency for "dragging its feet."[18] The union pleaded with OSHA to accelerate its analysis, and finally threatened litigation if such an analysis were not forthcoming.

OSHA finally completed a revised analysis and presented it to the court for the 1990 phase of *NGFA* v. *OSHA*.[19] The Fifth Circuit court lifted the stay on the one-eighth-inch standard around hazardous areas, effective August 1, 1990, and ordered OSHA to examine the feasibility of a facilitywide standard. OSHA Fire Protection Engineer Thomas H. Seymour noted the historic nature of the outcome: It was the first time that the conservative Fifth Circuit court upheld an OSHA regulation in its entirety.[20]

The current status of OSHA's grain dust rule making is something of a compromise between the positions of labor and industry. Labor seems to have been satisfied with the results of the rule making and litigation, although labor's advocate, the Public Citizen Litigation Group, expressed frustration that no facilitywide standard for sweeping appeared to be on the horizon.[21] OSHA's Seymour credited public participation for helping to develop a better rule than OSHA proposed originally, since the final rule was easier to enforce.[22] Finally, OSHA was preparing a new interrogatory for publication in the *Federal Register* to collect comments on expanding the standard. The National Grain and Feed Association, which arguably had put its money where its mouth was and invested in programs to design and operate modern grain elevators more safely, has been portrayed as insensitive to employee safety. Nevertheless, as the industry predicted, recent explosions have involved less loss of life,[23] attributed not to sweeping but to improved operations, the need for which industry officials conceded all along.

REGULATION SUSTAINING MINOR SUBSTANTIVE CHANGE: EPA'S PROPOSED REVISION OF THE HAZARD RANKING SYSTEM

The second category—regulatory concepts that were subjected to the OIRA clearance process and eventually emerged with minor substantive change—

includes an indeterminate number of proposed regulations, depending on one's definition of minor substantive change. OIRA sometimes insisted vehemently on the substitution of one word for another—e.g., *financial* in place of *economic*—and appears to have believed that a victory had been achieved when the change was made. Frequently, OIRA called for word changes or insertion or deletion of phrases or sentences in the preamble of the proposed regulation, which rather effectively altered the apparent purpose and thrust of the policy. Whether changes in the preamble constitute a substantive change is a legitimate focus of debate, but OIRA's demands for such changes and its satisfaction in securing them suggest that the changes must have some degree of substance (if we assume the behavior is rational).

In this section, we shall recount the emergence of a revision to EPA's Hazard Ranking System that would reduce the liability of alleged polluters in proportion to the amount of waste already removed from the disposal site. OIRA reportedly advocated that EPA institute this credit, and the provision is a part of the rule that was promulgated in December 1990.

In 1980, Congress enacted the Comprehensive Environmental Response, Compensation, and Liability Act (CERCLA).[24] The law established the Hazardous Substance Response Trust Fund, more popularly known as the Superfund.[25] The fund of $1.6 billion allowed the president to subsidize the cleanup of waste sites. The president delegated his authority to the administrator of EPA.[26] It thus became the administrator's duty to establish a National Oil and Hazardous Substances Pollution Contingency Plan (NCP)[27] detailing a list of sites targeted for earliest action. This was called the National Priority List (NPL).[28] There are over one thousand sites currently listed.

In order to implement NCP requirements, EPA adopted the Hazard Ranking System (HRS). This is a scoring process that assesses the relative danger associated with actual or potential damage at a waste site. Factors in the scoring process include toxicity of the waste substances, quantities of waste involved, and nearby population. Factors are weighted and combined according to a mathematical formula, producing an HRS score for the site. The higher a site's HRS score, the higher its place of ignominy on the NPL. The HRS score charged all the cumulative waste dumped at the site against the site, regardless of how much of the waste was removed by the polluter. Thus, if five hundred pounds of waste was originally dumped at the site, but one hundred pounds had been transported away, the five-hundred-pound quantity would be inserted into the formula. To some extent, the damage done by the one hundred pounds of removed waste might be irreversible (for example, it might have leached into groundwater), so the inclusion of it in the HRS score had some justification. Still, the irrevocable aspect was widely regarded to err on the side of risk aversion and to be deficient in its failure to encourage the removal of toxic waste.

Congress enacted the Superfund Amendments and Reauthorization Act of 1986 (SARA), which, in part, required EPA to study revisions in the HRS to more accurately assess the risk to health and the environment. An advance notice of proposed rule making was issued by EPA on April 9, 1987, and a public meeting apparently caused the HRS to come to OMB's attention. An EPA staff member recalled that OMB officials first broached the subject of credit for removed waste. It is not known what motivated OMB to advance the concept, but OMB was committed wholeheartedly to it. EPA thus acknowledged in the NPRM that the credit for removed waste was under consideration.[29] On December 23, 1988, EPA published a comprehensive NPRM to carry out the SARA mandate relative to revision of the HRS.[30] Among other changes, the NPRM called for a revision that would give credit for removal under some circumstances, thus reversing the risk aversion inherent in the existing inflexible provision. The proposal underwent OIRA review for eight months.

EPA and OMB engaged in discussions about the concept of the credit. Some were spirited, as the representatives of the two entities disagreed on some of the consequences of the revision. Indeed, internal disagreements within EPA created unpredictability in the agency's own position on the issue. Eventually, EPA submitted the draft of a regulation to OMB that would have provided some credit for removed waste. Officials of EPA acknowledged that OMB's review had an impact on the removal credit. "The rule has thousands of factors; [OIRA is] focusing on [that] one factor," one EPA staff member explained. "They have a valid argument," said another, "but it's not an inevitable one." When the final rule was published on December 14, 1990,[31] OMB's second period of review of the rule was concluded, after seven months.

Because the public comments came almost exclusively from industry, they were essentially congruent with OMB's view. EPA's public docket index for the NPRM (coded 105NCP-HRS) shows very scarce involvement from organizations that could be considered environmental advocacy groups. None of these comments pertained to the provision relating to the credit for removal of hazardous waste. But the comments from industry reinforced OMB's call for the credit and inspired further EPA analysis on the subject.

Although an internal debate within EPA concerning the credit for removed waste seems to have been ongoing, the EPA staff people opposing the concession to industry obtained no support from the political environment. The notion that removed waste may have already done undetected but irreversible damage generated no action from environmental groups, and thus—when the final rule was promulgated—the relaxed provision was included. In championing the relaxation of the HRS algorithm, and bolstered by appeals for change from industrial associations, OMB created a minor substantive change that was clearly in the spirit of the cost-benefit criterion of Executive Order 12291. Insofar as the credit provides some market-type incentive for polluters to clean up their own mess, the change may be just the kind of remedy that 1970s economists envisioned when they called for more extensive regulatory reform through presidential leadership.

REGULATION THAT WAS UNDERMINED: EPA'S NSPS FOR STATIONARY-SOURCE NITROGEN OXIDE EMISSIONS

The third category—regulatory concepts that were subjected to the OIRA clearance process and never emerged—includes an indeterminate number of cases, partly because of the uncertainty of the definition of major substantive change and partly because regulatory officials have some incentives to conceal instances in which planned rule making was distorted or terminated because of OMB disapproval.

This was the case for the aborted attempt of EPA regulators to promulgate a regulation creating a New Source Performance Standard (NSPS) for nitrogen oxide (NO_x) emissions from stationary pollution sources. Like an airplane falling from the sky and disappearing from radar monitors, the regulatory design vanished from the public policy agenda. Limited documentation indicates that OMB opposition caused dispirited EPA regulators to concede the issue.

The Clean Air Act Amendments of 1970 created an extensive program to restrain the rise in air pollution.[32] The amendments revised the original Clean Air Act, which, prior to EPA's creation, had been administered by the Department of Health, Education, and Welfare. The amendments required EPA to designate "criteria pollutants." The key provisions include the National Ambient Air Quality Standards (NAAQS), State Implementation Plans (SIP) that implemented the NAAQS, and NSPSs that applied to large, new stationary sources of emissions regardless of existing ambient air quality. The NSPSs were defined in the statute as those that reflected "the degree of emission limitation achievable through the application of the best system of emission reduction which (taking into account the cost of achieving such reduction) the Administrator determines has been adequately demonstrated."[33]

In 1979, EPA personnel concluded that it would be appropriate to control emissions of nitrogen oxide from *large* internal combustion engines in such facilities as electric power generators, oil-drilling rigs, pipelines, and various other huge engines at stationary sources. On July 23 of that year, EPA developed two limits—seven hundred parts per million (ppm) for previously unregulated engines fired by natural gas and six hundred ppm for diesel engines. The proposal was awaiting action within the agency when the change of administrations occurred and the Reagan administration called in many pending rules for review. Under this arrangement, EPA sent a somewhat different recommendation to OMB under which the revision would apply only to diesel and dual-fired engines. EPA had come to realize that the best technology for achieving a 40 percent reduction (138,000 tons) in nitrogen oxide emissions from natural-gas-fired engines might result in an *increase* in carbon monoxide (CO) of 309,000 tons. Because these facilities tended to be located in densely populated areas whose traffic was already causing elevated carbon monoxide levels and because many of their facilities might have been forced into noncompliance with carbon monoxide limits, EPA backed off on the part of the proposal that would have revised the NSPS criterion involving nitrogen oxide as it applied to natural-gas-fired engines.

In the summer of 1981, OMB signalled EPA that the proposal to revise the nitrogen oxide NSPS was unacceptable. OMB said that EPA's decision to exclude natural-gas-fired engines from the proposal made the remaining proposal, which would reduce emissions by 22,000 tons at a cost of $500 per ton, too trivial to promulgate. OMB also observed that many of the diesel engines were located in sparsely populated areas whose air quality problems were relatively modest. Late in 1982, a meeting involving representatives of EPA and OMB had the long awaited proposal on the agenda; OMB officials reasserted the position that the narrower scope of the proposal made it more trouble than it was worth. An EPA memorandum reported:

> This package has been at OMB for a long time, and [OIRA desk officer] Geoff[rey] White argued that we really only had an option of finalizing the standard for diesel engines and natural gasoline engines or natural gasoline engines alone. His reasons for this were that the natural gasoline was the most cost effective of the two regulations and the increase in CO which was emitted could be overcome by additional regulation in the mobile source area for $41 per ton. He claimed that this is a figure he received from the EPA. We explained to Geoff that it was impossible to apply additional regulations to mobile sources and also that there were other nonquantifiable reasons for our recommendation to proceed only with the regulation of the diesel in-

> ternal combustion engines. Gail Coad agreed that if we would send a memo to her outlining these nonquantifiable reasons she would approve the package for release. Some of these items which will be included in the memo are: (1) regulating one internal combustion engine and not the other will not cause competitive disadvantages, (2) promulgating the regulation for natural gasoline engines will cause a significant increase in CO emissions and could trigger PSD [prevention of significant deterioration requirements, involving additional monitoring and mandated pollution control equipment] in certain nonattainment areas, and (3) diesel engines are located in urban areas compared to natural gasoline which are usually in rural areas, etc.[34]

In mid-1983, OMB notified EPA of its irrevocable disapproval.

With its rejection by OMB, the proposal disappears from the pages of history. Environmental groups had little or nothing to say about the birth and death of the proposal to revise the nitrogen oxide NSPS criteria. Although many EPA personnel passionately supported the proposal and defended it repeatedly to OMB, the inattention of advocacy groups doomed the "orphan" regulatory proposal, and it has been all but forgotten. In the absence of any support from interest groups, Congress, and the courts, the idea was clearly vulnerable to the regulatory clearance process.

ANALYSIS OF THE CASE STUDIES

The preceding case studies are intended to illustrate some of the general rules that have governed the review of regulations at OMB pursuant to Executive Order 12291. The activities, behaviors, and outcomes we observed in the case studies are summarized in table 8.1.

The regulation clearance process unquestionably enabled the president and his agents to exert substantial control over rule making at the expense of other authorities; nevertheless, *efforts by interest groups, Congress, or the courts to overcome presidential opposition to a given regulatory policy remained viable.* In cases involving a lack of interest by these competitors, OMB was able to draw regulatory officials into negotiations where it could get some things while giving up other things. The revised NSPS for stationary sources of nitrogen oxide is an example of an "orphan" rule, adopted by no one and thus vulnerable to a successful OMB "veto." But where intense involvement by interest groups ignited Congress or (perhaps with less durable results) the judicial branch, the illumination of OIRA activities tended to prove embarrassing to OMB and to result in a snowball effect that overwhelmed OIRA's

Table 8.1
Activities, Behaviors, and Outcomes Observed in Case Studies

	OSHA Grain Dust	EPA Hazard Ranking Score Revision	EPA Nitrogen Oxide NSPS Revision
Fate of regulation	Virtually no change	Minor substantive change	Elimination
Status of rule making	Essentially complete	Complete	Terminated
Political advantage	Congress and courts predominate, after mobilization by advocacy groups	OMB exerts influence bolstered by business associations	OMB prevails over internal EPA faction
Due process	OMB seeks unobstrusive influence, is overcome through exposure of its activities	OMB seeks influence; no interest groups challenge OMB through due process	OMB seeks influence; no interest groups are known to challenge OMB through due process
Delay	About 8 years	About 1 year	Permanent
Concern for compliance costs	OSHA's studies show interest in compliance costs, although studies are oriented toward justifying the proposed rule	EPA is motivated to consider that compliance costs of existing rule exceed benefits	EPA offers modifications reflecting awareness of trade-offs, but defends cost-effectiveness of remaining provisions; remaining provisions are defeated
Rationality	OSHA seeks to demonstrate link between hazard and remedy through extensive studies by consultants	EPA recognizes that transporting hazardous waste from a waste site may reduce hazard, so regulatory action may be obviated	EPA recognizes that reducing NO_x emissions in natural-gas-fired engines may result in more CO emissions; withdraws provision covering such engines

ambitions. It is thus extremely difficult to find well-documented instances of proposed rules that were permanently undermined by OMB, because those who had incentives to document the cases usually also had the incentive and desire to expose OIRA activities and to find allies in the other branches of government. This led to reversals of OMB's decisions. Rourke has written:

> While many observers have argued that Reagan's tenure in the White House restored the power of the presidency, it can also be said to provide a striking picture of the resourceful way in which groups opposed to changes that a White House is trying to make can stonewall a President's efforts to alter policies to which they are deeply attached.[35]

Although in other contexts federal government officials have been extremely candid and helpful to researchers, my efforts and those of other researchers to extract information from officials about cases in which OMB caused a regulatory proposal to die provoked a kind of *fear*, even panic. The personnel in regulatory agencies perceived any revelation that they divulged information about such cases to be the one unforgivable sin that would bring down the unrelenting wrath of the Executive Office of the President. Many staff members refused to talk at all and others insisted on anonymity as I researched this category of cases. OMB preferred that regulatory personnel observe a pact of *secrecy*. Thus, I was impeded in preparing the preceding material by a reluctance to talk on the part of officials. Other research efforts that attempt to learn about regulatory proposals killed by OMB would be similarly impeded. It is doubtful that an accurate record of these instances will ever be available. Numerous interview statements by regulatory officials and critics of OMB suggest that only "orphan" regulations, which find little support among interest groups, tended to be liquidated behind the scenes. This is precisely what happened to the proposed revision in the NSPS for stationary sources of nitrogen oxide. Consistent with the observation about fear of reprisals, no regulatory officials were willing to provide much information about that episode.

Many of the efforts of OIRA desk officers were *oriented toward minor, even trivial, changes* in the text of proposed regulations. Many agency officials have remarked about a desk officer's passionate defense of a request (or demand) that one word be replaced by a near synonym, or that the preamble be slightly altered while the regulation itself remained intact. Agency officials described the behavior as though it were idiosyncratic. One might speculate that OIRA desk officers created their own "science of regulation" on which they stake their professional identities and reputations. This commitment to a scientific paradigm for regulatory design would explain the passion for certain words and formulations in the text of regulations, oriented, as such a science would be, to consistency and uniformity.

Insofar as many cases fall into the first category of regulations that eventually emerged with virtually no OIRA-imposed change, the clear overriding result of regulatory clearance has been *delay*. After twelve years of experience with Executive Order 12291, regulatory officials clearly saw delay as the paramount result. In 1982, Lettie M. Wenner determined that the major effect of litigation was to delay administrative action rather than prevent it.[36] In the Reagan-Bush era, delays may have been due to lengthy internal review in OIRA, or to congressional hearings and/or litigation, or to all of these combined. OSHA's grain dust rule making was suspended for years because of the clearance process, while the revision of the Hazard Ranking System was held up for about a year. Regulatory officials express frustration and even alarm about the extent of harm they perceive to have been done while they await the opportunity to enforce the rules they deem necessary for the health and welfare of the public.

The case studies also show that agencies carried out cost-benefit analyses rather faithfully, reflecting *sensitivity to compliance costs*. OSHA sponsored at least two such analytical studies on grain dust before developing a rule. EPA was accommodating toward OMB's proposal that the Hazard Ranking System be revised to allow a credit for waste transported from a waste site. Undoubtedly, this sensitivity changed the tone of regulations throughout the federal government.

Executive Order 12291 does appear to have contributed a factor of *rationality* to rule making. All of the cases reflect agency efforts to produce regulations that make sense. In the grain dust case, OSHA examined the structure and operations of grain elevators to ensure that costly housekeeping methods were genuinely useful and necessary. In the HRS revision case, EPA was hospitable to the argument that waste carted away might conceivably have been eliminated as a menace to health. In the nitrogen oxide case, EPA limited the scope of its own proposed regulation when it saw that the effect of reducing nitrogen oxide emissions from natural-gas-fired engines would be an increase in carbon monoxide. Surely those who deemed that complaints by economists in the 1970s about inefficient, irrational regulations had validity can find some comfort in this noteworthy development.

9 Implications for Regulatory Reform

SUCCESSES OF THE REAGAN REGULATORY STRATEGY

The Nixon, Ford, and Carter reforms and the visions of economists for more efficient regulation, which had been merely a sideshow, were embellished and took on new life as President Ronald Reagan unleashed a determined assault on the regulatory system. The results were so extensive that even a Franklin Roosevelt or a Louis Brownlow might have been impressed.

The Regulatory Program issued by the Office of Management and Budget (OMB) for 1988–89 provided a statement of outcomes which the Reagan administration proudly claimed as improvements arising from the Reagan reform. OMB touted these accomplishments: (1) requiring justification of regulatory proposals; (2) reducing real and significant risks (rather than imagined risks claimed by entities with axes to grind); (3) harnessing market incentives; (4) revising uniform quality standards (to allow manufacturers to offer lower-quality products for end-uses not requiring high-quality products); (5) using performance standards in place of expensive engineering standards; (6) exchanging private rights or obligations among regulated parties; (7) promoting federalism and reducing burdens on state and local governments; and (8) streamlining regulatory procedures.[1]

OMB claimed that regulatory reform achieved savings and other benefits for the public and for regulated entities. The Council of Economic Advisers reported that airline deregulation has delivered $15 billion of benefits annually to airlines and travelers. Trucking deregulation is saving over $30 billion per year, while railroad deregulation is saving $15 billion.[2]

Despite some validity, the criticism that Reagan's strategy failed to guarantee a permanent increment in the power of the presidency does not take into account the fact that the voters who elect a president want to benefit promptly from the implementation of his and their policy preferences. With the possible exception of a few obsessed historians and political scientists, no voters cast their ballots for a presidential candidate in the hope that he will generate a permanent enhancement of the prestige and power of the presidency. Reagan demonstrated the use of political appointments to bring immediate benefits to his supporters, rather than long-lasting advantages to his successors. Although his successors owe Reagan no debt of gratitude for leaving a statutory legacy of regulatory reform behind, they can appreciate the lesson of how to tame an otherwise unresponsive bureaucracy. Elizabeth Sanders wrote that "when the dust has settled, it is likely that Reagan will have had more influence on the bureaucratic state than any other president except [Franklin D.] Roosevelt."[3]

The popular models of policy making in the pre-Reagan period reflected limited presidential involvement. The subgovernment model of the "iron triangle" suggested that each policy area was dominated by congressional committees, executive agencies, and interest groups that specialized in policy making in the respective area. The "iron triangle" approach was challenged by Hugh Heclo, who posited the existence of policy-specific "issue networks," which encompass very large numbers of participants, thus diluting the power of any one individual or institution.[4] Neither of these models posit that the president has much of a role to play. As political appointees seemed poised, for the first time, to resist clientele influence, and there were chilling threats of managerial reprisals from the Executive Office of the President (EOP), the iron triangle—if there ever was such an alliance—was reshaped into an "iron rectangle," with the EOP as a conspicuous participant.[5] The White House flexed its muscles and invaded the iron triangles (or issue networks), an accomplishment worthy of the Reagan Revolution.

As Verkuil observed, much of the literature about the politics of regulatory agencies became outdated as Reagan and his aides catapulted OMB to a position of superiority over all other agencies. Reagan's accomplishment "is the administrative law story of the decade," Verkuil wrote in a review of the 1980s. Not only have the agencies, congressional committees, and interest groups been delimited, but the strategy centering on the Office of Information and Regulatory Affairs (OIRA) eclipsed the significance of the involvement of the judicial branch.[6]

The advocates of Reagan-style regulatory relief who continue to tout the program as a watershed in federal regulation can point to evidence verifying that it brought valuable benefits to Reagan's constituency and circumscribed the power of federal agencies oriented toward autonomy. The results will continue to shape how regulations develop in Washington, D.C.

FAILURES OF THE REAGAN REGULATORY STRATEGY

The Reagan regulatory reform program had numerous detractors. Some represented progressive opinion, which felt that the interests of laborers, consumers, and disadvantaged groups were imperiled. But nonpartisan observers also raised criticism of the program, evaluating the Reagan approach as a missed opportunity to resolve the state of crisis in regulation.[7]

Inequities and Deprivation of Due Process

There were widespread suspicions that the Reagan regulatory relief program was oriented toward providing a more favorable regulatory climate for business interests, and that the means for fashioning this climate were deliberately shrouded in secrecy. Indeed, these claims were supported by extensive anecdotal evidence of OIRA's involvement and—in some cases—unrepentant admissions. Public interest groups found a less sympathetic response from previously supportive bureaucrats, who now pleaded with the activists to be understanding of the new pressures to which regulators were subject. Reagan administration officials reinforced the appearance of favoritism with declarations bluntly expressing the intention to relieve business of many regulatory burdens. OIRA officials James C. Miller III and Jim J. Tozzi crowed about their ability to subdue executive agencies without creating evidence of their involvement. The predictable result was doubts about the administration's sense of fair play. Members of Congress and leaders of interest groups were all affected by these doubts. "There seems little doubt... that the Reagan strategy has undermined public confidence in regulatory institutions. It has politicized regulatory administration [and] undercut the relationship between Congress, agencies, and the executive office in regulatory policymaking and implementation."[8]

The provocation, which seemed deliberate on OMB's part (since otherwise it would have to be considered unspeakably clumsy), sullied the reputation of regulatory reform. Some members of Congress were ready to pounce automatically on reform efforts should statutory proposals for centralized review be again solicited by the Republican administration.

The savings and loan crisis—arguably the worst public scandal in United

States history[9]—revealed extensive concern in many governmental institutions for the fortunes of well-connected individuals. The seeds for the disaster were sown in 1980, so it is unjust to blame the Reagan administration for the entire episode. During a congressional conference on the proposed Depository Institutions Deregulation and Monetary Control Act of 1980, an initiative of the Carter administration, representatives of California's savings and loan associations agreed to withdraw their objections to the bill if the limit on insurance deposits were raised from $40,000 to $100,000 per account.[10] Congress enacted the bill with this embellishment. Because the average depositor had about $6,000 in savings accounts, a $100,000 limit was surely a service to relatively wealthy depositors and to owners and managers of savings and loans. The direct effect of the additional insurance was to greatly increase the national government's contingent liability. This change might logically have been accompanied by more vigilant government scrutiny. Instead, the 1980 law initiated a process in which government regulation was relaxed while savings and loan activities became more discretionary and experimental. For example, under the 1980 law, a six-year phaseout of ceilings in deposit interest rates began and the development of longer-term savings instruments was encouraged. The Garn–St. Germain Depository Institutions Act of 1982 provided more flexibility to savings and loans by allowing them to make short-term consumer loans, issue credit cards, and make loans on commercial real estate.[11]

OMB's deregulation fervor entered the picture as the office cut staffing for the relevant regulatory agencies. OMB director David A. Stockman sought to cap the number of examiners at the Federal Home Loan Bank Board at seven hundred and examiners' starting salary at $13,500. In 1984, Stockman's deputy, Constance Horner, explained to Bank Board chairman Edwin J. Gray that deregulation meant fewer, not more, examiners.[12]

Once the constraints that had limited savings and loans to fixed-rate home mortgages were lifted, and the cap on savings interest rates abolished, speculators rushed in to purchase troubled savings and loans or to obtain charters for new ones. In many cases, the new owner would invest depositors' funds in the owner's own commercial real estate escapades. Office buildings and condominiums sprouted up, far beyond the demand for such improved properties. The free fall of property values in many states was accelerated by this useless activity. However, savings and loan owners relied on accounting scams, aided and abetted by some of the nation's most prominent and respected accounting firms, and encouraged by Reagan administration officials, to conceal the grim financial results of the disastrous investments made with depositors' funds. This concealment could occur because the government has traditionally allowed banks to suppress their financial reports. Those few regulatory officials who dared to challenge mismanagement and fraud on the part of savings and loan officials were often intimidated by members of Congress, who intervened on behalf of owners in their states and congressional districts. As the house of cards collapsed, the American taxpayers discovered how much they would have to pay on insured accounts in failed savings and loans. The public also learned about Charles Keating Jr., head of the Lincoln Savings and Loan Association, and a coterie of senators and representatives who had challenged regulatory officials trying to put the brakes on Lincoln's mounting losses.

> In 1986 the beneficiaries of [Keating's] significant largess were Sens. John McCain and Dennis DeConcini of Arizona, Sens. Timothy Wirth and William Armstrong of Colorado, Sen. Mack Mattingly of Georgia, Sen. John Glenn of Ohio, Sen. Alan Cranston of California, Sen. Chic Hecht of Nevada, Sen. Donald Riegle of Michigan, and congressmen too numerous to mention, with special emphasis on the Arizona delegation, Chip Pashayan of California, and Doug Bernard of Georgia.[13]

Mayer provides this example of interference by the senators.

> [Bank Board chairman Gray attended a meeting at] DeConcini's office, where four senators (Riegle did not attend this meeting) told him they had reason to believe the regulators were picking on Keating. They also said they had doubts about the direct-investment regulation, which might not be legal. Why didn't Gray suspend the regulation until the courts ruled? In return, Keating would promise to redirect his thrift and make lots of home mortgages.
>
> Several senators have denied that this is what was said, but this is what Gray told his staff when he returned from the meeting. Cranston, after publicly calling Gray a liar, later admitted to reporters that maybe something a little like what Gray said happened did happen.[14]

Senator Glenn is quoted as instructing bank examiners, "To be blunt, you should charge them [i.e., Lincoln Savings and Loan] or get off their backs." Senator Riegle demanded to know, "Where's the smoking gun? Where are the losses?"[15] Gray recalls:

> When it came to thrift matters in the Congress, the U.S. League [of Savings Institutions] and many of the affiliates were the de facto government. What

> the League wanted, it got. What it did not want from Congress, it had killed.... Every single day that I served as Chairman of the Federal Home Loan Bank Board, the U.S. League was in control of the Congress as an institution.[16]

Time and again, the regulators had to back off, leaving the savings and loan owner/speculators to make more reckless investments. Meanwhile, healthy savings and loans found their deposit insurance premiums on the rise, as the corrupt, collapsing thrifts drained the insurance fund of the Federal Savings and Loan Insurance Corporation.

Conservative, antiregulation theorists blame government involvement in the banking industry for the debacle. They say that the $100,000 deposit insurance decoupled the risk-reward linkage: wealthy depositors could place their savings into the shakiest savings and loans and earn extravagant interest rates while having the security of guaranteed government payments on principal and interest if—as seemed likely—the thrift collapsed. Deposits flowed from healthy, prudently managed savings and loans to the precarious institutions.

Progressive advocates of regulation tend to blame Reagan and George Bush for their cutbacks on regulatory staff. Representative Jim Leach (R-Iowa) is willing to distribute the blame between both parties and the two branches of the government: "This was disproportionately a liberal Democratic problem in Congress. It's also a Republican regulator problem and a Reagan philosophical problem. But legislatively, it was a Democratic problem."[17]

It is reasonable to view the savings and loan fiasco as an example of the "rich-get-richer" phenomenon so characteristic of the 1980s. Walter Fauntroy, the District of Columbia's delegate in the House of Representatives, inquired of Bank Board chairman M. Danny Wall at a January 6, 1989, hearing of the House Banking Committee:

> [Q. Fauntroy] Did I understand you to say that [Ronald] Perelman [a protégé of notorious junk bond dealer Michael Milken], in return for $315 million cash, received tax benefits of $897 million?
>
> [A. Wall] It might not work out that way.
>
> [Q.] But it might?
>
> [A.] Yes, it might.
>
> [Q.] I have just one question for you, Mr. Wall.

[A.] Yes?

[Q.] *Why is it only white folks who get that kind of deal?*[18]

Unreliability of Public Support

Deregulation began to look like a "stacked deck," which served to undermine the legitimacy of presidential involvement in regulation. Social scientists report that one of the best explanations for compliance with laws is the belief that the laws are legitimate.[19] There is no desire to comply with regulations emerging from a "black box."

The Reagan regulatory reform program seemed to possess less legitimacy than the regulations themselves. A 1979 survey conducted by *Public Opinion* reflected the popularity of regulating many aspects of business,[20] confirming a 1978 Harris poll indicating that consumers were willing to pay extra for environmental controls and nutritional labeling.[21] Public support for social regulation shadowed the Reagan administration's contention that it was protecting the public against regulations. "We will be lucky," Weidenbaum sighed, "if, in January 1984, we will be back to where we were in January 1981 in terms of the public's attitude toward statutory reform and social regulation."[22] Reagan was never successful in selling "relief" from social regulations to the United States public. Edwards reported the final results:

> Ronald Reagan was certainly interested in policy change and went to unprecedented lengths to influence public opinion. Nevertheless, numerous national surveys of public opinion have found that support for regulatory programs and spending on health care, welfare, urban problems, education, environmental protection, and aid to minorities has *increased*, not decreased, during Reagan's tenure.[23]

In the final analysis, the administration's claims to have operated in the public interest raised questions about why public support was not sustained, and why the administration gave up on public support after the program's early months. The public's continuing ambivalence was reflected in 1988 and 1990 surveys that show that 57 percent of the public believed that regulation did more harm than good,[24] while 70 percent considered current environmental regulations to be "not strict enough," and 41 percent had the same assessment of consumer protection regulation.[25] Reagan's and Bush's antiregulation rhetoric may have had the effect the two presidents sought: Surveys conducted by the Advisory Commission on Intergovernmental Regulation (ACIR) in 1987 and 1992 reveal that the public's faith in federal regulation declined substantially more than their faith in state and local regulation.[26]

More remarkable was the emerging ambivalence of the business community, the intended first-line beneficiary of regulatory relief. The United States Chamber of Commerce eventually developed discriminating taste—embracing some OIRA actions while holding others at arm's length. The National Federation of Independent Business concluded that the costs of OIRA review exceeded the benefits. On the micro level, individual firms, having been led to believe that they were being ushered into the Promised Land of laissez-faire, bitterly resented the remaining enforcement actions and interpreted such actions as discriminatory and disproportionate. Eads and Fix concluded that the regulatory relief program came "most conspicuously to grief" in the enforcement arena. In the end, it appears that the most devoted constituency for regulatory relief consisted entirely of Reagan, Bush, and the Executive Office of the President.

Patterns of Defective Analyses

Reagan's regulatory reform program was founded on the principle that the benefits of a regulation must exceed the costs. But economic and social problems do not carry preprinted price tags, and the costs and benefits of regulations designed to resolve those problems are not associated with definite values. The process of calculating costs and benefits involves speculation, estimation, and subjectivity. A study conducted in 1978 by the Senate's Committee on Governmental Affairs found that the benefits of regulations in the health, safety, and environmental areas are especially difficult to quantify. The Subcommittee on Oversight and Investigations of the House Interstate and Foreign Commerce Committee also issued a report in the late 1970s demonstrating that cost estimates for the same proposal vary greatly because of inaccurate measurements. Observers noticed that cost/benefit calculations were directly related to the motivations of the authors of the studies.[27]

The nature of the Reagan program—introduced as it was to effect deregulation and "relief"—created automatic doubt about OIRA's capacity for neutral analysis. There is no evidence that OIRA—which touted its expertise in regulatory analysis as superior to that of the agencies—ever developed scientific guidelines for formulating dependable cost-benefit analyses. Indeed, OIRA desk officers reported that their cost-benefit evaluative criterion involved a "laugh test": If they read a proposed regulation that made them laugh, they disapproved it.[28] While Reagan's 1980 campaign offered the promise that laughable regulations would be disallowed, even progressive Democrats had a basis to claim their rights established in statutes mandating health and safety regulation and the opportunity for due process in soliciting such regulation. The administration's analytical approach could not inspire confidence among broad constituencies, thus leaving the reputation of regulatory analysis vulnerable to cynicism and skepticism.

Perpetuation of Burdens on State and Local Governments

Although Reagan's "New Federalism" was purportedly intended to bolster the viability of state and local governments in the federal system,[29] the needs of these lower levels of government were for the most part neglected. According to David B. Walker, a continuing series of preemptions and grant conditions produced such mandates as the unpopular tandem truck regulation and the ban on teenage drinking, and more conditions attached to welfare programs. The Reagan administration rarely consulted state and local governments when developing programs having intergovernmental impacts.[30] The ACIR commented that "regulatory reform" had not and could not supplant the need for a "principled approach" to the problem of federal regulatory supervision of lower-level governments within the framework of federalism.[31]

An Unstable Outcome

To some who embraced President Reagan's vow to reform the regulatory system and thus obtain the benefits of reform foreseen by 1970s economists, the regulatory reform program was a broken promise. According to Gregory B. Christiansen and Robert H. Haveman, regulatory relief could not arrest the rate of inflation.[32] Goodman and Wrightson found no significant change in national environmental policy.[33] Steiner concluded that the program was effecting only a "marginal diminution" in the volume of regulation.[34] Each time OIRA thwarted a regulatory proposal disliked by conservative, probusiness constituents, it merely seemed to be a one-time victory portending no further progress in regulatory reform.

Abandoning legislative change as the vehicle for regulatory reform, the Reagan administration settled on a two-part strategy: first, relying on political appointees to bring regulatory relief through hierarchical control, and second, using the president's constitutional power to execute laws and require the opinions of his department heads. This strategy was ill fated, say Richard A.

Harris and Sidney M. Milkis, because administrative institutions and procedures were designed to promote regulation, not to impede them. As a result, the social regulatory process was insulated from the type of assault organized by Reagan's lieutenants.[35] Accordingly, the gains made by the Reagan strategy were limited and may be temporary. Moreover, while future presidents have been taught how to realize a political advantage through bureaucratic control, the same information in the hands of a progressive Democratic president could give conservatives cause for regret.

Goodman and Wrightson make the telling point that Reagan, determined not to repeat the "errors" of his predecessors who on occasion let upstart regulators gain the upper hand, made the fateful decision to adopt a no-compromise posture. This intransigence led to the inability to attract legislation from Congress.[36] Therefore, President Reagan left no regulatory legacy in the United States Code. What he won can be neglected by any successor who prefers to expend his political capital elsewhere. Agencies no longer subjected to heavy-handed OMB pressure to prepare cost-benefit analyses can be expected to abandon the function without ceremony.

An even more severe implication for the long-term objective of regulatory reform is the result of the mischief of administration officials who flaunted favoritism as a desired value. Vice presidential counsel C. Boyden Gray's "Hall of Flags" speech, which specifically invited business people to use the Task Force and OIRA as a special appeals court; OIRA administrator Miller's self-description as the "toughest kid on the block"; OIRA deputy administrator Tozzi's "no fingerprints" process, and his threats that recalcitrants would pay a price all served to intimidate the bureaucracy. That was their intention. But these expressions and tactics alienated Congress, interest groups, and the public. The concept of regulatory reform became an embarrassment. The obstacle to reform created by memories of the mischief of Reagan's top officials is one of the most unfortunate remnants of the Reagan Revolution.

IMPLICATIONS FOR FURTHER ATTEMPTS AT REGULATORY REFORM

The Reagan administration made a fateful decision to forgo laborious attempts to institutionalize the program in statute, opting instead for an aggressive management strategy. Thus, as the Reagan era drew to a close, the United States Code contained no record of Reagan's regulatory reform. The only record consisted of executive orders and OMB circulars—a house of straw that any successor could raze at will or merely neglect. As an activity conducted in the "zone of twilight" between legislative and executive power,[37] the regulatory review program's questionable status in our constitutional system makes it an illegitimate offspring.

What about the prospect, then, for permanent statutory institutionalization of presidentially coordinated centralized review? It is this issue that raises the most serious questions about the legacy of the Reagan and Bush administrations in the regulatory arena. The heavy-handed bluster used to get the attention of the potentially recalcitrant bureaucracy attracted the attention of other actors as well. Congress, the courts, interest groups, labor unions, and even individuals were repelled by the appearance of a rogue government establishment that was unfettered by laws. This public relations debacle has given OIRA, OMB, and the very concept of presidentially coordinated regulatory review a bad name that will endure. Members of Congress can be expected to evoke the memory of the early Reagan days whenever the issue is brought back to it.

10 Regulatory Review After Reagan

THE BUSH ADMINISTRATION: "HITTING THE GROUND LIMPING"

A Problem with the "Vision Thing"

Ronald Reagan, his circle of conservative ideologues, and a Republican Senate majority roared into Washington in late 1980 with the clear intention of engaging in bold confrontation with progressive Democratic legislators, progressive interest groups, and the purportedly antibusiness bureaucracy. The Reagan Revolution is often characterized as a radical movement because it planned a real departure from the regulatory state and welfare state, which had been either championed or conceded by every president from 1933 to 1980.

Reagan's mandatory retirement and George Bush's accession to the presidency resulted in a suspension of the antiregulation fervor that had emanated from the White House for eight years. There are several reasons why the Reagan Revolution could not extend into the Bush era.

First, Bush was preparing to face the second consecutive Congress in which both houses had Democratic majorities, in contrast to the Republican majority in the Senate that Reagan enjoyed from 1981 until 1987. Second, Bush's instincts led him toward conciliation, a trait that in childhood earned him the nickname, "Have Half."[1] Third, because of their perception that Bush's 1988 campaign against Democratic candidate Michael S. Dukakis had been unforgivably malicious, congressional Democrats vowed to deprive Bush of any semblance of a honeymoon period. Fourth, the activist bureaucracy that awaited Reagan in 1981 had been redirected in the Reagan years,[2] so that Bush inherited a less zealous and, in some ways, dispirited executive branch.

Fifth, Bush himself had a long history as a bureaucrat, and approached civil servants with an attitude of respect, far different from the scorn for the bureaucracy that Reagan expressed freely.[3] Sixth, Bush's eight-year-old habit of reciting Reaganesque conservative ideology in fact disguised a moderate, status quo core.[4] Seventh, public opinion, which was impatient with government regulation in the late 1970s and early 1980s, no longer condoned the conservative assault on regulation. In a November 1991 survey conducted by Peter Hart Research Associates, Americans ranked "reduced government safety and environmental regulations" as the least desirable of sixteen ways to revive the economy.[5] Eighth, the heavy-handed tactics that marred Reagan's regulatory reform effort now promised to shadow any effort by Bush, as Democratic legislators and progressive activists were poised to oppose aggressive regulatory reform as a reflex; indeed, a movement for *reregulation* was gaining strength.[6]

As a result of these conditions, the Bush administration adopted an approach of restraint—that is, the effort to redefine the role of the federal government was decidedly limited. With a sympathetic tone, Rockman explains that "George Bush was elected as a Republican essentially to continue the Reagan agenda in a somewhat more tempered way."[7] Less charitably, columnist Tom Wicker described President-elect Bush as a man who "has hit the ground limping."[8]

One signal that the Bush administration had no energetic strategy in its domestic policy was the announcement that Bush and his aides did not intend to exploit the traditional honeymoon period. (As mentioned above, the Democrats were already on record as promising to deprive Bush of a honeymoon anyway.) Bush said:

> There's a general thrust, and President Reagan set that. They asked me the other day about "the one hundred days." I said, "we don't have to put it in terms of one hundred days. We're not coming in to correct the ills of the past, we're coming in to build on a proud record that has already been established."[9]

Duffy and Goodgame explain that Bush had little use for confrontation in his domestic policy, because he preferred to hold his political capital in reserve for his real interest—foreign policy.

> [Bush] had judged that an attempt to confront a Democratic Congress with a distinctly Republican program would only insure four years of stalemate, undermine the bipartisan cooperation that he would need to score the for-

> eign policy successes that he craved, and risk reducing him to a failed, one-term president.... Bush would coopt the Democrats through compromise, to neutralize any big domestic issue on which they might gain partisan advantage: the environment, education, civilian research. Bush also, of course, would develop wedge issues, including crime and racial hiring quotas, to distinguish himself and other Republicans from the Democrats. And all along he would work to distinguish himself in the field where his strongest interest and expertise lay and where he enjoyed the greatest latitude for individual initiative: foreign policy.[10]

Bush's appointments of administration officials reflected his lack of interest in ideological manipulation of the executive branch. Some of his appointments were consistent with his "kinder and gentler" commitment: For example, to head the Occupational Safety and Health Administration (OSHA), he selected Gerald F. Scannell, a former director of OSHA's Office of Standards, clearly a supporter of workplace safety regulation.[11] To head the Environmental Protection Agency (EPA), he hired William K. Reilly, a committed environmentalist. Bush also nominated "aggressive regulators" to head the Food and Drug Administration and the Securities and Exchange Commission.[12] Simultaneously, he hired several senior staff members who would balance the proregulation appointees; Secretary of the Interior Manuel Lujan, for example, was seen as an opponent of forceful environmental regulation. In general, Bush's appointees could be characterized as practical, civil, cautious, and conciliatory. "They like to face problems and solve them, using a few shared values—prudence, marketplace wisdom, compassion in word if not in [deed]—as their guide.... He has hired few crusaders.... If previous administration's decision makers had something they wanted to do, Bush's prefer simply to do something."[13] These appointments were in sharp contrast to Reagan's appointments of ideologues, who created acrimony and embarrassment in the early years of the Reagan administration. Bush's appointments of moderates who were neither programmed nor inclined to undermine the missions of their respective agencies defused the tension between political appointees and civil servants that was common in previous administrations, especially Reagan's.[14]

But as Bush improved the climate of the executive branch, he sent it inadequate signals about what he wanted it to do in regulatory policy. Referring to the Task Force on Regulatory Relief that he chaired during his tenure as vice president, he announced, somewhat cryptically, that "that work has got to continue."[15] He also explained: "My philosophy is this: that when it comes to necessary regulation of business, I'm committed to letting the States take the lead, not the Federal Government."[16] Bush issued no executive orders for regulatory reform, until his January 1992 moratorium decision. Bush's aides seemed indifferent to opportunities to use the Office of Information and Regulatory Affairs (OIRA) to further develop presidential control of the executive branch.[17]

In these ways, Bush baffled observers looking for a coherent regulatory policy from the captain of the Reagan administration's regulatory reform efforts, and squandered the opportunity to continue the momentum his predecessors had generated in expanding presidential influence over regulation.

In the closing years of the Reagan administration, the regulatory review process settled into a routine. Under Reagan's last OIRA administrator, S. Jay Plager, a less confrontational approach had been adopted that contrasted sharply with the early Reagan-era leadership of Office of Management and Budget (OMB) director David A. Stockman, OIRA administrator (later OMB director) James C. Miller III, and OIRA deputy administrator Jim J. Tozzi. Upon Plager's appointment to the Federal Circuit of the Court of Appeals, OIRA deputy administrator James B. MacRae Jr. assumed the position of acting administrator. MacRae, a civil servant, continued to act in that capacity until the end of the Bush era, ensuring that only a modest level of provocation would occur. An official of the Department of Education said in a September 1992 interview that the relationship between his agency and OIRA was "stable," as might have been expected.

What might not have been expected was the impressive growth in regulatory activity in the first three years of the Bush administration. Some advocates of regulatory reform, who lamented and even anticipated a listless Bush-era regulatory review program,[18] raised protests against the loss of momentum of one of the centerpieces of the Reagan Revolution. One reporter described the first two and one-half years of the Bush administration as a "regulatory renaissance" of resumed rule-making activity, and cited the "complaints by business groups and conservatives who were an important part of President Bush's political coalition in 1988."[19] Regulatory agency staffing increased by 20 percent from 1985 to 1991.[20] The *Federal Register*, which contained 73,258 pages in 1980, dropped to 50,502 pages in 1985, but increased to 57,972 pages in 1991, indicating a recovery of regulatory activity under Bush. The number of regulations increased by 17 percent in the Bush era compared to the Reagan era.[21] Bush's regulatory expenditures in real dollars exceeded President Jimmy Carter's.[22] One of the administration's policies most troubling to advocates of deregulation was Bush's support of the Clean Air Act of 1990, which ran nearly eight hundred pages and involved about $30 million in implementation costs. However, after Bush took credit for justifying his "Environmental President" moniker by shepherding the Clean Air Act of 1990 through Congress, his aides proceeded to undermine implementation of the law by the EPA.

Council on Competitiveness

Within days of his inauguration, Bush established the Council on Competitiveness to continue the work of the Reagan-era Task Force on Regulatory Relief. Just as Vice President Bush had chaired the task force, so Bush appointed Vice President Dan Quayle to chair the council. On February 9, 1989, in a supplement to Bush's "Address on Administrative Goals Before a Joint Session of Congress," transmitted to Congress with the FY90 budget, Bush declared:

> The Council will review regulatory issues as may be referred by the President, bearing on competitiveness. In reviewing regulatory matters, the Council will be continuing the work of the former President's Task Force on Regulatory Relief—chaired in the Reagan Administration by then Vice President Bush.[23]

The council was designed to work with OIRA to perpetuate cost-benefit analysis and to coordinate development of legislative and administration initiatives to reduce the costs of regulations. Insofar as Quayle was clearly searching for a vehicle to become "a leading player in the Bush administration,"[24] one might have expected him to seek a visible leadership role at the vanguard of regulatory reform. Inscrutably, for many months, the council worked in obscurity and with no apparent zeal. This lethargy can be illustrated by Marshall Goodman's account of a caller to Vice President Quayle's office. The caller requested information about the Council on Competitiveness, chaired by Quayle, and was told that nobody in the office was familiar with the project![25] Unlike the early history of the Reagan task force, a time when the White House was eager to tout its contemplated impact, the introduction of the council was scarcely publicized. Senators John Glenn (D-Ohio), Carl M. Levin (D-Mich.), and Herbert H. Kohl (D-Wis.) and Representative John Conyers Jr. (D-Mich.) discovered as much when they contacted Quayle's office requesting information about the council, and received a small collection of fact sheets and press releases in response.[26] In November 1991, Senators Glenn, Levin, Kohl, and Joseph I. Lieberman (D-Conn.) questioned OIRA acting administrator MacRae and, according to a *Washington Post* reporter, received answers startlingly reminiscent of Reagan-era regulatory reform. In the reporter's paraphrasing:

> Yes, the [Council on Competitiveness] does advise [OIRA] on regulatory matters.
>
> No, [MacRae] cannot think of an instance when his staff turned down the advice.
>
> Yes, his staff communicates orally with the council.
>
> No, these communications are not recorded in any form.[27]

The council boasted an influential membership. As of summer 1991, the members were White House Chief of Staff John Sununu, Attorney General Richard Thornburgh, Secretary of the Treasury Nicholas Brady, Council of Economic Advisers (CEA) chairman Michael Boskin, OMB director Richard Darman, and Secretary of Commerce Robert Mosbacher.[28] Beginning in the last half of 1991, the Council on Competitiveness made its presence felt in an apparent effort to protect the administration's relationship with its constituency in the business community. The council restored the emphasis on cost-benefit analysis.[29] The council collaborated with the Food and Drug Administration in preparing new rules to shorten the duration of the drug approval process.[30] The EPA experienced déjà vu as its rule-making decisions were regularly reversed by the council.[31] The charges of secrecy and ex parte contacts that hounded the regulatory review program during the Reagan era resumed in earnest; indeed, they had been well rehearsed since 1981.

Contemporaneous with Bush's announcement of the moratorium, designed to restore Bush's reputation as a deregulator, the Council on Competitiveness increased its activity level. Quayle's prominence grew as the council became the ultimate appeals court within the administration, with the exception of the Oval Office, where few officials wanted to put their rivalries on display. "I'm the last stop before the president," Quayle said. "I have not had a decision appealed from the Competitiveness Council to the president."[32]

While Quayle and the council's staff basked in the publicity they were generating, they were circumspect in disclosing details about the council's operations, leaving outsiders—including members of Congress—to guess about them.[33] Reminiscent of OIRA deputy administrator Tozzi's boast in the early months of the Reagan administration, Quayle aides cited their knack for leaving "no fingerprints" in the wake of their regulatory review activities.[34] The glare of outside scrutiny was most annoying as council executive director Allan Hubbard fought off accusations of conflict of interest that would lead to his withdrawal from council activities in January 1992.

The open door policy to industry representatives that was the focus of controversy for the task force during the Reagan era was perpetuated by the council. "When [businesses] feel like they are being treated unfairly, they come to us," Hubbard said in 1991. However, Hubbard maintained that the council was neutral and had no preconceived agenda. In addition to complaints from industry, the council also received requests for intervention filed by OIRA in cases of disputes with agencies, or by agencies in cases of disputes with OIRA or other agencies.[35] Given Bush's preference that disputes among his aides not be elevated to the Oval Office, Quayle's decisions in the council on such disputes were final.

This finality convinced critics that the council exercised inordinate power. To Representative Henry Waxman (D-Calif.), the council was a "shadow government." Because Quayle's council enjoyed Bush's "total confidence," a former administration official explained, "nobody can touch these guys." In the summer of 1990, the council reportedly prescribed over one hundred changes in proposed regulations for carrying out the Clean Air Act, apparently setting off a flurry of negotiations between the council and EPA.[36] OIRA and the council disapproved an EPA regulatory proposal on recycling; EPA's Reilly appeared before the council in December 1990 and "got rolled," according to David D. Doniger, senior attorney of the Natural Resources Defense Council.[37]

The Subcommittee on Health and the Environment of the House Committee on Energy and Commerce held hearings in 1991 and 1992 to investigate the role of the Council on Competitiveness in interfering with implementation of the Clean Air Act of 1990. Although Bush himself had advocated the law's enactment, the council wrote over one hundred revisions to weaken EPA's proposed permit regulation, according to subcommittee chairman Waxman. The regulation would have been a key device for implementing the law, Waxman explained, but the council had vitiated EPA's draft regulation. He also complained: "A thorough examination of how EPA has done in meeting the deadlines of the new law tells a more disturbing tale. Of the 16 important actions that EPA is required by law to take by November 15, 1991—tomorrow—the agency has completed zero, not even one."[38]

Dean Cornelius M. Kerwin of American University observed that the council differed from the Reagan-era task force in that the task force carried out retrospective reviews of regulations, whereas the council acted as a "super-OMB" review operation, exacerbating the problem of depriving citizens of their right to due process.[39] Cass R. Sunstein, a lawyer in the Office of Legal Counsel in the Department of Justice during the Reagan administration, expressed doubts about the legality, under the Constitution and the Administrative Procedure Act, of the council's clear superiority over the discretion of agency officials.

> President Reagan's administration was exceptionally careful to ensure fidelity to the two simple practices that substantive communications with outsiders have to be disclosed and that the ultimate decision is for the agency head. It is unfortunate that there are new reasons for concern that President Bush's administration has violated the procedures assembled so carefully by the Reagan administration in conjunction with Congress and members of the public.... If it is the case that the Council [on] Competitiveness has been making these decisions and displacing the decisions of the [EPA], then the [council] has been behaving illegally, and its behavior should not be tolerated by Congress or by the President himself.[40]

Administration officials and their sympathizers disputed the portrait of the council as an entity vested with absolute power. From the beginning, Quayle predicted that the council would be "something of a clearinghouse."[41] Asked in late 1991 about the volume of regulatory issues reviewed by the council, Quayle replied, "Whew, quite a few." Administration officials were more specific, estimating that fifty cases had been processed in the preceding year.[42] Of course, fifty cases is a minuscule proportion of the total number of regulations generated by agencies each year. "While environmental and consumer groups have criticized the council as being anti-regulatory, some conservatives say the office... has proved to have little muscle. In fact, there has been an unabated growth in Federal regulations during the Bush Administration."[43] The debate was an indication that regulatory advocates could not accept any restraint placed on the discretion of agency officials, while advocates of deregulation were determined to continue to send signals to agencies that regulatory activity should be limited and judicious. But agency officials inevitably outnumbered the administration officials responsible for regulatory review. Says one of those administration officials: "No rule is ever completely killed—it's always in someone's computer."[44]

The growth in regulatory activity generated criticism by antiregulation leaders that Bush had become the "regulatory president." Concerned that he might forfeit some of his conservative, probusiness support, Bush took the initiative against regulation in his State of the Union address on January 28, 1992, when he announced a moratorium on new regulations for ninety days—a period that was extended twice.[45] In the State of the Union message, Bush instructed agency heads to conduct a "top-to-bottom" review of existing regulations to identify those that were restraining business activity. The administration proceeded to write new rules designed to reverse the effect of regulations already on the books. For example, rules restricting interstate banking were countered with new rules intended to relax the restrictions.[46]

Many laws required that certain regulations be issued, often with scheduling deadlines, and President Bush's moratorium order could not interfere with such mandated rules. Therefore, only rules issued upon the agency's discretion could be restricted. Bush permitted rules in that category to be processed in spite of the moratorium if the agency declared that delay in promulgation would unreasonably impair the public interest. Rules affecting workplace hazards of an urgent nature were specifically exempted from the moratorium.[47] EPA administrator Reilly emphasized that regulations required by the Clean Air Act would not be affected. "We do not propose to contravene the will of Congress."[48] Over time, the moratorium exceptions seem to have expanded, so that more regulations were getting through, according to one department official who requested anonymity.

For the agencies, the moratorium represented another level of scrutiny that proposed regulations had to undergo. All such proposals were already reviewed by OIRA to measure cost-benefit merit and consistency with the president's regulatory policies. At the highest levels of the Department of Agriculture, for example, a proposed regulation was reviewed to determine if it could be submitted during the moratorium because it was urgent and had no undue impact on the economy.

INTERACTION BETWEEN THE EOP AND AGENCY OFFICIALS

Cooperation

Agency officials exhibit cooperative postures toward OIRA because of fears that noncompliance may result in acts of revenge from the president or OMB; partners in federal government exchange relationships prefer accommodation to a fight to the finish.[49] Agency heads continued to exhibit this preference during the Bush administration:

> Agency heads say they are often told by the council [on Competitiveness] to change regulations. And in Congressional testimony Administration officials have been unable to name an instance in which an agency head overruled the... council. As one top official with the [EPA] put it, "We go up there and negotiate, and so far we have come away with many of the things we want. But not all.[50]

Agencies also cooperated with the EOP by voluntarily suppressing their own flow of regulatory submissions, thus contributing to President Bush's deregulation campaign. Said one official, his department "is picking the big ones now."

When Bush announced the first moratorium in January, EPA's Reilly said that the moratorium and regulatory review "would be used by us to redouble our efforts, to ensure that what we do is sensitive to the economy."[51] Even when Reilly found himself in conflict with the Council on Competitiveness or OIRA, he publicly put the best face on the interaction. He would state that he "voluntarily withdrew" a proposal that he had been ordered to bury, and would publicly defend the decision to withdraw it.[52]

Bargaining and Conflict

While in chapter 5 we described widespread compliance to EOP regulatory policies by agencies, we also contended that agencies will display resistance at the point that they perceive their missions to be imperiled by demands from the president's aides. Reactions to perceived threats run the gamut from resolve to frustration and from acts of evasion to overt conflict.

Regulatory agencies attempt to bargain as their first step. There may be concessions to be extracted from OMB. EPA's Reilly was reported to be adept at this. "The Reilly style is to fight for every inch of environmental progress, then retreat at the last minute when he calculates he has extracted the most he can get from the administration. His style rankles some Bush domestic-policy advisers, who question whether he is a team player."[53] Reilly expressed his resolve this way: "They have no authority to direct me in how I'll administer the law."[54] Jo Anne B. Barnhart, assistant secretary for children and families at the Department of Health and Human Services, asserted, "We are *not* in the business of writing regulations that are in direct defiance of Congress."[55]

Notwithstanding EPA's declaration of hegemony over environmental rule making, OIRA and the council persisted in their efforts to direct such activity, leading to frustration at the agency. "We have a pretty clear sense from EPA that they're not happy, but their hands are tied and they feel they don't have the power to stand up to the council," Representative Waxman said.[56]

Frustration may lead to defiance, expressed as evasion and leaks to influential outsiders. Reilly "hasn't hesitated to use the media," said former Bush administration economist Robert Hahn.[57] Some agencies evaded OIRA control by establishing "unofficial" procedures without using the rule-making process. Regulated parties who do not comply with "unofficial" procedures suffered penalties or the loss of licenses and approvals, just as they did when actual regulations were disobeyed—but the difference, of course, is that the standards were not submitted to OMB.[58]

When all of these preconfrontation steps were exhausted, eyeball-to-eyeball conflict was the remaining, and perhaps unavoidable, event. When this conflict involved an agency and OIRA, OIRA sometimes escalated the dispute to the Council on Competitiveness, where the agency representatives were likely to find themselves the object of an ambush.

One especially heated confrontation involved air pollution regulations proposed by EPA under the Clean Air Act of 1990. EPA had bargained for the proposals, reaching an agreement with Bush's counsel, C. Boyden Gray, and CEA chairman Boskin. Subsequently, the Council on Competitiveness disapproved the regulations. A showdown was scheduled for the council's April 3, 1992, meeting. Hours before the scheduled start of the meeting, EPA received a memo from the council claiming that the Department of Justice was siding with the council. Reilly realized that the turnout for the council meeting would be lopsided in favor of administration officials hostile to EPA's position. Reilly boycotted the meeting, which was then canceled.[59] An April 26 meeting that Quayle, Reilly, and other officials attended reached no resolution; for once, Reilly appeared ready to take the controversy to the president.[60] In the wake of Bush's 1992 reelection defeat, Reilly acknowledged that his ongoing conflict with senior White House officials damaged Bush's campaign and overshadowed Bush's environmental record.[61]

Former OMB director Miller attributed some of the more unpleasant clashes to OIRA acting administrator MacRae's status as a civil servant. "That civil servant is talking to a political appointee who is confirmed by the Senate ... and does not take kindly to being told what to do by a civil servant."[62] Bush's one attempt to appoint a permanent OIRA administrator was thwarted when a Senate committee held up the confirmation process.

CONGRESSIONAL ACTIVITY DURING THE BUSH ERA

In the 101st Congress (1989–1991), bills for reregulation found a sympathetic audience.

> During the 101st Congress numerous pieces of reregulation legislation were introduced. For example, the National Association of Broadcasters ... pushed for a reconsideration of the 1984 Cable Communications Policy Act, which virtually deregulated the cable industry. Broadcasters asked Congress and the Bush Administration to force community cable systems to carry all

> local broadcast channels licensed by the [Federal Communications Commission]. Indeed, on June 7, 1990, the Senate Commerce Committee voted 18-1 in favor of legislation that would reregulate the rates for basic tier cable service, a practice that was outlawed by the 1984 act.... Congress also moved to place new regulatory restrictions on the security markets..., introduced numerous bills attempting to reregulate the savings and loan industry..., sought to repeal antitrust exemptions for the insurance industry..., and initiated several bills that sought to develop a mandatory seafood inspection system.[63]

Since 1981, some members of Congress have perceived the regulatory review process as constituting a threat to the separation of powers and/or as undermining consumer, environmental, and occupational safety legislation of interest to them. The complaints tapered off in the later years of the Reagan administration, as OIRA's review process was subjected to new procedures countenanced by key members of Congress. As the Bush administration's dormant deregulatory inclination reawakened in 1991, the criticism was also reactivated. In the fall of 1991, Browning reported: "Lawmakers at all levels [Congress and state legislatures] accuse the Administration of trying to subvert Congress on a wide range of issues by directing executive branch agencies to write regulations that substitute conservative ideology for legislative intent."[64] The Council on Competitiveness was the main target, eclipsing OIRA. The council "borders on corruption,"[65] said Representative Gerry Sikorski (D-Minn.), and its activities amounted to "treason." Waxman called it "sinister." Representative Gerry E. Studds (D-Mass.) portrayed the council as "Orwellian." The council is a "polluter star chamber," said Representative George Miller (D-Calif.).[66]

The council invited anger by refusing to provide information about its activities requested by several congressional committees.[67] A Senate Governmental Affairs Committee report complained: "The Council has thus far refused to honor requests of this and other congressional committees to obtain basic information as to its organizational structure, staff, budget, activities, decisional and review criteria, and contacts with Federal agencies and outside groups."[68] The Bush administration exacerbated the tension between itself and Congress by repudiating most of the procedural compromises governing OIRA operations that were hammered out in negotiations between OMB and Congress, most of them in 1986. By returning to the secrecy and mystery for which OIRA officials showed preference in the early 1980s, the administration unnecessarily provoked angry reaction from Congress.

In their attempts to take the veil off the regulatory review process, congressional committees launched investigations and held hearings. For example, Conyers announced that the House Government Operations Committee would investigate the Council on Competitiveness, looking at alleged conflicts of interest and other matters.[69] Waxman's Subcommittee on Health and the Environment in the House Committee on Energy and Commerce held a year-long series of hearings on the council.[70] Representative John D. Dingell (D-Mich.), chairman of the Oversight and Investigations Subcommittee of the House Energy and Commerce Committee, obtained records of contacts between EPA and OMB and published the documents, over the objections of EPA and the subcommittee's Republican minority members.[71]

Other congressional reaction has included acts of revenge, such as Glenn's delay of action on the nomination of Bush nominee James Blustein to the position of OIRA administrator, which led to Blustein's withdrawal and the perpetuation of the vacancy in OIRA's top position.

The more common type of congressional reaction has involved legislation designed to circumscribe the activities of the council and of OIRA. Apart from procedural prescriptions, members of Congress sought to undermine Quayle's and OIRA's authority by eliminating authorizations or appropriations in order to kill regulatory review through defunding. OIRA was not reauthorized in the 102d Congress. Nevertheless, OIRA's funding continued because of a clause in an earlier reauthorization that extended funding automatically in the absence of reauthorization. A recommendation by the House Government Operations Committee to deny a Council on Competitiveness appropriation was similarly ineffective in terminating the administration's activities. On July 1, 1992, the House of Representatives defeated, by a vote of 183 to 236, a Republican amendment to restore funding for the Council on Competitiveness.[72] The vote was merely symbolic since only $86,000—far less than the actual costs of operating the council—was explicitly eliminated (by an Appropriations Committee decision on June 25 to strike the funding). As usual, the administration was defiant. David C. Beckwith, spokesman for the vice president's office, called the actions "harassment." "The same Congressional critics who allege the council was operating illegally have abandoned that tactic in favor of political harassment," he declared. "The council will continue to uphold and enforce laws at the least possible cost to jobs, consumers and the economy."[73] The effort of Senator Glenn to terminate funding for the council failed as well, and the council's operations were unimpeded through the end of Bush's and Quayle's term.

REGULATORY REFORM AT THE END OF THE BUSH ERA

While advocates of progressive regulation were consistently critical of Reagan's and Bush's regulatory review programs, the business community was more discriminating. The business community found that some of the rogue aspects of regulatory review, such as the secretive and heavy-handed nature, involved embarrassing publicity, and business people did not want to be firmly associated with it. The listless regulatory policy prevailing during the first half of the Bush administration was another object of disdain. Business people greeted Bush's January 1992 moratorium order skeptically. Said Terry Hill, a spokesperson for the National Federation of Independent Businesses, "Ninety days doesn't mean a lot to a small business struggling along with the recession." Thomas D. Hopkins, author of a cost of regulation study for the United States Chamber of Commerce, said: "We are in a period during the Bush administration of substantial rises in regulatory costs. Stopping for a moment and taking a careful look at what's coming down the pipeline might be useful. But it does seem like it's too little and too late."[74] The Reagan-Bush regulatory review program was based on the justifiable notion that a central clearinghouse was necessary to preclude multiple regulations that contradict one another, or nonsense regulations, or other regulations that burden the economy without commensurate benefit. Regrettably, the program's reputation continued to be blotted by unnecessary "no fingerprints" secrecy that concealed the merits of review while creating nagging doubts about impropriety. These doubts were encouraged by reports that Quayle and council aides held closed-door roundtables with donors to the Bush-Quayle campaign from the business community in cities on Quayle's campaign itinerary.[75]

The confusing legacy left by Bush in the regulatory arena is a consequence of his lack of a defining mission in domestic policy. The candidate who promised no new taxes, reduced government spending, and regulatory reform proved to be "the biggest taxer, the biggest spender, and one of the most expensive regulators in American presidential history."[76] Republican pollster Frank Luntz complained:

> [Bush] blustered promises of no new taxes, but turned around and gave us the second highest tax increase in American history. He pledged the creation of 40 million new jobs, yet the number of jobless today is at a 10-year high. He vowed reductions in government regulation and interference, yet more businesses than ever are dying under the weight of red tape.[77]

Bush was well aware of concerns that he lacked vision; he referred with frustration to his problem with the "vision thing." Duffy and Goodgame report that Bush's public life had no focus in terms of a policy-oriented goal; rather, his determination to serve was an end in itself. Bush once explained his ambition to hold the presidency as being centered on "the honor of it all." This purposeless plan set the stage for an administration without direction.

> Here, finally, was "the vision thing": The image Bush saw when he imagined a better future for America was [for Bush himself to be] in the Oval Office through January 1997! Silly as it may sound, this revelation proved useful as "an organizing principle," in the recollection of one senior official, ... and "gave us a quiet, internal coherence that had been missing until then."[78]

Only in desperation, as his business constituency grew restless and the 1992 campaign approached, did Bush revive the regulatory relief effort, replacing his lackadaisical posture with a jarring attack on regulation, including a moratorium and an assault on the provisions of the Clean Air Act of 1990, whose passage he himself had championed. "Rigor, clear-eyed cynicism, and political self-interest... drove [Bush's] domestic policy.... All of domestic policy was subordinated to the goal of Bush's re-election, and almost everything that didn't fit was thrown overboard."[79] The jagged edges of the administration's approach to regulatory review continued to provoke Congress, with unfortunate effects. OIRA's undependable funding, which depressed the size of the staff of desk officers, exacerbated the length of the delay in completing each regulation.[80] And the administration's failure to secure legislation authorizing regulatory review left the entire process subject to the whim of the next administration.

TESTING THE DURABILITY OF PRESIDENTIAL INFLUENCE: THE DEMOCRATS REGAIN THE WHITE HOUSE

The penchant for secrecy that was apparent in the behavior of the Council on Competitiveness and the appearance of indifference to the environment provided the 1992 Democratic ticket—Arkansas Governor Bill Clinton and Senator Albert Gore Jr. (D-Tenn.)—with a ready-made issue to take to the electorate. Knowledgeable citizens had been exposed to 12 years' worth of reports about secrecy, due-process deprivations, favoritism to business interests, and biased analytical methods. Now, Clinton was promising to lift the veil of secrecy, to resolve suspicions of influence peddling by special interests, and to dissolve the shadowy Council on Competitiveness. "I am opposed to such a body when it acts in secret without any form of public oversight," candidate Clinton wrote.[81] The speculation that the election of a Democratic president would terminate the trend of increased presidential intervention in regulatory activity was encouraged by Clinton's and Gore's campaign rhetoric. Nevertheless, the new president was expected to continue the review and coordination of regulatory policy in the Executive Office of the President.[82] The pattern of many administrations in this century has been that they felt the necessity to restrain government spending and regulation in order to maintain a healthy economy. This historical consideration, along with Clinton's candid recognition that government policies of recent years, left unchecked, are threats to the nation's economy, indicated that he would develop his own mechanisms to control the growth of regulation on health, environment, and safety.[83] Another signal that Clinton might impose presidential control on regulation was his use of the Reagan Revolution of 1981 as a "role model" during the transition that followed the election of 1992 (albeit for the purpose of "undoing much of Reagan's legacy").[84] Similarly, the regulatory reform program in the Carter administration was relatively ineffective, and Clinton has been using that experience as a case study of mistakes that a new administration ought to avoid. For example, unlike Carter, Clinton limited the freedom of his appointees to name their own sub-cabinet appointees, relying on former South Carolina Governor Richard Riley to screen subcabinet appointees for loyalty.[85]

In many ways, early appearances suggested that Clinton's approach to regulatory policy would overlap the thrust of the Bush program.

> [Clinton's] aides insist he would break with the traditional Democratic approach of promulgating detailed rules that dictate how businesses must comply. "There's going to be an attempt to innovate," says Michael Waldman who handles regulatory issues for the campaign. . . .
>
> Actually, although the two men don't admit it, Mr. Bush and Mr. Clinton agree on the need for new techniques for regulation. Both would ease the industrial burden of pollution control by using market mechanisms in environmental regulations. For instance, Mr. Bush's Clean Air Act gave utilities flexibility in how they cut sulfur-dioxide emissions, blamed for acid rain, by letting them trade pollution "credits." Mr. Clinton wants to expand such trading to other areas, including efforts to head off global warming.[86]

In an act more important symbolically than substantively, Vice President Gore summarily carried out Clinton's promise to dissolve the Council on

Competitiveness. In other ways, however, Clinton showed an intention to use the power of his office to redirect the regulatory establishment, furthering a pattern that developed in the 1970s.

> Fewer than eight months after Al Gore gleefully announced that he was abolishing the Council on Competitiveness as his first act as vice president, he has adopted much of its purpose and some of its anti-regulatory rhetoric.[87]

The Clinton administration assessed the total cost of compliance with regulations to be $430 billion per year—9 percent of the nation's gross national product.[88] Clinton has called for the elimination of wasteful regulations. In the case of regulations that hamstring the rest of the bureaucracy, the administration has called for a reduction of 50 percent of those regulations in a three-year period.[89] Where Clinton's approach has differed from Reagan's is that Reagan denounced executive agencies as the source of waste and inefficiency, while Clinton and Gore have sought to draw career executives into a partnership that will reform the regulatory system. In this regard, Clinton's declarations echo those of Presidents Franklin D. Roosevelt, Harry S. Truman, and Dwight D. Eisenhower,[90] all of whom turned to public administration practitioners and scholars for guidance. (Clinton's opinion of civil servants resembles Bush's more than Reagan's; Bush and Clinton share a sense of respect for career bureaucrats.)

Structurally, the core of the regulatory review process appears all but indistinguishable from that which Reagan and Bush left behind. OIRA will continue to be the coordinator. Furthermore, Clinton's OIRA, like Reagan's OIRA, will compare proposed regulations with the president's policy preferences for consistency—a practice that, in the 1980s, drove progressive public-interest groups to distraction. Sally Katzen, who served as general counsel of the Carter-era Council on Wage and Price Stability and advocated deregulation in that capacity, is Clinton's OIRA administrator; she commented:

> This leads us to create—or resuscitate perhaps would be a better word—a meaningful planning process, so that agencies would be aware of the administration's priorities, would align their plans to the extent permitted by law with those priorities, and the public would have a sense of a coherent executive branch philosophy. We hope to provide guidance to the agencies as to what is expected of them so that there will not be any surprises.[91]

Katzen contended that Clinton values OIRA highly and is deeply concerned about reforming the regulatory system.

> From the time that my appointment was announced, the White House has made it abundantly clear that this was one of the most important positions in the administration and that regulation is an important component of economic policy, which was President Clinton's major issue during the campaign. If there is the perception that regulatory review is a low priority, I think with time it will change.[92]

Another similarity between the Reagan and Clinton techniques is the conspicuous involvement of the Office of the Vice President. Like Quayle, Gore appears to be the final arbiter of disputes between agencies and between an agency and OIRA.[93] Gore's influence over the regulatory system is part and parcel of Gore's mission to "reinvent government." In the course of redesigning the government, Gore's office published a report on its National Performance Review (NPR).[94] NPR is based on principles of Total Quality Management and on Osborne and Gaebler's book, *Reinventing Government*.[95] The NPR's assumptions emphasize innovative practices of corporate management (such as quality circles and customer-oriented marketing). The NPR report was critical of the red tape that strangles both citizens *and* bureaucrats. The report cited Clinton's promise to reduce the federal payroll by 252,000 employees and to cut waste. Clinton's Executive Order 12866,[96] which replaced Reagan's EO 12291 and EO 12498, limits OIRA's role to "significant regulatory actions," meaning those having an annual regulatory effect of $100 million or more or those raising other important issues. These other issues may involve inconsistencies with regulations of other agencies.

Undoubtedly, President Clinton would like to distinguish his record from Reagan's by leaving a legacy of reorganization and regulatory reform in the United States Code. The administration-backed Government Reform and Savings Act was split into pieces for consideration by seventeen House committees, then reassembled by the House Rules Committee.[97] Proposed legislation that would streamline federal procurement and encourage early retirements stalled in Congress before Thanksgiving 1993.

> White House Chief of Staff Thomas F. "Mack" McLarty says even though the administration did not meet its major legislative goals on reinventing government this year [1993], it won't be deterred from proposing other elements of the package in the fiscal 1995 budget and succeeding budgets.
>
> "This is an eight-year project," McLarty says. "You'll see us push this and push this." He says that the initiative may be "resharpened" during 1995 budget deliberations at the White House, but that large elements of reinventing government will stay on the Clinton agenda.[98]

Prospects for success of the Clinton-Gore initiatives were damaged by analyses developed at the Congressional Budget Office (CBO) projecting savings of $305 million, a small fraction of the administration's estimate of $5.9 billion over five years.

> CBO, for example, found the administration's "buyout" proposal, which would offer up to $25,000 to workers resigning or taking early retirement, would cost the federal retirement system $519 million over five years and consume about $2 billion of the funding that agencies receive in appropriations over the next five years.[99]

The conservative tone of the reinventing-government reform program—emphasizing efficiency, streamlining, rationality, and quality—is consistent with other conservative themes of the Clinton presidency (such as frequent revisitation of the issue of the federal deficit left behind by the Republican administrations). The Clinton-Gore program has the potential of rehabilitating the sullied reputation of regulatory review, and fulfilling the unrealized promises that Reagan's ambitious program appeared to offer. The irony is that Clinton, a moderate Democrat, may institutionalize regulatory reform far more effectively than the antiregulation Reagan, a conservative Republican. There seems to be no shift in political control that can obstruct the forward march of presidential influence in the regulatory arena.

11 Theoretical Frameworks

The framers of the United States Constitution adopted Montesquieu's concept of the separation of powers, and established three branches: The legislative branch makes laws, the executive branch administers those laws, and the judicial branch applies those laws to cases and controversies that arise subsequent to the laws' execution. The framers, anxious that any one branch's monopolization of its corresponding power might give it a license to exert dangerously untrammeled power,[1] also constructed a system of checks and balances. Many of these checks and balances violate the principle of separation of powers; for example, when the president vetoes an Act of Congress, he is wielding legislative power by voting "no." As Chief Justice Warren E. Burger wrote, the framers did not intend that the three branches be " 'hermetically' sealed from one another."[2]

If the separation of powers had been made absolute, the activities and processes described in the preceding chapters would not have occurred. Congress's decision to delegate quasi-legislative power to independent regulatory commissions (IRCs) and executive agencies was conceivable only within a system that accepts violations of separation of powers as practical and legitimate. As Bowers suggests, the delegation of legislative duties to the executive branch is conceivable only with the acceptance of a "shared powers" design allowing for regulatory agencies to be supervised and controlled concurrently by Congress and the president.[3] But Bowers and others are compelled to interpret the Constitution at this juncture in a way that accounts for what is a fait accompli—the systematic exercise of extensive lawmaking power by executive agencies. Rules for controlling the officials to whom rule-making authority has been delegated are inevitably extraconstitutional, and the development of law in this area was deemed a separate area of inquiry known as "administrative law." Melnick observes: "While few judges or law professors will admit it, administrative law is increasingly becoming a forum for resolving interbranch competition for control of the bureaucracy."[4]

In the absence of constitutional guidance, the three branches have waged a brisk competition that has few formal rules, in order to determine which branch would secure the most influence in shaping the regulatory policies developed by the IRCs and executive agencies. Congress has made its claim for influence with the understanding that the agencies and commissions are "arms of Congress" created by the legislature to make regulations because Congress does not have enough time to develop the volume of necessary regulatory policies. The White House has maintained that the president ought to manage the agencies and commissions because he is the chief executive, ultimately responsible for the execution of laws. Certain federal judges have proclaimed the authority to guide and control the agencies and commissions because, in the absence of constitutional guidance, the public needs to be protected against the exercise of arbitrary and capricious regulatory power.

The agencies and commissions—the focus of efforts by Congress, the White House, and many judges to achieve continuing influence in regulatory matters—have inherent institutional interests to promote and protect. Because Congress is the source of appropriations and authority, agencies and commissions have long been accustomed to taking cues from Congress and reaping rewards for being compliant. Most of the agencies and commissions also developed connections with clientele groups, which provided lobbying services in securing favorable legislation from Congress. Initiatives by the Executive Office of the President (EOP) to interpose itself in the regulatory process are generally disliked by agencies and commissions, because the interference threatens to disrupt their more propitious relationships. Sometimes, the agencies may resent judicial interference, but, according to Melnick, agencies may applaud judges' efforts if they keep the EOP at bay.[5]

The subtleties and informalities of the interactions between regulatory agencies and other government agencies are indicative of the inutility of the traditional approach of institutionalism in understanding these relationships. No organization chart could elucidate the tendencies of regulatory agencies to enlist patrons in Congress and interest groups, to refuse certain partnerships, and to resist oversight from hierarchical superiors. A focus on the stated missions of the institutions or their apparent interrelationships based on their location in the bureaucracy fails to yield a useful description of their actual working arrangements with other agencies or their influence on economic and social policy.

By the 1950s, institutionalism had fallen into disfavor, displaced by behavioralism. Behavioralists saw institutions as "empty shells to be filled by individual roles, statuses and values."[6] The approach of "role theory," for example, offered the explanation that an individual with preexisting values and behaviors who is installed in an office in an organization adopts new behaviors that he or she believes suitable for an incumbent in that role. Thus, a laborer who has long distrusted management and resisted its objectives may be promoted to a supervisory position and develop an authoritarian pattern of behavior relative to former peers. March and Olsen describe the transformation:

> [A new office-holder] determin[es] what the situation is, what role is being fulfilled, and what the obligations of the role in that situation are. When individuals enter an institution, they try to discover, and are taught, the rules. When they encounter a new situation, they try to associate it with a situation for which rules already exist.[7]

Agency theory emerged in the literature of private sector management. This theory uses the "principal-agent" model, based on a compact that involves a "principal," that is, a person or other entity that requires the services of an "agent," a skilled individual capable of satisfying the principal's needs. Having contracted with the agent, the principal has the ongoing concern that the agent not rank his or her own interests above those of the principal or concentrate on self-aggrandizing activity to the detriment of the principal's welfare. The principal's challenge is to establish incentives that motivate the agent to promote the principal's interests. The principal also has a need to monitor the agent's activities so that behaviors inconsistent with the principal's objective can be identified and adjustments to the incentive arrangement can be made with dispatch. This theory was originally conceived to apply to relationships between private employers and their employees or to relationships between patients and doctors, clients and accountants, etc. Principal-agent theory was adopted by some public administration scholars who considered bureaucrats to be the agents of the public, of the legislature that created the executive agencies and IRCs, of the chief executive, or of the coalition that succeeded in establishing an agency or policy. The principal may be "the coalition enacting a new policy and establishing a structure and process for implementing it," while the agent "is the bureau that is to implement the policy."[8] The original coalition has good reason to fear the agency's independent pursuit of its own institutional interests: Once the agency disrupts the delicate balance of interests that caused the coalition to cooperate in promoting the agency's creation, the coalition may shatter, thus exerting no further influence on the agency. Accordingly, the original coalition will advocate the enactment of a law that circumscribes the agency's discretion.[9] This specificity may also limit the ability of the president to issue to agency officials orders that do not serve the coalition's interests. Another approach would identify the president as the principal and his politically appointed agency heads as the agents. In this relationship, the president hopes to ensure that the agency heads will forgo institutionally profitable policies in favor of policies that are beneficial to the president and to the constituency that elected him. President Ronald Reagan, by most accounts, was especially successful in making the "agency" of his appointees more faithful to *his* interests than to the interests of the coalitions supporting the statutory missions of the institutions.

The focus on individual behavior, which became popular among political scientists in the 1950s, diverted attention away from institutions. However, by the late 1970s, some rational choice theorists rebelled against the perception that political activity results from separate, whimsical decisions made by individuals. Shepsle explains: "Politics takes place in context, often formal and official (as in a legislative, judicial, or bureaucratic proceeding) but often informal as well (as in a club or faculty meeting)."[10] The result was a new approach known as "the new institutionalism." It emphasized structure and procedures, and suggested that the rules and processes under which government activity takes place heavily influence policy. Because public officials recognize the importance of structure and procedures and fear upheavals in rules that may frustrate the expectations of the participants in the original compromise establishing an agency or policy, legislators and the president establish an "ex ante agreement... that limits the ability of each to engage in ex post opportunistic behavior."[11]

In describing the framework known as "structure-induced equilibrium," Shepsle writes, "I found it inconceivable that professional politicians would spend untold hours wrangling over matters of structure and procedure, and that institutional handbooks of rules were extremely fine-grained and ran to hundreds of pages and multiple volumes, if those rules were 'merely' minutiae and not the stuff of general theory."[12] He continues: "The idea of equilibrium contained in this concept is founded on the structural and procedural features of the process being modeled. Process is made explicit and is given definition (as an extensive form game) by institutional context."[13]

March and Olsen explain:

> Without denying the importance of both the social context of politics and the motives of individual actors, the new institutionalism insists on a more

> autonomous role for political institutions. The state is not only affected by society but also affects it. . . . Political democracy depends not only on economic and social conditions but also on the design of political institutions. The bureaucratic agency, the legislative committee, and the appellate court are arenas for contending social forces, but they are also collections of standard operating procedures and structures that define and defend interests. They are political actors in their own right.[14]

Many studies of political behavior with a sociological tone bring sociological role theory to bear on the subject at hand. Role theory is a compelling model because, as Heinz Eulau observes, the concept of role is the "coin of the realm in the social sciences."[15] Likewise, Talcott Parsons explains that "the conceptual unit of the social system is the role."[16] The concept of role suggests that a position (or "office") molds an office-holder's opinions regardless of the beliefs, values, and expectations that predated installation into the role.

Governments exercise power. Logically, then, the role of a public official involves the exercise of power. Many scholars have observed that those who play roles in the government system seek to maintain and enhance not only their own power but also that of successive incumbents in the role. For example, with respect to the president, Pious observes, "The incumbent always must defend the institution and leave it stronger than he found it, lest he be thought less than 'presidential.'"[17] Similarly, in describing the universal preoccupation of legislators with extending the influence of the legislatures in which they serve, Lord Bryce commented that "a weak magistrate [chief executive] comes after a strong magistrate, and yields what his predecessor has fought for; but an assembly holds all it has ever won."[18] Volumes have been written about the concern of jurists to preserve and extend the power of the judiciary, a behavioral characteristic typified by Chief Justice John Marshall's pronouncement that "it is emphatically the province and duty of the judicial department to say what the law is."[19] In this principle, he discovered the momentous power of judicial review.

Insofar as a role is part of a system that contains other roles, the power associated with one role must be understood in relation to other roles. Emerson explains that the obverse of power is dependency.[20] The power A wields relative to B is identical to B's dependency on A. In symbolic terms:

$$\mathbf{P}\,(AB) = \mathbf{D}\,(BA)$$

Sometimes, an incumbent of a role may have direct power over the incumbent of a second role (e.g., the president may dismiss the administrator of the

EPA without cause). In other instances, an incumbent of a role may exercise control of resources and benefits through which he exercises indirect power over the incumbent of a second role (e.g., the director of OMB may be able to induce EPA's administrator to carry out a policy or to refrain from carrying out a policy by virtue of OMB's dominance in compiling the executive budget).[21]

One might contemplate why, if some roles involve more power than others, the competition for power in the United States government system has not already ended in the conquest of less powerful by more powerful roles. For example, if the chairmen of substantive and appropriations subcommittees possess the power of life and death over heads of executive agencies,[22] why have these legislators not proceeded to the logical conclusion and transformed the executive branch officials into powerless vassals of the legislative branch?

The answer to the puzzle may be found within the framework of "exchange theory." To be sure, exchange theory provides for the more powerful actor to succeed in exacting compliance from the less powerful actor, but the more powerful actor is expected to offer his good will, his approval, or some other resource in return.[23] If this exchange did not take place, the less powerful actor would lack an incentive to remain in the role system (in fact, he would have an incentive to escape). In the extreme, if all incumbents of the less powerful roles were made to feel vanquished, and no other incumbents could be induced to occupy these roles for want of a rational incentive, the power of the more powerful (supposedly victorious) role incumbents would disappear. "To keep power," it has been said, "you have to give it away." There can be no power holder in the absence of a power recipient, as the equation above indicates. Hence, more powerful role incumbents must provide incentives for less powerful role incumbents. In other words, power is associated with costs as well as benefits, and dependency involves benefits as well as costs.

Blau's exchange theory model describes social exchange as a process underlying relations between groups as well as individuals. His concept makes this model especially valuable for this study of relations between institutions. Models can be constructed as effectively for conflicts between groups as for cooperative arrangements. This is helpful in studying a government system founded on conflict, that is, on checks and balances. As Corwin stated, the Constitution is an "invitation to struggle."[24]

In this work, I have preferred to analyze the relationships of regulatory agencies to other entities as "exchanges" of valued considerations. As March and Olsen write, "Politics can be portrayed as a system of voluntary exchange, a search for Pareto-optimal accommodations to prior preferences."[25]

The exchange model emphasizes the mutual dependency that keeps two entities engaged in social exchange. Entities enter into exchange for the purpose of enhancing the utility of their resources. This circumstance may occur, says Kenneth E. Boulding, when one party has too much of one commodity and too little of another, and therefore seeks out a second party whose situation is the reverse.[26] Through exchange, each can effect a better balance. This circumstance may also occur simply because the two parties have divergent attitudes—e.g., a "person who trades . . . an apple for a pear values the apple more than the pear."[27] Thus, two parties consent to a voluntary exchange, and paradoxically each believes it is better off than it was before the transaction.

Dependency is a state of affairs that the dependent normally wishes to ameliorate as much as possible. In the equation above, we saw that power is the reverse of dependency. A continuum may be used to illustrate the polarity and the intermediate points.

Total Dependency on the Environment ________________ *Insurmountable Power over the Environment*

This model shows power and dependency not as values in a dichotomy but as terminal points in a continuum. Therefore, the dependent party need not await a miracle to transform itself into a power holder; it may find it feasible to seek an incremental change to the right. Long-lasting exchange relationships, especially those symbolized by contractual arrangements, are inherently designed to reduce a party's desperate dependency on the environment and to bestow upon it the more powerful security of lasting partnerships.[28]

As long as an entity feels that the exchange relationship is beneficial, it will remain in the relationship. Homans's rule of "distributive justice" reveals that a party has certain expectations: "A man in an exchange relation with another will expect that the rewards of each man be proportional to his costs."[29]

Like any social mechanism, social exchange is wrapped in norms and customs. Gouldner observes that participants in social relationships recognize a need to reciprocate for benefits received, as a "starting mechanism" of social interaction; to violate this norm stops the flow of benefits.[30] And unlike strictly economic relationships, social exchange involves *unspecified* obligations, according to Blau.[31]

We should not interpret the fact that an exchange relationship rests on mutual dependency that requires each party to provide something of value to the other as meaning that there is always an equal relationship between the two parties. An equal relationship would be a rare coincidence. More commonly, one partner does wield more power than the other. To be sure, this power need not be violent or coercive. Some sociologists would disqualify transfers that involve coercive power as failing to conform to the exchange model. Others would label physically coercive power as "the polar case of power," an extreme application of the model. Says Blau: "Although the customer technically imposes his will upon the jeweler when he makes him surrender a diamond ring by paying for it, this situation clearly should not be confused with that of the gangster who forces the jeweler to hand over the ring at the point of a gun."[32] Instead, the "power" of the more powerful party is rooted in its capacity to bestow benefits, or *rewards*, on the more dependent party, and to terminate the flow of rewards as a punishment. The dependent party would be cognizant of the potential punishment, which would dissuade rebellious behavior. Lindblom observed that this kind of power is at its peak when the dependent party is made to believe that a disobedient act will result in an *automatic* penalty, such as excommunication from a church in instances of heresy, divorce, etc.[33]

What does the more powerful party stand to gain from the exchange relationship with the more dependent party? The more dependent party may be able to contribute its labor or intellect to the transaction. If the more powerful party is not in need of these resources, then the price the weaker party pays for the relationship may be respect, affection, and homage, which the stronger party would accept as gratification. In essence, the stronger party can name its own price. "People who become indebted to a person for essential benefits are obligated to accede to his wishes lest he cease to furnish these benefits."[34]

Exchange theory may be poignantly applicable to the relationship between specialized executive agencies and generalist government officials, such as the president and his staff and members of Congress. Blau describes how organizations—which arise for the purpose of mobilizing resources and conducting collective productive activity—departmentalize for the purpose of specialization. The central organization delegates authority to the departments, and the departments acquire some measure of autonomy. Thus—as Mosher has shown for the public sector[35]—the professional requirements of the specialized departments repeatedly conflict with the whole organization's administrative requirements. Blau explains:

> The executive departments and agencies constituting elements of a country's political organization sometimes come into conflict with each other

> and with the central government itself. This occurs because their policies are partly determined by the requirements their specialized functions impose and not exclusively by directives from the central political authority, which means that they have some autonomy. Disagreements among the different branches of the military establishment and between the military establishment and the Administration illustrate this point.[36]

We might add that the tension between the federal government's central administration—the president's own apparatus in the EOP, notably the White House Office and OMB—and the executive agencies can be considered another illustration of the sometimes cooperative and sometimes confrontational relationship often maintained between the generalist and specialist components of an organization. By making relatively few attempts to influence regulatory policy (until recent administrations), the White House exhibited an unusual deference to professional expertise. Recent administrations have sought to achieve some compatibility of objective between their overall policy intentions and the operation of regulatory agencies.

In the past three decades, the literature of political science and public administration has increasingly recognized that the institutional structures established by the Constitution and the statutes, and the chains of command that these structures imply, only mark the starting points for the bargaining, compromising, and accommodating that occur informally. These negotiations are inconsistent with the letter and spirit of the Constitution and laws, and have limited regard for public opinion. In contrast to the supremacy implied by the term "chief executive," the president finds that his subordinates often display the boldness to withhold their obedience to presidential orders, awaiting the signal that the White House is willing to negotiate. Neustadt wrote in 1980: "The [president's] power to persuade is the power to bargain. Status and authority yield bargaining advantages. But in a government of 'separated institutions sharing powers,' they yield them to all sides. . . . Command has limited utility; persuasion becomes give-and-take."[37]

Presidents and political appointees who have sought to extract spontaneous compliance from the bureaucracy have found the hard-line strategy to be counterproductive. First, "cracking the whip" on the bureaucracy, imposing one unwanted policy after another, requires an enormous amount of time from the president and his EOP staff. As Koenig explains: "Even more resistant [than Congress] to the President's quest for dominion over the executive branch is the giant bureaucracy itself, with its layers of specialists, its massive paper work . . . , lumbering pace, [and] addiction to routine."[38] Second, while in theory "the buck stops" at the Oval Office, there may still be some advantage for the president in allowing responsibility to be diffused, so that, in cases of policies that attract adverse publicity, he can appear blameless and can credibly intervene to resolve the controversy. Third, bureaucrats subjected to hostile commands may be able to take revenge by executing the orders automatically and literally. The literature indicates numerous instances of administrators who have done their superiors favors by advising against ill-advised actions, or who have ignored directives with explosive potential. Pfiffner offers an example: "A 'yes boss' attitude ... may be downright dangerous. One career executive remembers warning his newly appointed political boss that a sole source contract granted to the boss's former colleagues 'would not pass the smell test' in Washington. His boss did not grant the contract and later thanked him for the warning."[39] In the same vein, Secretary of the Treasury George P. Shultz protected President Nixon more effectively than did many of his other aides by simply ignoring or defying some of Nixon's orders that were minefields. The Internal Revenue Service had received an order from counsel John Dean to harass every person included on the infamous "enemies list." The IRS inquired of Secretary Shultz about the proper course of action. "I felt that this was something we had no business doing," Shultz remembered. "So I just told the IRS, 'Do nothing.' "[40]

The inherent power of career executives enables them to create difficulty for a president and to compel a president to offer concessions to reestablish a condition of peaceful coexistence. Rourke writes:

> Career subordinates have a formidable capacity to make trouble for executives in the outside community, ... and this threat requires political executives to exercise diplomacy in their dealings with these officials. Such diplomacy may sometimes lead a chief executive to call for improved salary and fringe benefits for an agency's staff as a means of purchasing their support for policy goals.[41]

Clinton Rossiter, too, noticed that the audience to which the president has the most difficulty "selling" his programs is not Congress, but rather the bureaucracy.[42] As a specific example, Rourke describes how President Nixon was forced to bargain with the Pentagon as he sought to implement his de-escalation program ("Vietnamization") in the Far East, and how other presidents have similarly been drawn to the bargaining table by the military.

> One of the best measures of an agency's strength in dealing with the president is the extent to which the White House has to bargain with it in order

> to secure its cooperation. During the withdrawal of American troops from Vietnam, President Nixon was obliged to make many concessions to the armed services in order to maintain their support for his troop-withdrawal program. Moreover, in order to secure Department of Defense acceptance of disarmament agreements being negotiated with the Soviet Union, the White House has often had to give strong support to the department's demand for the continued development of strategic weapons. One secretary of defense insisted in testimony before Congress that the department would oppose an arms-control agreement if the increased appropriations necessary to continue a weapons development program were not forthcoming. Recent administrations have thus been put in the paradoxical position of supplementing presentations of a disarmament treaty to Congress with a proposal for increased military appropriations.[43]

Accordingly, the relationship between the president and his subordinates is not that of the supremely powerful with the despairingly powerless, but a balancing of needs, interests, and conciliations between worthy competitors for leverage. Lindblom describes the relationship as a state of "mutual adjustment."[44] Pfiffner agrees that the "cycle of accommodation" works to the advantage of presidents, so that presidents' "distrust of career executives is misplaced."[45] Even Nixon's assistant to the president for domestic affairs, John D. Ehrlichman—who characterized the relationship of the White House and bureaucracy as an exercise in "guerilla warfare"—reevaluated the exclusion of career executives from policy deliberations as a "big mistake." "I did not encounter devastating problems with the bureaucracy," Ehrlichman recalled. "You have to remember that the career service is not a 'faceless, formless enemy.'"[46] Reagan aide Craig Fuller had a similar experience:

> My experience in the four years that I've been here is that... the relationship between the political appointee and the career people in the departments is very much a partnership.... I don't come at this with some notion that we have some norm of behavior among the career staff that is totally at odds or variance with the ideals of the political appointee.[47]

Waterman emphasizes the importance of a president selecting political appointees who can advocate the president's program to the bureaucracy and secure its support. "Appointees who support the president's program can help sell the president's agenda to civil servants and thereby can be useful in building bureaucratic support for the president's policies."[48]

It should be noted that the difficulty of superiors in securing compliance from subordinates is far from unique to the executive branch. Belcaster has uncovered the same phenomenon in the judicial branch.

> Just as the President oversees executive branch functions, the Supreme Court stands atop the judicial branch. And when the Supreme Court renders opinions, just as when the President speaks, one expects that functionaries within the respective branch listen. Although they are not mere functionaries, one expects appellate courts to respond properly when the Supreme Court pronounces. Thus, it is rare to hear the Supreme Court denounce an appellate court's behavior as "Monday morning quarterbacking."[49] . . . It is rarer still to hear the Court describe an appellate court as "Kafkaesque."[50] . . . One seldom reads such chastisements, because the Supreme Court so rarely suggests that its authority has been thwarted. . . .
>
> The D.C. Circuit's increasingly influential administrative "common law" conflicted with Supreme Court decisions, and, thereby, presented a de facto challenge to the hierarchy established by Article III. As head of the Article III [judicial] branch, the Supreme Court serves as the "guarantor of consistency in the law." . . . In some ways, however, the Supreme Court abdicated its responsibility as head of the judicial branch by enabling, rather than checking, the D.C. Circuit's independence. . . .
>
> Most commentators consider *Chevron* [i.e., *Chevron U.S.A., Inc., v. Natural Resources Defense Council, Inc.,*][51] a "watershed decision." In one swoop, the Supreme Court set aside its conflicting line of administrative law cases by announcing a rule that federal courts must follow when reviewing agency statutory interpretations. In doing so, the Supreme Court not only attempted to articulate a coherent rule to guide reviewing courts, the Court also sought to rein-in appellate courts, who, like the D.C. Circuit, were applying a variety of rules.[52]

Belcaster finds that the result, perversely, was a *decline* in the rate of affirmance of agency decisions by the D.C. Circuit Court in the first few years following the *Chevron* decision![53]

Finally, the competition between the executive and legislative branches was programmed by the Constitution. Referring to these two branches, Sundquist remarked, "The Constitution, in effect, put two combatants in the ring and sounded the bell that sent them into endless battle."[54] But this interbranch competition has been complicated by the bifurcation of the executive branch into a presidency and a bureaucracy that perceive conflicting interests, and by the durable alliance between many executive agencies and their corresponding congressional committees. When the president cannot resolve disputes with the bureaucracy, or when he initiates a campaign to subdue the bureaucracy through such devices as reorganization, Congress is virtually certain to weigh in.[55] The failure to compromise with the bureaucracy may, in fact, invite Congress to decide the issue. In that case, the president's party delegation may defend him or may opt instead to defend the institutional interests of the legislature (or the demands from members' congressional districts), to the president's detriment.

Although presidents "remain highly dependent on their party to move their legislative programs,"[56] they often find they lack support from their own party members. Franklin D. Roosevelt was so frustrated by the unwillingness of some Democrats in Congress to support his New Deal programs that he launched a futile campaign to overthrow them in their nomination contests.[57] President Carter offered this account of his frustration:

> I learned the hard way that there was no party loyalty or discipline when a complicated or controversial issue was at stake—none. Each legislator had to be wooed and won individually. It was every member for himself, and the devil take the hindmost! Well-intended reforms in the organization of Congress and of the Democratic party had undermined the power of party leaders.[58]

And while Reagan enjoyed amazing success in his efforts to unify Republicans in Congress and secure the votes of conservative Democratic legislators early in his first term, the coalition eventually dissolved—and even the exuberance of Republicans faded. Senate Republican leader Robert J. Dole (R-Kans.) reminisced: "The President was fresh [in 1981]. The Republican Senate was fresh. We were all finally committee chairmen and subcommittee chairmen. We knew we had to stick together. Now the bloom is gone."[59] By 1987, Reagan's percentage of votes won in Congress was the lowest recorded since *Congressional Quarterly* started keeping such records.[60]

In the past, presidents would try to bargain through the political parties, including congressional leaders and committee chairmen, who constituted a powerful oligarchy. But numerous developments have confused the picture: split control, decline of political parties, opportunities for "mavericks" to win party nominations through primary elections and other election reforms, and decentralization of power in Congress through progressive reduction of the power of party leaders and committee chairmen. Amidst these fragments have arisen special interest groups and the news media. Presidents have turned to both of these bodies—to the interest groups to lobby for presidential policies in Congress, and to the news media to send out appeals for support from the public. Mark A. Peterson describes how presidents have developed alliances with interest groups. "As the modern presidency draws more policy issues directly into the White House domain, the opportunity for groups to secure explicit communications with the president or presidential surrogates becomes an increasingly precious commodity. Presidents thus have something of value to offer cooperative group leaders."

Presidents also want something in exchange. They desire group actions that aid in accomplishing presidential objectives. Managing such efficacious relationships with the interest group system, however, requires a White House establishment capable of orchestrating exchanges that are conducive to promoting a particular president's interests.[61]

And, with respect to using the news media, Kernell describes presidents' inclination to "go public" to gain an advantage against Congress.[62]

Although Sundquist is quite justified in referring to the relationship between the executive and the legislative branches as an endless battle, one could just as convincingly claim that the Constitution placed the branches of government in a perpetual exchange relationship. The American system of checks and balances comprises a variety of institutional roles held in a delicate balance that is founded on protection of institutional self-interest.[63] Congress's restraint in patiently allowing the EOP to expand its centralized authority over regulatory agencies indicates its willingness to experiment with systems that may increase presidential power, as long as the legislature benefits as well. Arguably, these benefits might include the opportunity to transfer blame for failed programs to the president, the luxury of abdicating responsibility for unpopular but necessary decisions, and the establishment of a systematic policy control process that may improve the efficiency of government programs and provide more satisfaction to various constituencies. The Stigler-Peltzman theory holds that regulation is a commodity provided by "entrepreneurial politicians" who perceive an opportunity to realize some kind of gain by providing it.[64] Normally, the gain is the approval of consumers, producers, environmentalists, bureaucrats, and other constituencies that demand it.[65] Without recognizing this exchange opportunity, we would be hard pressed to explain why Congress opted to continue to appropriate funds for OIRA over the calls by some legislative leaders to prohibit the use of such resources for regulatory clearance, and why a substantial body of support in Congress for presidential involvement in regulatory oversight has lingered into the Clinton era. Clearly, Congress has expected to receive *something* in return for its relative magnanimity.

Conclusion

As a process aimed at restructuring the relationship between the presidency and the executive agencies, the executive agencies and Congress, and the executive agencies and the courts, the regulatory relief program generated some fascinating dynamics of organizational behavior. Early in the Reagan era, some observers predicted that the executive agencies would defy the president, pointing to literature that showed a succession of presidents bemoaning bureaucratic resistance to their directives. Some observers predicted that Congress would mobilize to terminate the regulatory relief process to protect Congress's relationship with the agencies it guarded so jealously. Even though the tight "partnership" between the executive agencies and the federal courts had been loosened somewhat by the Supreme Court, some observers still fully expected the courts to draw the line at secretive, ex parte regulatory review; advocates of social regulation called on the courts to treat the president as though he were any private citizen, and expected the courts to circumscribe the president's rapidly expanding role in the regulatory rule-making process.

The outcome of the Reagan initiative is that many of the "laws" of political science and public administration need to be reviewed and revised to account for the remarkable accommodation of the presidential demand for entry into the regulatory process. Surely in times of national emergency, presidents have been allowed and even called upon to expand their influence in order to implement new policies demanded by the public and Congress. In the case at issue here, where Reagan's supposed initiative for deregulation proved to be an ideologically based strategy to mold regulatory rule making into conservative, proindustry shape, the presidential initiative was *not* uniformly popular and *contradicted* many of the values held by Congress and the public. The preexisting models of public policy in this kind of situation did not account for the restraint of Congress and the courts or for the extensive compliance of executive agencies. I have used exchange theory to explain this restraint and compliance. It is apparent that the institutions of the national government, though they may compete with the presidency for influence, would not tend to derive satisfaction from weakness in the presidency, because they could not receive many benefits from a weak institution. Thus, when President Ronald Reagan offered a credible argument that the presidency up to that time had been all but frozen out of the regulatory process, the other institutions evaluated the contention carefully, and concluded that a weak presidency is a suboptimal condition for each of the components of the national government. I have provided evidence to indicate that the competing institutions tolerated the expanded role of the presidency and sought a new array of benefits as compensation. For Congress, the new benefits may have included a reduced exposure to blame for failed regulatory policies and the opportunity to file petitions in the regulatory review process as a service to influential constituents. For the judicial branch, the new benefits may have included a reduction in docket workload, since disputes could be resolved in another arena. For the executive agencies, the new benefits may have included the opportunity to bargain for various concessions (such as a larger budget or new legislation) and a more favorable appearance of democratic and managerial legitimacy.

The insertion of regulation analysis procedures into a mechanism that had long been inclined toward highly specified, deeply intrusive control of commerce and manufacturing is of historic importance. Future presidents and Congresses struggling with obstacles to productivity, prosperity, and competitiveness in world markets may be loath to dismantle the structures that were installed to promote economic rationality in regulation. Also of historic importance is Reagan's demonstration that a president has the capacity to reorient the executive branch if he strategically uses his appointment power and has the determination to call the agencies to account by applying his extensive statutory power to manipulate agency resource levels. The new literature of political science and public administration will need to reflect and explain these new procedures and new results if it is to illuminate the interactions of the national government and of its executive branch in the wake of the Reagan Revolution.

Notes
References
Index

Notes

INTRODUCTION

1. U.S., President, Executive Order, "Federal Regulation," *Federal Register* 46 (February 17, 1981): 13,193; U.S., Office of the Federal Register, *Code of Federal Regulations* [C.F.R.], 3, 1981 Compilation, p. 127; rpt. in *U.S. Code* [U.S.C.], title 5, §601 note (1988) and in U.S., President, *Public Papers of the Presidents of the United States: Ronald Reagan, 1981* (Washington, D.C.: GPO, 1982), pp. 104–08.
2. U.S., President, Executive Order, "Regulatory Planning Process," *Federal Register* 50 (January 8, 1985): 1036; 3 C.F.R., 1985 Comp., p. 323; rpt. in 5 U.S.C. §601 note (1988) and in U.S., President, *Public Papers of the Presidents of the United States: Ronald Reagan, 1985* (Washington, D.C.: GPO, 1988), 1:10–12.

CHAPTER 1

1. Quoted in "How There Came to Be Only One Telephone Company in Town" (Bell System advertisement), *National Review*, July 18, 1975, p. 768.
2. *Statutes at Large* 1 (1789): 29; *Statutes at Large* 1 (1789): 55, cited by Howard Ball, ed., *Federal Administrative Agencies: Essays on Power and Politics* (Englewood Cliffs, N.J.: Prentice-Hall, 1984), p. 5.
3. Richard M. Neustadt, "The Administration's Regulatory Reform Program: An Overview," *Administrative Law Review* 32 (Spring 1980): 129.
4. *Munn v. Illinois*, 94 U.S. 131 (1877).
5. Congress had delegated executive power to certain officials of the executive branch on previous occasions. For example, in 1790, Congress authorized the president to make rules and regulations for traders with the Indians. In 1813, the secretary of the treasury was authorized to make regulations to implement the Internal Revenue Administrative Act. Gary C. Bryner, *Bureaucratic Discretion: Law and Policy in Federal*

Regulatory Agencies (New York: Pergamon Press, 1987), pp. 10–11. Delegation of quasi-legislative power to the ICC was novel insofar as the agency was established specifically to concentrate on functions that were legislative in character.

6. James Q. Wilson, "The Politics of Regulation," in *The Politics of Regulation*, ed. James Q. Wilson (New York: Basic Books, 1980), p. 365.
7. Quoted in Marver H. Bernstein, *Regulating Business by Independent Commission* (Princeton: Princeton University Press, 1955), p. 265.
8. Kenneth J. Meier, *Regulation: Politics, Bureaucracy, and Economics* (New York: St. Martin's Press, 1985), p. 1.
9. The phrase appeared in Justice Oliver Wendell Holmes Jr.'s dissenting opinion in *Frank v. Mangum, Sheriff of Fulton County, Georgia*, 237 U.S. 309, 349 (1915): "Any judge who has sat with juries knows that in spite of forms they are extremely likely to be impregnated by the environing atmosphere." Over Holmes's objections, the court denied petitioner Leo M. Frank a writ of habeas corpus. Frank, whose death sentence was commuted to life in prison by Georgia's Governor John M. Slaton, was lynched by an anti-Semitic mob in Marietta, Ga., in 1915. In 1986 the Georgia General Assembly granted Frank a posthumous pardon.
10. George J. Stigler, "Public Regulation of the Securities Markets," *Journal of Business* 37 (April 1964): 117–41.
11. Said one official of the Civil Aeronautics Board, "Of course policy views are going to affect someone's opportunities. If a board member is consistently anticarrier, or opposes rate increases, he isn't going to have the carriers knocking down his doors to offer him employment." Quoted in Paul J. Quirk, *Industry Influence in Federal Regulatory Agencies* (Princeton: Princeton University Press, 1981), p. 153.
12. Marver H. Bernstein, "Independent Regulatory Agencies: A Perspective on Their Reform," *Annals of the American Academy of Political and Social Sciences* 400 (March 1972): 23. Subsequent scholarly works even rejected Bernstein's concession that regulatory agencies were originally founded in the public interest. In 1963, Gabriel Kolko advanced the "original intent" theory, concluding that regulatory agencies were designed from their inception to satisfy special interests. Kolko explains, for example, that the creation of the Food and Drug Administration can be attributed to the desires of the big meatpackers to eliminate price competition from small meatpackers. Gabriel Kolko, *The Triumph of Conservatism: A Reinterpretation of American History, 1900–1916* (Glencoe, Ill.: Free Press, 1963), pp. 98–100.
13. 430 F. 2d 891 (D.C. Cir. 1970).
14. David Vogel, "The 'New' Social Regulation in Historical and Comparative Perspective," in *Regulation in Perspective: Historical Essays*, ed. Thomas K. McGraw (Cambridge: Harvard University Press, 1981), p. 161.
15. A. Lee Fritschler, "The Changing Face of Government Regulation," in Ball, ed., *Federal Administrative Agencies*, p. 40.
16. Ralph Nader, *Unsafe at any Speed: The Designed-in Dangers of the American Automobile* (New York: Grossman Publishers, 1965).

17. H. Craig Petersen, *Business and Government*, 3d ed. (New York: Harper and Row, 1989), p. 377.
18. Cited ibid., pp. 380–88.
19. Murray L. Weidenbaum, *Business, Government, and the Public*, 3d ed. (Englewood Cliffs, N.J.: Prentice-Hall, 1986), pp. 23, 28–31, 179.
20. Cited in George A. Steiner and John F. Steiner, *Business, Government, and Society: A Managerial Perspective*, 3d ed. (New York: Random House, 1980), p. 160.
21. Meier, *Regulation*, p. 3.
22. Ibid.
23. Edward Paul Fuchs, *Presidents, Management, and Regulation* (Englewood Cliffs, N.J.: Prentice-Hall, 1988), p. 3.
24. Paul H. Weaver, "Regulation, Social Policy, and Class Conflict," in *Regulating Business: The Search for an Optimum*, ed. Donald P. Jacobs (San Francisco: Institute for Contemporary Studies, 1978), p. 200.
25. Fuchs, *Presidents, Management, and Regulation*, p. 3.
26. Fritschler, "The Changing Face of Government Regulation," p. 45.
27. Ibid.
28. George C. Eads and Michael Fix, *Relief or Reform? Reagan's Regulatory Dilemma* (Washington, D.C.: Urban Institute Press, 1984), p. 255; and Petersen, *Business and Government*, p. 376. See also chapter 9 of this book.
29. Michael D. Reagan, *Regulation: The Politics of Policy* (Boston: Little, Brown, 1987), p. 92.
30. Bernstein, *Regulating Business by Independent Commission*, p. 23, citing Louis Brownlow's testimony to the Committee on Labor and Public Welfare in the Senate, *Hearings on the Establishment of a Commission on Ethics in Government*, 82d Congress, 1st sess., June–July 1951, p. 213.
31. *Rathbun ("Humphrey's Executor") v. United States*, 295 U.S. 602 (1934).
32. U.S., Congress, Senate, Committee on Governmental Affairs, *Study on Federal Regulation*, vol. 5, *Regulatory Organization*, 95th Cong., 1st sess., December 1977, pp. 27–31.
33. Petersen, *Business and Government*, p. 366.
34. CAB *v. Delta Airlines*, 365 U.S. 316 (1961).
35. Eads and Fix, *Relief or Reform?* p. 14.
36. Committee for Economic Development, "Redefining Government's Role in the Market System," in U.S., Congress, House, Committee on the Judiciary, Subcommittee on Administrative Law and Governmental Regulations, *Regulation Reform Act of 1979*, part 1, 96th Cong., 1st and 2d sess., Nov. 7, 13, 16, 28, 1979; Dec. 3, 5, 10, 1979; Jan. 29, 1980; Feb. 1 and 5, 1980, p. 283. See also Edward F. Denison, "Effects of Selected Changes in the Institutional and Human Environment upon Output per Unit of Input," *Survey of Current Business* 58 (January 1980): 21–44.
37. Murray L. Weidenbaum, *Business, Government, and the Public*, 2d ed. (Englewood Cliffs, N.J.: Prentice-Hall, 1981), p. 344.

38. The panoply of studies that reported enormous levels of compliance costs drew fire from regulatory advocates—especially consumer, environmental, and labor activists. They criticized the methodologies used to estimate costs and to assess the impact on economic activity. One complaint was that Weidenbaum had attributed $665 per automobile to compliance costs by assuming that initial investment costs were incurred annually. Kathleen F. O'Reilly, executive director of the Consumer Federation of America, quoted in U.S., Congress, Senate, Committee on Governmental Affairs, *Hearings on Regulatory Reform Legislation*, part 1, 96th Cong., 1st sess., March 20; April 6 and 24; May 3, 4, 16, and 18, 1979, p. 1236. A second complaint was that Weidenbaum estimated compliance costs by simply multiplying administrative costs by twenty. A Congressional Research Service analysis by Julius W. Allen concluded that the Weidenbaum study had "enough questionable components to make the totals arrived at suspect and of doubtful validity." U.S., Library of Congress, Congressional Research Service, "Costs and Benefits of Federal Regulation: An Overview," July 19, 1978, pp. 1–6. A Congressional Research Service report concluded that compliance cost studies "tend to support the varied interest of the sponsor of the estimate or to fit the hypothesis of the individual making the estimate." U.S., *Regulation Reform Act of 1979*, part 1, p. 327. Dr. Nicholas A. Ashford, assistant director of the Center for Policy Alternatives at the Massachusetts Institute of Technology, agreed: "Agencies depend to a large extent upon industry data to derive estimates of compliance costs. I do not believe I am being too unkind in questioning the bias of those estimates." U.S., *Hearings on Regulatory Reform Legislation*, part 1, p. 1142. Some critics have complained that many compliance cost estimates—notably the Weidenbaum study—reported figures that included the cost imposed by economic regulation, but were then used to discredit social regulation. Weidenbaum's study counted all kinds of regulation—trucking, airline rate, and environmental regulation—and added the budgets of the Coast Guard and Customs Service, which are not usually deemed regulatory agencies. Ashford testimony, ibid., p. 1148, and testimony of Roy A. Schotland, ibid., p. 1239. Another objection, noted by Ashford, is that the compliance cost estimates have often ignored the "learning curve" effect by which industries and their workers learn to comply more efficiently over time. Overestimates inevitably result. Ibid., p. 1142. Critics object that many compliance cost estimates categorize transfers of wealth as costs, when the net value of such a transfer is arguably zero. See testimony of Schotland, ibid., p. 1235. Finally, critics dispute the conclusions of the compliance cost studies in terms of their assessment of impact of regulation on economic activity. The Council on Wage and Price Stability concluded that less than 0.75 percent of the Consumer Price Index can be connected to regulation, equivalent to less than 1 percent of the double-digit inflation of the 1970s. Cited in testimony of Ashford, ibid., pp. 1147–48.
39. Quoted in Bob Davis, "Cost of Regulation Isn't Easy to Figure, But Estimates Exist," *Wall Street Journal*, September 23, 1992, p. A6.
40. Quoted in U.S., Advisory Commission on Intergovernmental Relations, *Regulatory*

Federalism: Policy, Process, Impact and Reform (Washington, D.C.: GPO, February 1984), p. 11.

41. U.S., *Regulatory Federalism*, pp. 1, 9–10.
42. Vogel, "The 'New' Social Regulation," p. 158.
43. Weidenbaum, *Business, Government, and the Public*, 2d ed., p. 11.
44. More information about regulatory review in the Nixon, Ford, and Carter administrations appears in chapter 2.
45. Concerning the subgovernment model of the "iron triangle," see, e.g., Douglass Cater, *Power in Washington: A Critical Look at Today's Struggle to Govern in the Nation's Capital* (New York: Random House, 1964); and J. Leiper Freeman, *The Political Process: Executive Bureau-Legislative Committee Relations* (New York: Random House, 1965).
46. Weaver, "Regulation, Social Policy, and Class Conflict," pp. 196–99.
47. Alana Northrop, "The President and the Bureaucracy: Enemies, Helpmates, or Noncontenders," in *The Presidency in Transition*, ed. James P. Pfiffner and R. Gordon Hoxie (New York: Center for the Study of the Presidency, 1989), pp. 185–86.
48. Martha Derthick and Paul J. Quirk, *The Politics of Deregulation* (Washington, D.C.: Brookings Institution, 1985), p. 12.
49. Benjamin I. Page and Robert Y. Shapiro, "Effects of Public Opinion on Policy," *American Political Science Review* 77 (March 1983): 181, 188–89.
50. Northrop, "The President and the Bureaucracy," p. 184.

CHAPTER 2

1. Roger G. Noll, *Reforming Regulation: An Evaluation of the Ash Council Proposals* (Washington, D.C.: Brookings Institution, 1971), p. 36.
2. U.S., Congress, House, Committee on Energy and Commerce, *Presidential Control of Agency Rulemaking: An Analysis of Constitutional Issues That May Be Raised by Executive Order 12291*, report prepared for the use of the House Committee on Energy and Commerce, 97th Cong., 1st sess., June 15, 1981.
3. Testimony of Louis Brownlow in U.S., *Hearings on the Establishment of a Commission on Ethics in Government*, p. 213. See also U.S., *Study on Federal Regulation* 5:27–28.
4. James P. Pfiffner, "Can the President Manage the Government? Should He?" in *The Managerial Presidency*, ed. James P. Pfiffner (Pacific Grove, Calif.: Brooks/Cole Publishing Company, 1991), p. 2.
5. U.S., White House, President's Committee on Administrative Management, *Administrative Management in the Government of the United States*, January 8, 1937, p. 36.
6. Howard Ball, *Controlling Regulatory Sprawl: Presidential Strategies from Nixon to Reagan* (Westport, Conn.: Greenwood Press, 1984), p. 28.
7. Discussion of these observations may be found in Meier, *Regulation*, pp. 276–84; Steiner and Steiner, *Business, Government, and Society*, pp. 157–59, 163–71; and Weidenbaum, *Business, Government, and the Public*, 3d ed., pp. 15, 17, 180.

8. Joseph Cooper and William F. West, "Presidential Power and Republican Government: The Theory and Practice of OMB Review of Agency Rules," *Journal of Politics* 50 (November 1988): 868, citing the following: Harold Seidman and Robert Gilmour, *Politics, Position, and Power: From the Positive to the Regulatory State*, 4th ed. (New York: Oxford University Press, 1986); and Richard Nathan, *The Administrative Presidency* (New York: John Wiley and Sons, 1983).
9. Dwight A. Ink, "The President as Manager," *Public Administration Review* 36 (September/October 1976): 510, 513.
10. Ronald C. Moe, "Traditional Organizational Principles and the Managerial Presidency: From Phoenix to Ashes," *Public Administration Review* 50 (March/April 1990): 129–30, 133–34.
11. William F. West and Joseph Cooper, "Legislative Influence v. Presidential Dominance: Competing Models of Bureaucratic Control," *Political Science Quarterly* 104 (Winter 1989–90): 587.
12. James L. Sundquist, presentation before the National Capital Area Chapter of the American Society for Public Administration, November 18, 1986. An American Bar Association study found numerous instances in which Congress recognized the president's capacity to make case-by-case balancing judgments (especially in foreign policy matters). See U.S., Congress, Senate, Committee on the Judiciary, Subcommittee on Administrative Practice and Procedure, *Administrative Procedure Act Amendments of 1978*, 95th Cong., 2d sess., Sept. 12, 13, 20, and 21, 1978, p. 1149.
13. See G. Calvin Mackenzie, "Cabinet and Subcabinet Personnel Selection in Reagan's First Year: New Variations on Some Not-So-Old Themes," presented at annual meeting of the American Political Science Association, New York, September 1981; David M. Welborn, *The Governance of Federal Regulatory Agencies* (Knoxville: University of Tennessee Press, 1977); Florence Heffron with Neil McFeeley, *The Administrative Regulatory Process* (New York: Longman, 1983), p. 126; Meier, *Regulation*, p. 26; Seymour Scher, "Congressional Committee Members as Independent Agency Overseers," *American Political Science Review* 54 (September 1960): 911–20; Carol S. Greenwald, *Group Power: Lobbying and Public Policy* (New York: Praeger, 1977), p. 229.
14. Terry M. Moe, "Regulatory Performance and Presidential Administration," *American Journal of Political Science* 26 (May 1982): 200. Michael D. Reagan writes (*Regulation*, p. 74):

> The Teamsters Union, a dominant force in the trucking industry, is the only national union that supports Republican presidential candidates, notably Ronald Reagan. Reagan's first chairman of the ICC (1981–86), Reese Taylor, is a good example of the importance of the leverage over the IRCs that is provided to presidents through the appointment process, and the fact that the chair serves at the will of the president. A Utah lawyer with very strong connections to the trucking industry, Taylor espoused deregulation rhetori-

cally, but quickly made it clear in practice that he would go much slower and not as far with trucking deregulation, as what the "true believers" had hoped for.

15. Meier, *Regulation*, pp. 26–28.
16. Paul R. Verkuil, "Jawboning Administrative Agencies: Ex Parte Contacts by the White House," *Columbia Law Review* 80 (June 1980): 943.
17. U.S., *Study on Federal Regulation* 5:62. Not all independent regulatory commissions are restrained from filing lawsuits with their own counsel.
18. John R. Hibbing, "The Independent Regulatory Commissions Fifty Years After *Humphrey's Executor v. U.S.*," *Congress and the Presidency: A Journal of Capital Studies* 12 (Spring 1985): 59.
19. See U.S., *Study on Federal Regulation* 5:46, and Stephen J. Wayne, *The Legislative Presidency* (New York: Harper and Row, 1978), p. 72.
20. See Ball, *Controlling Regulatory Sprawl*, p. 18.
21. Lloyd N. Cutler and David R. Johnson, "Regulation and the Political Process," *Yale Law Journal* 84 (June 1975): 1410–11.
22. Michael E. Kraft and Norman J. Vig, "Environmental Policy in the Reagan Presidency," *Political Science Quarterly* 99 (Fall 1984): 438–39.
23. U.S., *Presidential Control of Agency Rulemaking*, pp. 3–4.
24. James R. Bowers, "Looking at OMB's Regulatory Review Through a Shared Powers Perspective," *Presidential Studies Quarterly* 23 (Spring 1993): 335.
25. U.S., Congress, Senate, Committee on Governmental Affairs, Subcommittee on Intergovernmental Relations, *Hearing on Oversight of the Office of Management and Budget Review and Planning Process*, 99th Cong., 2d sess., January 28, 1986, p. 253.
26. B. Dan Wood and Richard W. Waterman, "The Dynamics of Political Control of the Bureaucracy," *American Political Science Review* 85 (September 1991): 803.
27. Kraft and Vig, "Environmental Policy in the Reagan Presidency," p. 422.
28. *Youngstown Sheet and Tube Co. v. Sawyer*, 343 U.S. 579, 637 (1952).
29. Joel L. Fleishman and Arthur H. Aufses, "Law and Orders: The Problem of Presidential Legislation," *Law and Contemporary Problems* 40 (Summer 1976): 5.
30. William Hebe, "Executive Orders and the Development of Presidential Power," *Villanova Law Review* 17 (March 1972): 694.
31. Phillip J. Cooper, "By Order of the President: Administration By Executive Order and Proclamation," October 6–8, 1983, mimeo., pp. 5–6.
32. *Jenkins v. Collard*, 145 U.S. 546, 560–61 (1891), and *Maryland Casualty Co. v. United States*, 251 U.S. 342, 349 (1919).
33. *Youngstown v. Sawyer*, 579, 587.
34. *Amalgamated Meat Cutters and Butcher Workmen of North America v. Connally*, 337 F. Supp. 737, 755 (D.D.C. 1971).
35. *United States v. Eliason*, 41 U.S. (16 Peters) 291, 301, 302 (1842).
36. *Prize* cases, 67 U.S. (2 Black) 635 (1863). However, Lincoln's suspension of habeas

corpus was disapproved in *Ex parte Merryman*, 17 F. Cas. 144 (No. 9,487) (C.C.D. Md. 1861), as executive usurpation of a legislative power.

37. The "twilight" metaphor is Justice Jackson's in his concurring opinion in Youngstown, 637–38.
38. Fleishman and Aufses, "Law and Orders," p. 24.
39. Justice Jackson wrote: "When the President takes measures incompatible with the express or implied will of Congress, his power is at its lowest ebb, for then he can rely upon his own constitutional powers minus any constitutional powers of Congress over the matter. Courts can sustain exclusive presidential control in such a case only by disabling Congress from acting upon the subject." *Youngstown v. Sawyer*, 637–38.
40. *Peters v. Hobby*, 349 U.S. 331, 350 (1955).
41. Ruth P. Morgan, *The President and Civil Rights: Policymaking by Executive Order* (New York: St. Martin's Press, 1970), p. vii.
42. Cooper, "By Order of the President," p. 26.
43. Ibid., p. 5.
44. Eads and Fix, *Relief or Reform?* p. 45.
45. Ibid. For information on the involvement in regulation of presidents from Theodore Roosevelt to John F. Kennedy, see Morton Keller, "The Pluralist State: American Economic Regulation in Comparative Perspective, 1900–1930," in McGraw, ed., *Regulation in Perspective*, pp. 68–69, 78, 85; Marshall R. Goodman and Margaret T. Wrightson, *Managing Regulatory Reform: The Reagan Strategy and Its Impact* (New York: Praeger Publishers, 1987), p. 26; Ellis Hawley, "Three Facets of Hooverian Associationalism: Lumber, Aviation, and Movies, 1921–1930," in McGraw, ed., *Regulation in Perspective*, pp. 95–123; Robert R. Nordhaus, "Regulating the Regulators: A Legal (and Political) History," 1981, mimeo.; Hibbing, "The Independent Regulatory Commissions," p. 59; U.S., *Study on Federal Regulation* 5:73; Thomas Gale Moore, "Rail and Trucking Regulation," in *Regulatory Reform: What Actually Happened*, ed. Leonard W. Weiss and Michael W. Klass (Boston: Little, Brown and Company, 1986), p. 18.
46. Robert E. Litan and William D. Nordhaus, *Reforming Federal Regulation* (New Haven: Yale University Press, 1983), p. 67.
47. Eads and Fix, *Relief or Reform?* pp. 46–47.
48. Katherine L. Bernick, "Executive Branch Coordination: The Quality of Life Review," prepared for the American Bar Association's Commission on Law and the Economy, September 30, 1977, cited in Eads and Fix, *Relief or Reform?* p. 48.
49. John D. Ehrlichman, Domestic Council Study Memorandum No. 15, June 16, 1971, cited in Eads and Fix, *Relief or Reform?* p. 48.
50. Bernick, "Executive Branch Coordination," p. 18, cited in Eads and Fix, *Relief or Reform?* p. 49.
51. See Eads and Fix, *Relief or Reform?* pp. 46–50. See also Harold H. Bruff, "Presidential Power and Administrative Rulemaking," *Yale Law Journal* 88 (January 1979): 464–65.
52. Derthick and Quirk, *The Politics of Deregulation*, p. 45. See also Daniel J. Balz, "Sum-

mit Inflation Meetings Highlight More Questions than Answers," *National Journal Reports* 6 (October 5, 1974): 1503–05.

53. U.S., President, Executive Order, "Inflation Impact Statements," *Federal Register* 39 (November 27, 1974): 41501; U.S., Office of the Federal Register, *Code of Federal Regulations* [C.F.R.], 3, 1971–1975 Compilation, p. 926.
54. James C. Miller and Bruce Yandle, *Benefit-Cost Analysis of Social Regulations* (Washington, D.C.: American Enterprise Institute, 1979), p. 6.
55. Quoted in W. Kip Viscusi, "Presidential Oversight: Controlling the Regulators," *Journal of Policy Analysis and Management* 2 (Fall 1982): 159.
56. Ball, *Controlling Regulatory Sprawl*, p. 53.
57. Meier suggests that Carter "was perhaps the most active president in regulatory policy." Meier, *Regulation*, p. 25.
58. Interview by the author with David Plocher, staff attorney, OMB Watch, December 29, 1987.
59. Litan and Nordhaus, *Reforming Federal Regulation*, pp. 69–70.
60. U.S., President, Executive Order, "Improving Government Regulations," *Federal Register* 43 (March 24, 1978): 12661–65; 3 C.F.R., 1978 Comp., p. 152.
61. Fuchs, *Presidents, Management, and Regulation*, p. 52.
62. Ibid., p. 78.
63. Eads and Fix, *Relief or Reform?* p. 87.
64. Peter M. Benda and Charles H. Levine, "Reagan and the Bureaucracy: The Bequest, the Promise, and the Legacy," in *The Reagan Legacy: Promise and Performance*, ed. Charles O. Jones (Chatham, N.J.: Chatham House Publishers, 1988), p. 106.
65. Lloyd N. Cutler, "The Case for Presidential Intervention in Regulatory Rulemaking by the Executive Branch," *Tulane Law Review* 56 (April 1982): 833, 834–35. See also Stephen Breyer, *Regulation and Its Reforms* (Cambridge: Harvard University Press, 1982), p. 3.
66. Quoted in a written statement by Richard J. Leighton, chairman of the United States Chamber of Commerce Task Force on Administrative Procedure Act Reform, in U.S., Congress, Senate, Committee on the Judiciary, Subcommittee on Administrative Practice and Procedure, *Hearings on Regulatory Reform Legislation*, part 2, 96th Cong., 1st sess., June 13, July 18, 20, 25, and 26, 1979, p. 270.
67. U.S., *Hearings on Regulatory Reform Legislation*, part 1, p. 157.
68. Ibid., p. 292.
69. Edward Paul Fuchs, *Institutionalizing Cost-Benefit Analysis: Politics in the Regulatory Process, 1974–1981* (Ph.D. diss., University of Houston, May 1983), p. 177.
70. Ronald Reagan, "Statement on the Reduction of Federal Regulations," June 13, 1981, in U.S., *Public Papers: Ronald Reagan, 1981*, p. 512.
71. Seidman and Gilmour, *Politics, Position, and Power*, p. 127.
72. Susan J. Tolchin and Martin Tolchin, *Dismantling America: The Rush to Deregulate* (New York: Oxford University Press, 1985), p. 41.
73. See, e.g., statement of Representative Edward J. Markey (D-Mass.) in "Independent

Agencies—Independent from Whom?" (program presented by the Section of Administrative Law and Regulatory Practice, American Bar Association, Washington, D.C., October 14, 1988), *Administrative Law Review* 41 (Fall 1989): 491–532, at 495–96. See also chapter 9 of this book.

74. Fuchs, *Institutionalizing Cost-Benefit Analysis*, p. 178.
75. "As a general proposition," a congressional report notes, "Presidents have respected the independent status of the commissions. There is an expectation that, in discharging their adjudicatory functions in particular, those agencies should be free of interference or direction from the White House." U.S., *Study on Federal Regulation* 5:67.
76. See U.S., Congress, House, Committee on Energy and Commerce, Subcommittee on Oversight and Investigations, *Hearing on the Role of* OMB *in Regulation*, 97th Cong., 1st sess., June 18, 1981, pp. 94, 101.
77. Assistant Attorney General Larry Simms, "Proposed Executive Order on Federal Regulation," undated (stamped February 12, 1981), rpt. in U.S., *Hearing on the Role of* OMB *in Regulation*, pp. 151–61.
78. Benda and Levine, "Reagan and the Bureaucracy," p. 102. Emphasis deleted.
79. Goodman and Wrightson, *Managing Regulatory Reform*, p. 3.
80. See, e.g., Eads and Fix, *Relief or Reform?* pp. 254–55, 258–59. The editors' foreword to the book summarizes Eads and Fix's conclusion and predicts that the "early political results of regulatory relief" will eventually prove to be "a detour on the road to regulatory reform" (p. xiv).
81. Transmittal message from Ronald Reagan to the Congress in U.S., Office of Management and Budget, *Regulatory Program of the United States Government, April 1, 1987–March 31, 1988* (Washington, D.C.: GPO, June 1987), p. vii.
82. Goodman and Wrightson, *Managing Regulatory Reform*, p. 26.
83. Frank B. Cross, "Executive Orders 12,291 and 12,498: A Test Case in Presidential Control of Executive Agencies," *The Journal of Law and Politics* 4 (Winter 1988): 538–39.
84. U.S., Congress, Senate Committee on Environment and Public Works, *Office of Management and Budget Influence on Agency Regulation*, 99th Cong., 2d sess., May 1986, p. xi.
85. Antonin Scalia and Anne Brunsdale, "Deregulation HQ: An Interview on the New Executive Order with Murray L. Weidenbaum and James C. Miller III," *Regulation* 5 (March/April 1981): 22.
86. Quoted in Steven Mufson, "The Anonymous Face of Power," *Washington Post National Weekly Edition*, May 7–13, 1990, p. 6.
87. *Statutes at Large* 94 (1980): 2812.
88. U.S., *Hearing on the Role of* OMB *in Regulation*, p. 45.
89. U.S., *Regulatory Program of the United States Government*, pp. l–li.
90. U.S., Congress, Senate, Committee on Governmental Affairs, *Office of Management*

and Budget: Evolving Roles and Future Issues, 99th Cong., 2d sess., February 1986, p. xiii.

91. Benda and Levine, "Reagan and the Bureaucracy," p. 116. They are quoting U.S., Congress, Senate, Committee on Governmental Affairs, *Paperwork Reduction Act of 1980*, 96th Cong., 2d sess., 1980, p. 56.
92. U.S. Congress, *Congressional Record*, 99th Cong., 2d sess., vol. 132 (October 17, 1986): 33205.
93. Richard Curtis and Maggie Wells, *Not Exactly a Crime: Our Vice Presidents from Adams to Agnew* (New York: Dial Press, 1972), pp. 56, 128.
94. Paul C. Light, *Vice-Presidential Power: Advice and Influence in the White House* (Baltimore: Johns Hopkins University Press, 1984), p. 1.
95. A national security aide quoted Secretary of State Henry A. Kissinger as frequently pondering, "Maybe we ought to brief what's his name [i.e., the vice president]." Quoted ibid., p. 146.
96. Quoted in ibid., p. 8.
97. Ibid., p. 63.
98. Some accounts indicate that Kennedy gave Johnson the OEOB office in order to "keep closer tabs" on his former rival. Ibid., p. 392.
99. Ibid., p. 259.
100. Ibid., p. 63.
101. Eads and Fix, *Relief or Reform?* pp. 2–3, 118–19.
102. U.S., *Regulatory Federalism*, pp. 229–30.
103. Transcript of Hall of Flags Regulatory Reform Meeting, April 10, 1981, p. 22, printed in U.S., *Hearing on the Role of* OMB *in Regulation*, p. 92.
104. Interview by the author with anonymous OMB official.
105. Rich Grawey, majority staff counsel, Subcommittee on Manpower and Housing, House Government Operations Committee, to Chairwoman Cardiss Collins (D-Ill.), Hearing Memorandum, March 17, 1981, quoted in Ball, *Controlling Regulatory Sprawl*, p. 104.
106. U.S., Executive Office of the President, Presidential Task Force on Regulatory Relief, *Reagan Administration Regulatory Achievements*, August 11, 1983.
107. Interview by the author with John P. Schmitz, June 27, 1988.
108. John Hart, *The Presidential Branch* (New York: Pergamon Press, 1987), p. 123.
109. Benda and Levine, "Reagan and the Bureaucracy," p. 111.
110. Schmitz interview, June 27, 1988.

CHAPTER 3

1. Charles E. Lindblom, "The Science of Muddling Through," *Public Administration Review* 19 (Spring 1959): 79–88; David Braybrooke and Charles E. Lindblom, *A Strategy of Decision* (New York: Free Press, 1963).

2. See, e.g., Aaron Wildavsky, *The New Politics of the Budgetary Process*, 2d ed. (New York: HarperCollins, 1992), pp. 80–81.
3. Terry Eastland, *Energy in the Executive: The Case for the Strong Presidency* (New York: Free Press, 1992), p. 2. Kraft and Vig, reviewing the Reagan administration's environmental policy, interpret what they observed as a demonstration of "how an incoming presidential administration strongly committed to reversing previous policies can achieve systematic, nonincremental policy change." Kraft and Vig, "Environmental Policy in the Reagan Presidency," p. 416.
4. Quoted in Reagan, *Regulation*, pp. 130–31.
5. *U.S. Code* [U.S.C.], title 33, §701 (1988).
6. Fuchs, *Presidents, Management, and Regulation*, p. 6.
7. See U.S., *Hearings on Office of Management and Budget: Evolving Roles and Future Issues*, pp. 89–90.
8. William F. West, "Structuring Administrative Discretion: The Pursuit of Rationality and Responsiveness," *American Journal of Political Science* 28 (May 1984): 350.
9. U.S., *Hearings on Regulatory Reform Legislation*, part 1, p. 187.
10. *American Textile Manufacturers Institute, Inc., v. Donovan, Secretary of Labor*, 452 U.S. 490, 510–511 (1981).
11. U.S., *Hearings on Regulatory Reform Legislation*, part 1, p. 14.
12. Adapted from David L. Weimer and Aidan R. Vining, *Policy Analysis: Concepts and Practice*, 2d ed. (Englewood Cliffs, N.J.: Prentice-Hall, 1992), p. 260.
13. U.S., Congress, House, Committee on Interstate and Foreign Commerce, Subcommittee on Oversight and Investigations, *Federal Regulation and Regulatory Reform*, 94th Cong., 2d sess., October 1976, p. 180.
14. Reagan, *Regulation*, p. 127.
15. Emphasis added. U.S., *Hearing on Oversight of Office of Management and Budget Regulatory Review and Planning Process*, pp. 177–78. Michael E. Kraft ("The Use of Risk Analysis in Federal Regulatory Agencies: An Exploration," *Policy Studies Review* 1 [May 1982]: 667) reported that various federal regulatory agencies may be disposed toward or against risk assessment. He found that risk analyses are rarely "the determinative factor" in regulatory decisions.
16. U.S., *Hearings on Regulatory Reform Legislation*, part 1, pp. 1142–43.
17. Ibid. The point was validated by Douglas Costle, Charles Schultze, and John White in post-hearing testimony: "The state of the art for accurately calculating direct incremental costs is more advanced than the state of the art for valuing benefits." Ibid., p. 279.
18. James L. Wright, director of the United Auto Workers' Region IV, complained that practitioners of cost-benefit analysis were neglecting to calculate long-range costs associated with disease or injury. U.S., Congress, Senate, Committee on Governmental Affairs, Subcommittee on Energy, Nuclear Proliferation and Governmental Processes, *Hearing on Federal Regulation*, part 1, *Effect on the Automobile Industry*, 97th Cong., 1st sess., April 16, 1981, p. 153.

19. Some of the controversial techniques include the discounted future earnings approach and Viscusi's "willingness to pay" approach. The latter places a lower value on the lives of individuals who are engaged voluntarily in risky occupations. These approaches tend to make the lives of affluent individuals appear intrinsically more valuable than the lives of others, as Michael D. Reagan explains: "Greater value is placed on the life of a younger person than an older one, on a white-collar than a blue-collar worker, and on the lives of men over women, to the extent that a sex differential still exists in average salary levels. . . . Some may accept risky employment because it is the only thing available, rather than out of a personal calculation comparing wage and risk for a particular job." Reagan, *Regulation*, p. 126. See also W. Kip Viscusi, "Alternative Approaches to Valuing the Health Impacts of Accidents: Liability Law and Prospective Evaluations," *Law and Contemporary Problems* 46 (Fall 1983): 49–68.
20. U.S., Congress, Senate, Committee on Governmental Affairs, *Hearing on Regulatory Reform Legislation of 1981*, 97th Cong., 1st sess., May 12 and June 23, 1981, p. 245.
21. David D. Doniger, cited in Albert R. Matheny and Bruce A. Williams, "Regulation, Risk Assessment, and the Supreme Court: The Case of OSHA's Cancer Policy," *Law and Policy* 6 (October 1984): 444.
22. U.S., *Federal Regulation and Regulatory Reform*, p. 515.
23. Alan B. Morrison, "OMB Interference with Agency Rulemaking: The Wrong Way to Write a Regulation," *Harvard Law Review* 99 (March 1986): 1066.
24. Written statement by Nancy Drabble and Carolyn Brickey, Public Citizen's Congress Watch, in U.S., Congress, House, Committee on the Judiciary, Subcommittee on Administrative Law and Government Relations, *Hearings on Regulatory Procedures Act of 1981*, 97th Cong., 1st sess., March 24; April 2, 7, and 30; May 5, 7, 14, and 19; Sept. 10, 1981, p. 417, and written statement by Morton A. Myers, deputy director, Program Analysis Division, U.S. General Accounting Office, in U.S., Congress, House, Committee on the Judiciary, Subcommittee on Administrative Law and Governmental Relations, *Hearings on Regulation Reform Act of 1979*, part 1, 96th Cong., 1st and 2d sess., Nov. 7, 13, 16, 28; Dec. 3, 5, 10, 1979; Jan. 29; Feb. 1 and 5, 1980, p. 676. See also Thomas O. McGarity, "Regulatory Analysis and Regulatory Reform," *Texas Law Review* 65 (June 1987): 1305–06.
25. U.S., Congress, Senate, Committee on the Judiciary, *Hearings on Regulatory Reform*, part 1, 96th Cong., 1st sess., May 10 and 15, 1979, p. 106.
26. Bryner, *Bureaucratic Discretion*, p. 41.
27. Stan Crock, Christine Del Valle, and Michael J. Mandel, "What's Deadlier, a Toxic Workplace or Low Pay?" *Business Week*, April 13, 1992, pp. 100–01; and William A. Niskanen, "Straws in the Wind," *Regulation* 15 (Spring 1992): 7–9.
28. See statement of Senator Lloyd Bentsen (D-Tex.) in U.S., *Hearings on Regulatory Reform Legislation*, part 1, p. 292.
29. Eileen Siedman, "Why Not *Qualitative* Analysis?" *Public Administration Review* 37 (July/August 1977): 415. See also OMB Report, "Improving Government Regulations: A Progress Report," part 1, September 1979, rpt. in U.S., Congress, Senate,

Committee on Governmental Affairs, Subcommittee on Oversight of Government Management, *Hearing on Oversight of Agency Compliance With Executive Order 12044 "Improving Government Regulations"*, 96th Cong., 1st sees., October 10, 1979, p. 162.

30. See statement by Lester B. Lave in U.S., *Hearing on Regulatory Reform Legislation of 1981*, p. 253.
31. Grover Starling, *Strategies for Policy Making* (Chicago: Dorsey Press, 1988), p. 282.
32. U.S., *Hearings on Regulatory Reform*, part 1, pp. 2–3. See also statement by Barry M. Mitnick in U.S., *Hearings on Regulation Reform Act of 1979*, part 2, Nov. 7, 13, 16, 28, 1979; Dec. 3, 5, 10, 1979; Jan. 29, 1980; Feb. 1 and 5, 1980, p. 1161.
33. U.S., *Hearings on Regulation Reform Act of 1979*, part 2, p. 1162.
34. See, e.g., Joel D. Aberbach, "The President and the Executive Branch," in *The Bush Presidency: First Appraisals*, ed. Colin Campbell, S.J., and Bert A. Rockman (Chatham, N.J.: Chatham House Publishers, 1991), pp. 223–25. At a meeting on April 29, 1973, Assistant to the President John D. Ehrlichman complained bitterly to President Richard M. Nixon: "We have no discipline in the bureaucracy." Nixon added, "We never fire anybody. We never reprimand anybody. We never demote anybody. We always promote the sons-of-bitches that kick us in the ass." Quoted in Richard P. Nathan, *The Plot That Failed: Nixon and the Administrative Presidency* (New York: John Wiley and Sons, 1975), p. 69.
35. James P. Pfiffner, "Nine Enemies and One Ingrate: Political Appointments during Presidential Transitions," in *The In-and-Outers: Presidential Appointees and Transient Government in Washington*, ed. G. Calvin Mackenzie (Baltimore: Johns Hopkins University Press, 1987), p. 72.
36. Francis E. Rourke, "Executive Responsiveness to Presidential Policies: The Reagan Presidency," *Congress and the Presidency* 17 (Spring 1990): 2–3.
37. Mackenzie, "Cabinet and Subcabinet Personnel Selection." Also quoted in Pfiffner, "Nine Enemies and One Ingrate," p. 72.
38. Bert A. Rockman, "The Style and Organization of the Reagan Presidency," in Jones, ed., *The Reagan Legacy: Promise and Performance*, p. 16.
39. Quoted in Eads and Fix, *Relief or Reform?* p. 139.
40. Benda and Levine, "Reagan and the Bureaucracy," p. 108.
41. Quoted in Bryner, *Bureaucratic Discretion*, p. 66.
42. Quoted in Dick Kirschten, "Team Players," *National Journal*, February 19, 1983, p. 385.
43. Quoted in Elizabeth Drew, "A Reporter at Large," *New Yorker*, March 16, 1981, pp. 91–92. Terry M. Moe also indicates that the Reagan transition team "wanted partisans located deep within the established bureaucracy, even if expertise was lacking." Terry M. Moe, "The Politicized Presidency," in *The New Direction in American Politics*, ed. John Chubb and Paul Peterson (Washington, D.C.: Brookings Institution, 1985), p. 260.
44. Quoted in Tolchin and Tolchin, *Dismantling America*, p. 41.
45. Francis E. Rourke, "Presidentializing the Bureaucracy: From Kennedy to Reagan," in Pfiffner, ed., *The Managerial Presidency*, p. 130.

46. Benda and Levine, "Reagan and the Bureaucracy," pp. 109–10.
47. Quoted in ibid., p. 110.
48. Quoted in ibid., p. 111.
49. Patricia W. Ingraham and Carolyn R. Ban, "Models of Public Management: Are They Useful to Federal Managers in the 1980s?" *Public Administration Review* 46 (March/April 1986): 154.
50. Murray L. Weidenbaum, "Regulatory Reform Under the Reagan Administration," in *The Reagan Regulatory Strategy: An Assessment*, ed. George C. Eads and Michael Fix (Washington, D.C.: Urban Institute Press, 1984), p. 33.
51. Edie N. Goldenberg, "The Permanent Government in an Era of Retrenchment and Redirection," in *The Reagan Presidency and the Governing of America*, ed. Lester M. Salamon and Michael S. Lund (Washington, D.C.: Urban Institute Press, 1984), p. 390.
52. Rockman, "The Style and Organization of the Reagan Presidency," p. 10.
53. Dr. John Hernandez, a candidate for the position of EPA administrator, was interviewed by two aides to OMB director David A. Stockman. Fred Khedouri, OMB's budget director for the EPA, "leaned over in his chair, and kind of quiet like, but dead serious, asked [Hernandez], 'Would you be willing to bring EPA to its knees?' " Hernandez "just demurred," Hernandez recalls, and the job went instead to Anne Gorsuch Burford. Quoted in Burford's autobiography, Anne Burford with John Greenya, *Are You Tough Enough?* (New York: McGraw-Hill, 1986), pp. 83–84.
54. Eads and Fix, *Relief or Reform?* p. 255.
55. Charles H. Levine and Rosslyn S. Kleeman wrote, "The success of the Reagan administration in using political appointees to control the administrative machinery of government is a lesson that is unlikely to be lost on future presidencies." In "The Quiet Crisis of the Civil Service: The Federal Personnel System at the Crossroads" (Washington, D.C.: National Academy of Public Administration, December 1986), p. 29.
56. Reagan gave regulatory policy a priority comparable to the priority his administration assigned to tax, budgetary, and monetary policy in revitalizing the U.S. economy. Editors' foreword in Eads and Fix, *Relief or Reform?* p. xiii.
57. Goodman and Wrightson, *Managing Regulatory Reform*, p. 2.
58. Quoted in Marshall R. Goodman, "A Kinder and Gentler Regulatory Reform: The Bush Regulatory Strategy and Its Impact," paper presented at the annual meeting of the Southern Political Science Association, Atlanta, November 8, 1990, p. 10.
59. Quoted in U.S., *Hearing on Oversight of the Office of Management and Budget Regulatory Review and Planning Process*, p. 107.
60. See Benda and Levine, "Reagan and the Bureaucracy," p. 102.
61. Goodman and Wrightson, *Managing Regulatory Reform*, p. 73.
62. Interview by the author with Jacquelyn Y. White, June 13, 1988.
63. Morton Rosenberg, "Congress's Prerogative Over Agencies and Agency Decisionmakers: The Rise and Demise of the Reagan Administration's Theory of the Unitary Executive," *George Washington Law Review* 57 (January 1989): 628–29.

64. Meier, *Regulation*, p. 3.
65. Interview by the author with Dr. Wendy L. Gramm, November 16, 1988.
66. Morrison, "OMB Interference with Agency Rulemaking," 1064.
67. Bryner, *Bureaucratic Discretion*, p. 109.
68. Interview by the author with Scott H. Jacobs, June 29, 1988.
69. Christopher C. DeMuth and Douglas H. Ginsburg, "White House Review of Agency Rulemaking," *Harvard Law Review* 99 (March 1986): 1084.
70. Remarks before the United States Chamber of Commerce, Washington, D.C., December 6, 1984, quoted in [David Plocher], OMB *Control of Rulemaking: The End of Public Access* (Washington, D.C.: OMB Watch, August 1985), p. 13.
71. "Memorandum on the Regulatory Planning Process" (January 4, 1985), in U.S., *Public Papers of the Presidents: Ronald Reagan, 1985*, 1:12.
72. DeMuth and Ginsburg, "White House Review of Agency Rulemaking," p. 1085.
73. Morrison, "OMB Interference with Agency Rulemaking," p. 1064.
74. U.S., White House, *Economic Report of the President and the Annual Report of the Council of Economic Advisers* (Washington, D.C.: GPO, 1982), p. 147.
75. Eads and Fix, *Relief or Reform?* p. 211.
76. Interview by the author with an official in the Department of Health and Human Services.
77. Quoted in U.S., *Office of Management and Budget Influence on Agency Regulations*, pp. 19–20.
78. Interview by the author with HHS official.
79. Interview by the author with EPA official.
80. Interview by the author with anonymous Washington consultant.
81. Interview by the author with Dr. Odelia C. Funke, chief of the Regulation Management Branch, EPA Office of Policy, Planning and Evaluation, June 30, 1988.
82. Interview by the author with Samuel W. Fairchild, senior desk officer, OIRA Commerce and Lands Branch, November 10, 1988.
83. Interview by the author with S. Jay Plager, November 15, 1988.

CHAPTER 4

1. George C. Eads, "Harnessing Regulation: The Evolving Role of White House Oversight," *Regulation* 5 (May/June 1981): 19.
2. U.S., Congress, House, Committee on Government Operations, Subcommittee on Manpower and Housing, *Hearings on Office of Management and Budget Control of* OSHA *Rulemaking*, 97th Cong., 2d sess., March 11, 18, and 19, 1982, p. 179.
3. U.S., *Hearing on the Role of* OMB *in Regulation*, p. 9.
4. Quoted in Erik D. Olson, "The Quiet Shift of Power: Office of Management and Budget Supervision of Environmental Protection Agency Rulemaking Under Executive Order 12,291," *Virginia Journal of Natural Resources Law* 4 (Fall 1984): 43.
5. Interview by the author with an OSHA official.

6. Quoted in Kim Masters, "Lawyers Search for Keys to New Regulatory Power Center," *Legal Times*, February 23, 1981, p. 11.
7. Interview by the author with Thomas Rollins, June 17, 1988.
8. Quoted in Richard W. Waterman, *Presidential Influence and the Administrative State* (Knoxville: University of Tennessee Press, 1989), p. 131.
9. Reagan, *Regulation*, p. 130.
10. Interview by the author with OIRA staff member.
11. Interview by the author with Jefferson B. Hill, June 24, 1988.
12. Testimony in U.S., Congress, Senate, Committee on Governmental Affairs, *Hearings on Reauthorization of* OMB*'s Office of Information and Regulatory Affairs*, 101st Cong., 2d sess., Feb. 21, 22, 1990, p. 30.
13. Rowland Evans Jr. and Robert D. Novak, *Nixon in the White House* (New York: Random House, 1971), p. 12.
14. Herbert Kaufman, *The Administrative Behavior of Federal Bureau Chiefs* (Washington, D.C.: Brookings Institution, 1981), pp. 117–19, 122. See also Kaufman, *The Forest Ranger: A Study in Administrative Behavior* (Baltimore: Johns Hopkins University Press, 1960), chapter 6.
15. Hill interview.
16. Eads and Fix, *Relief or Reform?* p. 88.
17. Ibid.
18. [Plocher], OMB *Control of Rulemaking*, p. 25.
19. OMB Watch, "Douglas H. Ginsburg Backgrounder," October 30, 1987, mimeo., p. 2.
20. Quoted in Thomas O. McGarity, "Regulatory Reform in the Reagan Era," *Maryland Law Review* 45 (Spring 1986): 262.
21. Ball, *Controlling Regulatory Sprawl*, pp. 77–78. The six consumer safety and health agencies are the Consumer Product Safety Commission; the Food and Drug Administration; the Antitrust Division; the Federal Railroad Administration; the National Highway Traffic Safety Administration; and the Bureau of Alcohol, Tobacco, and Firearms.
22. Hill interview. The phenomenon of horror stories is described in Christopher H. Foreman Jr., *Signals From the Hill: Congressional Oversight and the Challenge of Social Regulation* (New Haven: Yale University Press, 1988), p. 47.
23. The president must "take Care that the Laws be faithfully executed." Article 2, §3.
24. See chapter 6.
25. Burford with Greenya, *Are You Tough Enough?* pp. 82–83.
26. Quoted in Oliver A. Houck, "President X and the New (Approved) Decisionmaking," *The American University Law Review* 36 (Winter 1987): 545.
27. *Hearing on the Role of* OMB *in Regulation*, p. 5.
28. Statement of May 8, 1986, rpt. in Goodman and Wrightson, *Managing Regulatory Reform*, pp. 190–91.
29. U.S., *Hearing on Oversight of the Office of Management and Budget Regulatory Review and Planning Process*, pp. 4, 49.

30. Ibid., p. 174.
31. Ibid., p. 10.
32. Peter Behr, "If There's a New Rule, Jim Tozzi Has Read It," *Washington Post*, July 10, 1981, p. A21.
33. Interview by the author with anonymous agency official, 1988.
34. Interview with HHS official.
35. From a column in the *Cleveland Plain Dealer*, July 26, 1982, quoted in Alliance for Justice, "Contempt for Law: Excluding the Public from the Rulemaking Process" (Washington, D.C.: Alliance for Justice, 1983), p. 1.
36. *National Law Journal*, April 27, 1981, quoted in Eads, "Harnessing Regulation," p. 26.
37. Quoted in Tolchin and Tolchin, *Dismantling America*, pp. 65–66.
38. 627 F. Supp. 566 (D.D.C.).
39. U.S., *Hearing on Oversight of the Office of Management and Budget Regulatory Review and Planning Process*, pp. 91–92.
40. Olson, "The Quiet Shift of Power," p. 64 n. 324.
41. Interview by the author with anonymous Washington consultant, November 14, 1988.
42. Houck, "President X and the New (Approved) Decisionmaking," p. 545.
43. Quoted in Tolchin and Tolchin, *Dismantling America*, p. 77.
44. Testimony of Gary D. Bass Before the Subcommittee on Legislation and National Security of the House Government Operations Committee, July 25, 1989, mimeo., pp. 10–11.
45. Interview by the author with Patrick M. McLain, November 17, 1988.
46. OMB Watch, *Monthly Review*, May 1988, p. 2.
47. Viscusi, "Presidential Oversight," p. 161.
48. Bryner, *Bureaucratic Discretion*, p. 17.
49. [Plocher], OMB *Control of Rulemaking*, p. i.
50. U.S., *Hearings on Office of Management and Budget Control of* OSHA *Rulemaking*, p. 350.
51. Quoted in Pete Earley, "What's a Life Worth? How the Reagan Administration Decides for You," *Washington Post Magazine*, June 9, 1985, p. 36.
52. Quoted in Houck, "President X and the New (Approved) Decisionmaking," p. 536, from a report in the *Environmental Reporter*.
53. U.S., *Hearings on Office of Management and Budget Control of* OSHA *Rulemaking*, p. 350.
54. For accounts of these allegations, see U.S., Congress, House, Committee on Energy and Commerce, Subcommittee on Oversight and Investigations, *Hearings on* EPA*'s Asbestos Regulations: A Case Study of Interference in Environmental Protection Agency Rulemaking by the Office of Management and Budget*, 99th Cong., 1st sess., April 16, 1985, p. 482; and John Sibbison, "Whose Agency is It, Anyway? How OMB Runs EPA," *Washington Monthly*, December 1985, p. 21.
55. Interview by the author with Robert P. Bedell, November 9, 1988.
56. Bryner, *Bureaucratic Discretion*, p. 117.

57. U.S., *Hearings on Oversight of the Office of Management and Budget Regulatory Review and Planning Process*, pp. 108–09.
58. The change from experimental to permanent status resulted from an agreement involving Senators Carl Levin (D-Mich.) and Durenberger and OMB officials. See chapter 6.
59. OMB Watch, "Paperwork Reduction: The Quick Fix of 1986" (Washington, D.C.: OMB Watch, November 1986), p. 2.
60. Quoted in Goodman, "A Kinder and Gentler Regulatory Reform," p. 22.
61. 48 Fed. Reg. 13666, at 13668 (March 31, 1983).
62. Interview by the author with Treasury official.
63. 29 C.F.R. §1926.59; 52 Fed. Reg. 31852 (August 24, 1987).
64. *United Steelworkers of America v. Auchter*, 763 F. 2d 728 (3d Cir.).
65. 819 F. 2d 1263 (3d Cir.).
66. Memorandum from Randy S. Rabinowitz, counsel for International Union, United Auto Workers, "OMB Paperwork Review of OSHA's Formaldehyde Standard," January 29, 1988.
67. Both are reported at 855 F. 2d 108 (3d Cir. 1988).
68. Morrison, "OMB Interference with Agency Rulemaking," p. 1064.
69. Interview with OSHA official.
70. Ibid.
71. Ibid.
72. U.S., Office of Management and Budget, *Regulatory Program of the United States Government, April 1, 1990–March 31, 1991* (Washington, D.C.: GPO, Aug. 3, 1990), p. 647.
73. U.S., Congress, Senate Committee on Environment and Public Works, *Office of Management and Budget Influence on Agency Regulations*, 99th Cong., 2d sess., May 1986, p. xv.
74. "EPA Charges OMB 'Grossly' Exceeds Deadlines in Reviewing Clean Air Rules," *Inside the Administration*, July 18, 1985, p. 10.
75. "OMB to Cut Backlog on Air Act Regs in Response to EPA Concern Over Delay," *Inside the Administration*, August 1, 1985, p. 11.
76. 627 F. Supp. 566 (D.D.C.).
77. Funke interview.
78. Public Law 98-616; *Statues at Large* 98 (1984): 3221.
79. Interview by the author with OIRA desk officer, 1988.

CHAPTER 5

1. *Rathbun ("Humphrey's Executor") v. United States*, 295 U.S. 602 (1935).
2. U.S., White House, President's Committee on Administrative Management, *Administrative Management in the Government of the United States*, January 8, 1937, p. 36.
3. See chapter 6 for a discussion of Congress's influence. The influence of clientele

groups is chronicled, e.g., in Theodore J. Lowi, *The End of Liberalism: The Second Republic of the United States*, 2d ed. (New York: W. W. Norton and Co., 1979), and David B. Truman, *The Governmental Process: Political Interests and Public Opinion*, 2d ed. (New York: Albert A. Knopf, 1971). The influence of agency personnel is discussed later in this chapter.

4. See Frederick C. Mosher, *Democracy and the Public Service*, 2d ed. (New York: Oxford University Press, 1982).
5. DeMuth and Ginsburg, "White House Review of Agency Rulemaking," p. 1085. See also Bryner, *Bureaucratic Discretion*, p. 16.
6. See U.S., *Hearing on Oversight of Agency Compliance With Executive Order 12044*, p. 162; and U.S., *Hearings on Regulatory Reform Legislation*, part 1, p. 290.
7. U.S., *Hearing on Federal Regulation*, part 1, *Effect on the Automobile Industry*, p. 26.
8. Quoted in Murray L. Weidenbaum, *The Future of Business Regulation: Private Action and Public Demand* (New York: AMACOM, 1979), p. 116.
9. U.S., *Hearing on Role of OMB in Regulation*, p. 101.
10. "Independent Agencies—Independent from Whom?" *Administrative Law Review* 41 (Fall 1989): 504.
11. U.S., *Hearings on Regulatory Procedures Act of 1981*, pp. 730–31. In 1988, IRS officials did not seem to feel that their agency was still exempt from the process, however.
12. Interview by the author with Richard S. Carro, associate general counsel for legislation, litigation, and regulation, Department of the Treasury, June 21, 1988.
13. "Treasury Obtains Secret Agreement to Limit OMB Review Under E. O. 12498," *Inside the Administration*, May 3, 1985, p. 6, emphasis deleted.
14. "OMB Now a Regulator in Historic Power Shift," *Washington Post*, May 5, 1981, p. A1. Cited in U.S., *Regulatory Federalism: Policy, Process, Impact and Reform* pp. 196–97. OMB's decision to forgo pre-promulgation review of EO 12291 among affected agencies departed from what had become the standard three-stage procedure for circulating executive orders before promulgation. John F. Cooney, former assistant general counsel in OMB's Office of the General Counsel, stated that generally "an agency would not attempt to propose a controversial policy through the Executive order process that had not previously been pre-cleared with other affected agencies, because the triple circulation process insures that any unresolved agency objections will be elicited, and they will bring the process to a halt until the objections are resolved." Letter to the author, October 29, 1991. Observers who attended a conference entitled, "Politics and Science of Garbage: Exploring Waste Management Policies in America," in Washington, D.C., on June 13, 1991, report that President Bush's counselor C. Boyden Gray (a coauthor of EO 12291) and Miller described the February 17, 1981, meeting with agency attorneys in their keynote statements at the conference. As Gray and Miller described the shock that had overcome the agency attorneys at the February 17 meeting, they could not conceal their amusement, and apparently had no desire to do so.

15. David A. Stockman, *The Triumph of Politics: How the Reagan Revolution Failed* (New York: Harper and Row, 1986), p. 103.
16. "Commerce Dept. Files 'Objections' to Tedious OMB Demands Under E. O. 12498," *Inside the Administration*, April 26, 1985, p. 4.
17. Interview with OSHA official.
18. In the Proposed Rules Section, 5,347 documents appeared in 1980, followed by only 3,862 documents in 1981, and 3,240 in 1988. Data were compiled and provided by Ruth C. Pontius, senior editor, Office of the Federal Register, National Archives. Pontius cautions that "documents" include removals of material from the Code of Federal Regulations, various amendments, and other forms, and do not represent new rules only. Interview by the author with Ruth C. Pontius, August 7, 1991.
19. Olson, "The Quiet Shift of Power," p. 50.
20. Rollins interview. See also Pete Earley, "What's a Life Worth?" *Washington Post Magazine*, June 9, 1985, pp. 11–13, 36–37.
21. Gerd Winter, "Bartering Rationality in Regulation," *Law and Society Review* 19, no. 2 (1985): 219–50.
22. Interview with OSHA official.
23. Morrison, "OMB Interference with Agency Rulemaking," 1069–70.
24. *Motor Vehicles Mfrs. Ass'n. v. State Farm Mut. Auto. Ins. Ass'n.*, 463 U.S. 29, 51 (1983).
25. *Public Citizen v. Steed*, 733 F. 2d 93, 102 (D.C.Cir. 1984).
26. *New England Coalition on Nuclear Pollution v. Nuclear Regulatory Commission*, 727 F. 2d 1127, 1131 (D.C.Cir. 1984).
27. *United Steelworkers of America v. Auchter [I]*, 763 F. 2d 728, 743 (3d Cir. 1985).
28. Cited in James Q. Wilson, "The Rise of the Bureaucratic State," *The Public Interest* 41 (Fall 1975): 80. "At the level of the social group, . . . competition between two groups produces similarities between them." David Frisby, *Georg Simmel* (Chichester, England: Horwood Limited, 1984), p. 81. Georg Simmel maintains that conflict with another group promotes mobilization of membership and internal cohesiveness. Because each partner to the conflict prefers to participate in a conflict whose mechanics are compatible with its internal structural instruments, the organizations of the two partners in the same conflict may tend to converge over time. See Lewis A. Coser, *The Functions of Social Conflict* (Glencoe, Ill.: Free Press, 1956), pp. 87–88, 90, 95, 121, 123, and 129. Rourke observes: "The way that both the president and Congress have . . . had to bureaucratize their own operation in order to control the bureaucracy illustrates the contagion effect of bureaucracy. Institutions that carry on extensive and continuing interaction with bureaucratic organizations are eventually compelled to hire their own bureaucrats to assist them in performing this task." Francis E. Rourke, *Bureaucracy, Politics, and Public Policy*, 3d ed. (Boston: Little, Brown and Company, 1984), p. 195. A Nixon "insider" observed in 1972: "Every President wants his own men—this President especially. Distrustful of bureaucracy, Mr. Nixon has built a kind of defense against it—and in doing so, he has built his own bureaucracy." Quoted in

"Nixon's Top Command: Expanding in Size, Power," *U.S. News and World Report*, April 24, 1972, p. 74.

29. Interview by the author with Stuart Miles-McLean, environmental protection specialist, Office of Regulatory Management and Evaluation, EPA's Office of Policy, Planning and Evaluation, August 23, 1991.
30. See Bryner, *Bureaucratic Discretion*, p. 125.
31. Interview with OSHA official.
32. Interview by the author with Lawrence A. Finfer, program analyst, Office of Program Analysis, Department of the Interior, August 27, 1991.
33. Interview by the author with Kenneth C. Depew, general attorney, Division of Regulations Management, Department of Education, August 26, 1991.
34. Interview by the author with Keith J. Collins, director of economic analysis staff, USDA, August 26, 1991.
35. Morrison, "OMB Interference with Agency Rulemaking," p. 1065.
36. McGarity, "Regulatory Reform in the Reagan Era," pp. 262–63.
37. Quoted in Waterman, *Presidential Influence and the Administrative State*, pp. 123–24.
38. Ibid., p. 125.
39. Cited in "OSHA Lax on Safety Laws, Group Says," *Atlanta Journal*, December 10, 1991, p. A3.
40. Eads and Fix, *Relief or Reform?* pp. 191, 193–95, 200. Meier determined that there was a cause and effect relationship between President Reagan's criticism of OSHA and a subsequent cutback of OSHA's enforcement activities. Meier, *Regulation*, pp. 26–28.
41. Frederic A. Eidsness Jr., "An Administration Sold on Clean Water" [letter to the editor], *New York Times*, November 9, 1982, p. A30.
42. Tolchin and Tolchin, *Dismantling America*, p. 80.
43. Quoted in Bryner, *Bureaucratic Discretion*, p. 157.
44. Seidman and Gilmour, *Politics, Position, and Power*, pp. 142–43.
45. Interview by the author with James J. Delaney, principal deputy assistant secretary of defense (reserve affairs), Department of Defense, June 16, 1988. Delaney also attributed PHS's insubordination to its insatiable appetite for funds. "The Public Health Service's travel budget is bigger than the U.S. Coast Guard's entire budget. . . . It could utilize the entire budget of the U.S. government and still ask for more."
46. Robert A. Rogowsky, "Sub Rosa Regulation: The Iceberg Beneath the Surface," in *Regulation and the Reagan Era: Politics, Bureaucracy and the Public Interest*, ed. Roger E. Meiners and Bruce Yandle (New York: Holmes and Meier, 1989), p. 218.
47. Steven Waldman, "Regulation Comes Back," *Newsweek*, September 12, 1988, p. 44.
48. Terry M. Moe, "Regulatory Performance and Presidential Administration," p. 200.
49. U.S., *Hearing on the Role of* OMB *in Regulation*, p. 94.
50. Recorded at OMB Bulletin 85-9, Suppl. 1.
51. [Plocher], OMB *Control of Rulemaking*, pp. 14–15.
52. Funke interview.
53. OIRA economist John F. Morrall III concluded that Department of Transportation

rules were "83 times more cost-effective than those of OSHA and 40 times more cost-effective than those of EPA." Morrall, "A Review of the Record," *Regulation* 10 (November/December 1986): 25–34, at 32. Burford supported the principle of reducing compliance costs, but refused to delegate her and her appointees' authority to the regulatory analysis staff, thus neutralizing it. See Thomas F. Walton and James Langenfeld, "Regulatory Reform under Reagan—The Right Way and the Wrong Way," in *Regulation and the Reagan Era*, p. 57.

54. U.S., *Hearings on Regulatory Procedures Act of 1981*, p. 280.
55. These include FCC's Office of Plans and Policy, the Office of Engineering and Technology, the Office of General Counsel, the Office of the Managing Director, and the Information Resources Branch.
56. Interview by the author with Terry D. Johnson, June 27, 1988.
57. Quoted in "Independent Agencies—Independent from Whom?", p. 500.
58. Carro interview.
59. Interview with Treasury official.
60. Alliance for Justice, "Contempt for Law," p. 8.
61. 21 U.S.C. §348(c)(3)(A) (1982).
62. Bryner, *Bureaucratic Discretion*, p. 188.
63. Tolchin and Tolchin, *Dismantling America*, p. 80.
64. Funke interview.
65. Interview by the author with John F. Gallivan, Public Health Service regulation officer, June 28, 1988.
66. Alliance for Justice, "Contempt for Law," p. 8.
67. *Aqua Slide 'N' Dive v. Consumer Product Safety Commission*, 569 F. 2d 831 (5th Cir. 1978). See also Rogowsky, "Sub Rosa Regulation," p. 211, and Bryner, *Bureaucratic Discretion*, pp. 148–49, 152, 154–55.
68. Fuchs, *Institutionalizing Cost-Benefit Analysis*, p. 178.
69. Reagan-era ICC chairman Heather J. Gradison's renomination encountered resistance in the Senate from senators who objected to the deficient implementation of deregulation. Her apparently imminent defeat motivated her to resign instead. "ICC Chairman Quits, Avoids Reconfirmation Fight," Associated Press report printed in *Florida Times-Union*, May 26, 1989, p. A-22.
70. Fuchs, *Institutionalizing Cost-Benefit Analysis*, p. 178.
71. *New England Coalition on Nuclear Pollution v. Nuclear Regulatory Commission*, 727 F. 2d 1127 (D.C.Cir. 1984). The court found the NRC's action arbitrary and capricious. Ibid., p. 1130.
72. Interview by the author with FCC official.
73. See, e.g., *United Steelworkers of America v. John A. Pendergrass [II]*, 855 F. 2d 108 (3d Cir. 1988).
74. See chapter 3.
75. Interview by the author with economic regulatory commission official.
76. FCC Rules, part 73.

77. Interview by the author with anonymous official. See also Norman Blank, "Reagan-Fowler Meeting in Fall Held 'Improper,'" *Washington Post*, February 3, 1984, pp. D1–D2, and photo in *Washington Post*, February 9, 1984, p. B6.
78. Wood and Waterman, "The Dynamics of Political Control," p. 823.
79. Bryner, *Bureaucratic Discretion*, p. 67.
80. U.S., *Hearing on Oversight of the Office of Management and Budget Regulatory Review and Planning Process*, pp. 251–52.
81. Interview by the author with Lawrence J. DeNardis, November 19, 1986. DeNardis was exasperated by OMB's interference in an annual revision by the secretary of HHS of Diagnostic-Related Group (DRG) reimbursements based on the Health Care Financing Administration's prospective-pricing plan. When OMB, which wanted no increase at all, vetoed the secretary's intention to increase DRG rates by 1.5 to 2.0 percent in the spring of 1986, a compromise settlement of 0.5 percent was reached. However, Congress was lobbied by the hospital industry and it terminated the secretary's power to set DRG reimbursement rates. DeNardis complained that, "because of OMB meddling, the secretary lost his most strategic role for 'making a difference'" in terms of correcting inefficiency.
82. Interview by the author with Jo Anne B. Barnhart, November 12, 1986.
83. Delaney interview.
84. Walton and Langenfeld, "Regulatory Reform under Reagan—The Right Way and the Wrong Way," pp. 41, 57.
85. White interview.
86. Interview by the author with OIRA desk officer.
87. U.S., *Hearing on Oversight of the Office of Management and Budget Regulatory Review and Planning Process*, p. 250.
88. U.S., *Hearings on EPA's Asbestos Regulations*, p. 3.
89. James L. Sundquist's presentation to American Society for Public Administration's National Capital Area Chapter, November 18, 1986.
90. Interview by the author with Richard A. Eisenger, December 24, 1987.
91. OMB officials have characterized OMB as a mere "watchpuppy," according to Marshall R. Goodman in a presentation related to his paper, "A Kinder and Gentler Regulatory Reform."
92. Jacobs interview.
93. Interview with HHS official.
94. Interview with OSHA official.
95. Interview with HHS official.
96. Quoted in Reagan, *Regulation*, p. 165.
97. Interview with Barry J. White, June 22, 1988.
98. Interview with FCC official.
99. Quoted in Reagan, *Regulation*, pp. 161–62.
100. McGarity's interview of April 23, 1984, with Houston, cited in McGarity, "Regulatory Analysis and Regulatory Reform," *Texas Law Review* 65 (June 1987): 1243–1333, at 1269.

101. Ibid., pp. 1264–65, 1269, 1330. McGarity's observations were echoed by Judith Segal, director of the Policy and Programs Planning Staff, USDA Food Safety and Inspection Service, in McGarity's interview of March 15, 1984, cited ibid., p. 1265.
102. McGarity's interview of April 4, 1983, with Patrick H. Cody, acting director, Regulatory Impact and Executive Correspondence Staff, Program Planning and Development, USDA Agricultural Stabilization and Conservation Service, cited ibid., p. 1263.
103. Scalia and Brunsdale, "Deregulation HQ," p. 22.
104. Christopher C. DeMuth in U.S., *Hearings on Office of Management and Budget Control of* OSHA *Rulemaking*, p. 315.
105. U.S., *Regulatory Program of the United States Government, April 1, 1987–March 31, 1988*, p. xxi.
106. Jacobs interview.
107. Fairchild interview.
108. Plager interview.
109. *Hearings on* EPA*'s Asbestos Regulations*, p. 28.
110. Carro interview.
111. Olson, "The Quiet Shift of Power," p. 41.
112. Ibid., p. 50.
113. Funke interview.
114. Goodman and Wrightson, *Managing Regulatory Reform*, p. 73.
115. Quoted in Howard Ball, "Presidential Control of the Federal Bureaucracy," in *Federal Administrative Agencies*, p. 222.
116. Bryner, *Bureaucratic Discretion*, pp. 188, 191, 197.
117. Ibid., p. 157.
118. Gail Bingham and James Laue, "Disagreeing About the Rules: Negotiation and Mediation," EPA *Journal*, March 1988, pp. 17–19. See also Daniel J. Fiorino, "Regulatory Negotiation as a Policy Process," *Public Administration Review* 48 (July/August 1988): 764–72.
119. Charles E. Ludlam, "Undermining Public Protections: The Reagan Administration Regulatory Program" (Washington, D.C.: Alliance for Justice, 1981), p. 33.
120. Bryner, *Bureaucratic Discretion*, p. 143.
121. See, e.g., Steiner and Steiner, *Business, Government, and Society*, p. 166. A memorable case study about the "right to comply" is S. Prakash Sethi, "Sears Roebuck and Company versus Attorney General of the United States," in *Up Against the Corporate Wall*, 4th ed., ed. S. Prakash Sethi (Englewood Cliffs, N.J.: Prentice-Hall, 1982), pp. 330–64.
122. Interview by the author with Jefferson B. Hill, chief of the Commerce and Lands Branch, OIRA, November 26, 1991.
123. "The result of [OSHA's] approach to safety regulation [during its first two years] is that the agencies have all too often set standards for what seem to be frivolous hazards." Nina Cornell, Roger Noll, and Barry Weingast, "Regulating Safety," in *Setting National Priorities*, ed. Henry Owens and Charles Schultze (Washington, D.C.: Brookings Institution, 1976), p. 502. OSHA's and President Carter's term for non-

sense regulations was "nitpicking rules," and steps were taken in 1978 to eliminate nearly one thousand of them at OSHA. President Carter's Regulatory Reform Message, March 26, 1979, rpt. in *Regulatory Reform Legislation*, part 1, p. 164. Objecting to Federal Trade Commission plans to impose new restrictions on television advertisements aimed at children, *The Washington Post*, on March 1, 1978, editorialized that the commission had become the "National Nanny." See also Steiner and Steiner, *Business, Government, and Society*, p. 165.

124. Bryner, *Bureaucratic Discretion*, p. 144.
125. McGarity, "Regulatory Analysis and Regulatory Review," pp. 1263–65, 1269, 1330.

CHAPTER 6

1. See, e.g., Joel D. Aberbach, *Keeping a Watchful Eye: The Politics of Congressional Oversight* (Washington, D.C.: Brookings Institution, 1990); Morris P. Fiorina, *Congress: Keystone of the Washington Establishment*, 2d ed. (New Haven: Yale University Press, 1989); Joseph P. Harris, *Congressional Control of Administration* (Washington, D.C.: Brookings Institution, 1964); and Morris S. Ogul, *Congress Oversees the Bureaucracy: Studies in Legislative Supervision* (Pittsburgh: University of Pittsburgh Press, 1976).
2. Rourke, *Bureaucracy, Politics, and Public Policy*, p. 43. See also idem, "Presidentializing the Bureaucracy: From Kennedy to Reagan," in *The Managerial Presidency*, ed. Pfiffner, p. 125.
3. Harris, *Congressional Control of Administration*, pp. 279, 284–94.
4. Michael W. Kirst, *Government without Passing Laws: Congress's Nonstatutory Techniques for Appropriations Control* (Chapel Hill: University of North Carolina Press, 1969), p. 193. Indeed, no verbal cue seems to be necessary at all. "Should discontinuities occur between legislative preferences and bureaucratic activities, Congress controls resources, legislation, and appointments. Bureaucracies are aware of this and are cautious to avoid alienating legislative principals. Thus Congress does not have to engage in active and continuous oversight to [effect] political control. Rather, 'anticipative responses' assure that administrative decisions will be consistent with congressional preferences." Wood and Waterman, "The Dynamics of Political Control," p. 803.
5. Harris, *Congressional Control of Administration*, p. 2.
6. See *Immigration and Naturalization Service v. Chadha et al.*, 462 U.S. 919, 942 n. 13 (1983).
7. Barbara Hinkson Craig, *Chadha: Story of an Epic Constitutional Struggle* (New York: Oxford University Press, 1988), pp. 149–50 and 160.
8. Martin D. Kohout, "Absence of Legislative Veto Has Unexpected Result," *PA Times*, April 29, 1988, p. 1.
9. 462 U.S. 919 (1983).
10. West and Cooper, "Legislative Influence v. Presidential Dominance," p. 593.
11. Chadha, p. 953 n. 16.

12. Plocher interview.
13. Louis Fisher, "Judicial Misjudgments About the Lawmaking Process: The Legislative Veto Case," *Public Administration Review* 45 (November 1985): 706. For further discussion about the evolution of the character of legislative vetoes after the Chadha decision, see Barbara Hinkson Craig, "Wishing the Legislative Veto Back: A False Hope for Executive Flexibility," in *The Fettered Presidency: Legal Constraints on the Executive Branch*, ed. L. Gordon Crovitz and Jeremy A. Rabkin (Washington, D.C.: American Enterprise Institute for Public Policy Research, 1989), p. 195.
14. Quoted in Kohout, "Absence of Legislative Veto," p. 1.
15. Crovitz and Rabkin, "Introduction," in Crovitz and Rabkin, ed., *The Fettered Presidency*, p. 1. But, in the same volume, Fisher denies that micromanagement is a new phenomenon, instead tracing it back to the beginning of the republic. "Micromanagement is a relatively new word to express a very old complaint: intervention by Congress in administrative details." Fisher, "Micromanagement by Congress: Reality and Mythology," p. 139.
16. U.S., White House, *Regulatory Reform: President Carter's Program* (1980), p. 1, quoted in Ball, ed., *Federal Administrative Agencies*, p. 2.
17. American Bar Association spokesperson Lloyd N. Cutler maintained that Congress should willingly divest its power to veto regulations and should cede it to the president, explaining that Congress would never have delegated regulatory authority away if it were capable of shaping regulatory policy. Quoted in U.S., Congress, Senate, Committee on the Judiciary, Subcommittee on Administrative Practice and Procedure, *Hearings on Administrative Procedure Act Amendments of 1978*, 95th Cong., 2d sess., Sept. 12, 13, 20, and 21, 1978, p. 349. Brookings Institution economist Lester B. Lave criticized congressional attempts to write detailed regulations into statutes (as in the automobile emission standards of the Clean Air Act). Quoted in U.S., *Hearings on Regulatory Reform Legislation of 1981*, p. 245. Bryner characterized congressional oversight as "ad hoc and sporadic, unlike the routinized nature of White House oversight." Bryner, *Bureaucratic Discretion*, p. 204.
18. Plager interview.
19. Quoted in Charles O. Jones, "Meeting Low Expectations: Strategy and Prospects of the Bush Presidency," in *The Bush Presidency*, ed. Campbell and Rockman, p. 58.
20. Foreman, *Signals From the Hill*, pp. 146–47.
21. Robert S. Gilmour, "Congressional Oversight: The Paradox of Fragmentation and Control," *The Bureaucrat* 10 (Fall 1981): 38.
22. James L. Sundquist, "Congress and the President: Enemies or Partners?" in *Congress Reconsidered*, 1st ed., ed. Lawrence C. Dodd and Bruce I. Oppenheimer (New York: Praeger Publishers, 1977), pp. 222–43. See also idem, *The Decline and Resurgence of Congress* (Washington, D.C.: Brookings Institution, 1981), pp. 156–58, 369–72, 397–98, 427–39, 447–56.
23. See, e.g., Kirst, *Government without Passing Laws*, pp. 132–33.
24. One example is a demand by Representative Joe Evins (D-Tenn.) that Federal Trade

Commission chairman Caspar Weinberger protect the interests of three commission employees affiliated with Evins's "old-boy network." In an act of defiance rarely seen in such interactions, Weinberger reacted by summarily firing the employees. See Randy I. Bellows, "A Failing Agency: The Federal Trade Commission," in *Public Management in a Democratic Society*, ed. Robert B. Reich (Englewood Cliffs, N.J.: Prentice-Hall, 1990), pp. 134–36.

25. Christopher H. Pyle and Richard M. Pious, *The President, Congress, and the Constitution* (New York: Free Press, 1984), pp. 156–57.
26. Louis Fisher, *The Politics of Shared Power: Congress and the Executive* (Washington, D.C.: Congressional Quarterly Press, 1981), pp. 108–09.
27. U.S., *Hearings on Regulatory Reform Legislation*, part 1, p. 269.
28. McLain interview.
29. Goodman and Wrightson, *Managing Regulatory Reform*, p. 20.
30. Eads and Fix, *Relief or Reform?*, p. 255.
31. U.S., *Hearings on* EPA*'s Asbestos Regulations*, 427.
32. See Craig, *Chadha*, pp. 215, 222–23.
33. U.S., Congress, Senate, Committee on Governmental Affairs, Subcommittee on Energy, Nuclear Proliferation, and Governmental Processes, *Hearing on Federal Regulation*, part 3, 97th Cong., 1st sess., July 2, 1981, p. 115.
34. U.S., *Hearing on Role of* OMB *in Regulation*, p. 7.
35. Seidman and Gilmour, *Politics, Position, and Power*, pp. 142–43.
36. *Public Citizen Health Group et al. v. Tyson*, 796 F. 2d 1479 (D.C. Cir. 1986).
37. Plocher interview.
38. OMB Watch, "Regulatory Review: OMB's New Public Disclosure Rules" (Washington, D.C.: OMB Watch, June 24, 1986), p. 3.
39. Plocher interview.
40. Goodman and Wrightson, *Managing Regulatory Reform*, pp. 192–93.
41. Quoted in OMB Watch, "Paperwork Reduction," p. 3.
42. Interview by the author with Roger L. Sperry, former professional staff member, Senate Governmental Affairs Committee, November 7, 1988.
43. Interview by the author with Margaret T. Wrightson, October 9, 1991.
44. Plocher interview.
45. OMB Watch, "Regulatory Review: OMB's New Public Disclosure Rules," p. 3.
46. Sperry interview.
47. Goodman and Wrightson, *Managing Regulatory Reform*, pp. 192–93.
48. The memorandum is rpt. in U.S.,*Regulatory Program of the United States Government, April 1, 1987–March 31, 1988*, pp. 605–07.
49. Chiles said,

> The Committee amendment to require advise [*sic*] and consent of the Senate in the selection of the Administrator of OIRA is designed to strengthen accountability to Congress. During development of the 1980 Paperwork

> Act the Senate agreed to President Carter's request to drop the idea of Senate confirmation of the head of OIRA in exchange for his support of a separate authorization and appropriation account for the office's activities. This administration chose not to abide by what I regard the language of the act to mandate. A separate appropriation account consistent with the separate authorization has not yet been created. In addition, the issue of how resources have been used and what resources are needed to accomplish the ambitious strategy Congress incorporated in the 1980 Act has been a point of continuing contention between the administration and OIRA's oversight committees in the House and Senate. The 1986 amendments will require Presidential appointment and Senate confirmation of the head of OIRA in the future. They retain the language which I believe mandates a separate appropriations account. They also require a reporting by function of how resources are to be used by OIRA which will be tied to the annual budget process. Accountability to Congress will be strengthened by these steps.

U.S., Congress, Senate, Committee on Governmental Affairs, *Federal Management Reorganization and Cost Control Act of 1986*, Calendar No. 744, S.Rept. 99-347, July 31 (legislative day July 28), 1986, pp. 123–24.

50. OMB Watch, "Regulatory Review: OMB's New Public Disclosure Rules," cover page.
51. Ibid., p. 5.
52. Ibid., pp. 7, 9.
53. According to Robert S. Gilmour, a professional staff member in the Senate Governmental Affairs Committee, some negotiations involved Gramm and the committee's staff, while others involved OMB director Miller and Senators Roth and Mark O. Hatfield (R-Ore.). Communication with author, October 1991.
54. *Statutes at Large* 100 (1986): 1783-317.
55. Goodman and Wrightson, *Managing Regulatory Reform*, p. 194.
56. Gramm interview.
57. *Statutes at Large* 98 (1984): 3221.
58. Funke interview; and Miles-McLean interview. As an example of a "deadline hammer," see *U.S. Code*, title 42, §6924(f)(3) (1988), rpt. from *Statutes at Large* 98 (1984): 3221, 3229.
59. Rollins interview.
60. Roger G. Noll, "Regulation After Reagan," *Regulation* 12, 3 (1988): 13–14.
61. U.S., *Office of Management and Budget Influence on Agency Regulations*, p. v.
62. U.S., *Hearings on Office of Management and Budget: Evolving Roles and Future Issues*, p. ix.
63. Miller vowed that the administration would continue to review regulations even if OIRA were gutted legislatively. "We will do it [regulatory review] in the White House. If [Congress takes] the office out of the White House, we will do it in the Justice Department. If [Congress takes] the office out of the Justice Department, we will do

it in Commerce." Quoted in OMB Watch, "Paperwork Reduction: The Quick Fix of 1986," p. 4.

64. Fairchild interview.
65. U.S., *Hearings on Reauthorization of OMB's Office of Information and Regulatory Affairs*, p. 10.
66. Ibid., p. 11.
67. U.S. Congress, Senate, Committee on Governmental Affairs, *Regulatory Review Sunsine Act*, 102d Cong., 2d sess., February 25 (legislative day January 30), 1992, S.Rept. 102-256, p. 2.
68. U.S., Congress, Senate, *Journal of the Senate of the United States*, 101st Cong., 1st sess., p. H-29.
69. Goodman, "A Kinder and Gentler Regulatory Reform," pp. 24–26.
70. "The Reregulation President" [editorial], *Wall Street Journal*, June 17, 1991, p. A10.
71. Elizabeth A. Palmer, "White House War on Red Tape: Success Hard to Gauge," *Congressional Quarterly Weekly Report*, May 2, 1992, p. 1156.
72. Robert D. Hershey Jr., "Quayle Says Rules Review Saving U.S. $10 Billion," *New York Times*, April 3, 1992, p. A16.
73. Morrison, "OMB Interference with Agency Rulemaking," pp. 1071–72.
74. Paul R. Verkuil, "Jawboning Administrative Agencies," pp. 988–89.
75. James T. O'Reilly and Phyllis E. Brown, "In Search of Excellence: A Prescription for the Future of OMB Oversight of Rules," *Administrative Law Review* 39 (Fall 1987): 443.

CHAPTER 7

1. See, e.g., *Goldberg v. Kelly*, 397 U.S. 254 (1970); *Matthews v. Eldridge*, 424 U.S. 319 (1976); *Office of Communications of United Church of Christ v. FCC*, 359 F. 2d 994 (D.C.Cir. 1966); *Home Box Office, Inc. v. FCC*, 567 F. 2d 9 (D.C.Cir.), cert. denied, 434 U.S. 829 (1977).
2. In *United States v. Florida East Coast Ry. Co*, 410 U.S. 224 (1973), the court ruled that the Interstate Commerce Commission—which had been in the habit of conducting formal proceedings for rule making but had recently reverted to informal notice and comment procedures—was acting appropriately pursuant to the Interstate Commerce Act. In *Vermont Yankee Nuclear Power Corp. v. Natural Resources Defense Council, Inc.*, 453 U.S. 519 (1978), the court rebuked the Court of Appeals for the D.C. Circuit for "engrafting [its] own notions of proper procedures upon agencies entrusted with substantive functions by Congress."
3. To use Richard Funston's language, the Supreme Court's "yea-saying" power is more important than its "nay-saying" power. Funston, "The Supreme Court and Critical Elections," *American Political Science Review* 69 (September 1975): 809.
4. *Field v. Clark*, 143 U.S. 649, 692 (1892).
5. *Wayman v. Southard*, 23 U.S. (10 Wheat.) 1, 43 (1825).
6. *Houston, East and West Ry. v. United States*, 234 U.S. 342, 355 (1914).

7. *A. L. A. Schechter Poultry Corp. v. United States*, 295 U.S. 495 (1935).
8. *Gray v. Powell*, 314 U.S. 402, 412 (1941).
9. *Amalgamated Meat Cutters and Butcher Workmen of North America v. Connally*, 337 F. Supp. 737, 755 (D.D.C. 1971).
10. Fleishman and Aufses, "Law and Orders," p. 25.
11. Lowi, *The End of Liberalism*, pp. 297–98.
12. Kenneth Culp Davis, *Administrative Law Treatise*, 2d ed. (San Diego, Calif.: By the author, 1978), 1:151, 153, 206–08. Davis cites approvingly a New York case in which a state court ruled that "an administrative agency is forbidden from exercising its discretionary power without first detailing standards or guides to govern the exercise of that discretion." *Nicholas v. Kahn*, 47 N.Y.2d 24, 389 N.E. 2d 1086, 1091 (1979). Quoted in Davis, *1982 Supplement to Administrative Law Treatise* (San Diego, Calif.: K. C. Davis Pub. Co., 1982), p. 24.
13. In *Arizona v. California*, 373 U.S. 546, 626 (1963), Justice John M. Harland, joined by Justices Potter Stewart and William O. Douglas, warned that delegation may amount to "unrestrained authority" raising "the gravest constitutional doubts." According to OMB Watch senior attorney David Plocher, Chief Justice William H. Rehnquist has written dissenting opinions that appear to suggest a return to the Schechter rule. Plocher interview.
14. Theodore L. Becker, *The Impact of Supreme Court Decisions* (New York: Oxford University Press, 1969), p. 18. In the second edition (1973), Becker took note of friction between President Richard M. Nixon and the Warren Court on issues of civil liberties. The Nixon and Reagan court appointments neutralized the ideologically oriented source of friction in the Reagan and Bush administrations.
15. *Immigration and Naturalization Service v. Chadha* 462 U.S. 919 (1983).
16. McLain interview. Craig and Gilmour state that "in the late-1980s, the court signaled a possible retreat from any . . . presumption that it would stand guardian at the boundaries of constitutional departments. . . . The court now defers to self-enforcement of the political system in separation-of-powers decisions." Barbara Hinkson Craig and Robert S. Gilmour, "The Constitution and Accountability for *Public* Functions," *Governance: An International Journal of Policy and Administration* 5 (January 1992): 50. They cite *Morrison v. Olson*, 487 U.S. 654 (1988); *Humphrey v. Baker*, 848 F. 2d 811 (D.C.Cir. 1988); and *Mistretta v. United States*, 488 U.S. 361 (1989).
17. See, e.g., *Myers v. United States*, 272 U.S. 52 (1926); *Buckley v. Valeo*, 424 U.S. 1 (1976); *Northern Pipeline Construction Co. v. Marathon Pipe Line Co.*, 458 U.S. 50 (1982); *Bowsher v. Synar*, 478 U.S. 714 (1986); and the *Chadha* decision.
18. See, e.g., *Rathbun ("Humphrey's Executor") v. United States*, 295 U.S. 602 (1935); *Wiener v. United States*, 357 U.S. 349 (1958); *Nixon v. Administrator of General Services*, 433 U.S. 425 (1977); *Thomas v. Union Carbide Agric. Prod. Co.*, 473 U.S. 568 (1985); and *Commodity Futures Trading Commission v. Schor*, 478 U.S. 833 (1986).
19. Morton Rosenberg, "Congress's Prerogative Over Agencies," 631, 643–44. Entin writes, "The limited utility of judicial review in legislative-executive conflicts has been

demonstrated numerous times.... Some commentators, most notably Dean [Jesse H.] Choper, have suggested that the judiciary refrain from deciding constitutional conflicts between Congress and the President." Jonathan L. Entin, "Congress, the President, and the Separation of Powers: Rethinking the Value of Litigation," *Administrative Law Review* 43 (Winter 1991): 33–35. Choper's analysis appears in his book, *Judicial Review and the National Political Process: A Functional Reconsideration of the Role of the Supreme Court* (Chicago: University of Chicago Press, 1980), pp. 260–379.

20. Bryner, *Bureaucratic Discretion*, p. 204. Note, however, that evidence from the judiciary's meticulous review of the Federal Energy Regulatory Commission's natural gas regulations establishes a case study of unusually insistent judicial demands for unattainable analytical standards. An energy shortage in the 1990s with extensive implications for the economy is on the horizon, according to Richard J. Pierce Jr., "The Unintended Effects of Judicial Review of Agency Rules: How Federal Courts Have Contributed to the Electricity Crises of the 1990s," *Administrative Law Review* 43 (Winter 1991): 7, 22–23, 26.
21. Judge David Bazelon of the United States Court of Appeals for the District of Columbia Circuit announced the dawning of "a new era in the history of the long and fruitful collaboration of administrative agencies and reviewing courts," in which courts would demand more procedural guarantees. *Environmental Defense Fund v. Ruckelshaus*, 439 F. 2d 584, 598 (D.C.Cir. 1971). The "partnership metaphor" was described in Daniel D. Polsby, "*F.C.C. v. National Citizens Committee for Broadcasting* and the Judicious Use of Administrative Discretion," in *The Supreme Court Review, 1978*, ed. Philip B. Kurland and Gerhard Casper (Chicago: University of Chicago Press, 1978), p. 34.
22. *Sierra Club v. Costle*, 657 F. 2d 298, 405–406 (D.C.Cir. 1981).
23. John D. Ehrlichman, Nixon's assistant to the president for domestic affairs, complained, "We only see them [political appointees] at the annual White House Christmas party; they go off and marry the natives." Quoted in Richard P. Nathan, *The Plot That Failed*, p. 40. The generic concept of "going native"—i.e., "becoming influenced by people on the wrong side of the organizational boundary"—is described in Daniel Katz and Robert L. Kahn, *The Social Psychology of Organizations* (New York: John Wiley, 1966), p. 51.
24. Alan B. Morrison, "Presidential Intervention in Informal Rulemaking: Striking the Proper Balance," *Tulane Law Review* 56 (April 1982): 897–902. The direct quotation appears p. 890. The "procedural interventionist" approach was proposed by the ABA's Committee on Law and the Economy and approved by the ABA annual meeting in August 1979. See also Cutler, "The Case for Presidential Intervention," pp. 830–48.
25. Bryner, *Bureaucratic Discretion*, pp. 204–05.
26. Plocher interview.
27. Plocher interview, updated on November 26, 1991.
28. U.S., *Study on Federal Regulation* 5:27.
29. The case of *Kendall v. United States*, 36 U.S. (12 Pet.) 524 (1838), barred a presi-

dential order which would have restrained the postmaster general from executing a legislative duty. The case of *Accord, United States ex rel. v. Shaughnessy*, 374 U.S. 260 (1954), establishes that the president cannot always "override or revise the officer's interpretation of his statutory duty."

30. Strauss emphasizes the president's prerogative to "require the Opinion, in writing, of the principal Officer in each of the Executive Departments." Art. 2, §2, part 1, of the Constitution, discussed in Peter L. Strauss, "The Place of Agencies in Government: Separation of Powers and the Fourth Branch," *Columbia Law Review* 84 (April 1984): 648–50, 662–67. According to Itzhak Zamir, the president's authority to control the branch he heads was established with the acquiescence of the other two branches in the second half of the nineteenth century. Itzhak Zamir, "Administrative Control of Administration Action," *California Law Review* 57 (October 1969): 867, 873. Cross maintains that a structural analysis of the Constitution forbids any conclusion that either Congress or the agencies might possess rule-making authority, and by process of elimination, calls for the conclusion that the authority belongs to the president. Frank B. Cross, "Executive Orders 12,291 and 12,498," *The Journal of Law and Politics* 4 (Winter 1988): 504–05.
31. *Chevron, U.S.A., Inc., v. Natural Resources Defense Council, Inc.*, 467 U.S. 837, 865 (1984).
32. Remarks by Chief Judge Patricia Wald in "The Contribution of the D.C. Circuit to Administrative Law," *Administrative Law Review* 40 (Fall 1988): 519.
33. *International Ladies' Garment Workers Union v. Donovan*, 722 F. 2d 795, 828 (D.C.Cir. 1983).
34. *American Textile Manufacturers Institute v. Donovan, Secretary of Labor*, 452 U.S. 490 (1981).
35. Ball, *Controlling Regulatory Sprawl*, p. 89.
36. Robert V. Zener, "The 'Cotton Dust' Standard," *Legal Times*, July 13, 1981, p. 13.
37. *Lead Industries Ass'n. v. Environmental Protection Agency*, 647 F. 2d 1130, 1150 (D.C.Cir. 1980), cert. denied, 449 U.S. 1042 (1980).
38. Cases reaffirming the supremacy of the statutory deadlines include *State of Illinois v. Gorsuch*, 530 F. Supp. 340 (D.D.C. 1981); *Sierra Club v. Gorsuch*, 551 F. Supp. 785 (N.D.Cal. 1982); *Environmental Defense Fund v. Gorsuch*, 713 F. 2d 802 (D.C.Cir. 1983); *State of New York v. Gorsuch*, 554 F. Supp. 1060 (S.D.N.Y. 1983); and *Natural Resources Defense Council v. Ruckelshaus*, 14 ELR 20817, 21 ERC 1953 (United States District Court, D.D.C., September 14, 1984). In *Environmental Defense Fund v. Lee M. Thomas, Administrator, U.S. Environmental Protection Agency, et al.*, 627 F. Supp. 566 (D.D.C. 1986), Judge Thomas A. Flannery objected that OIRA was violating section 8(a)(2) of EO 12291—the provision declaring that the order is invalid for purposes that violate statutes—by holding up proposed regulations beyond statutory deadlines for issuance of the rules.
39. *Meyer v. Bush*, Civil Action No. 88-3112 (1991).
40. William A. Niskanen, "Straws in the Wind," *Regulation* 15 (Spring 1992): 9.

41. Steve Bronstein, "OSHA air-quality rules toppled," *Atlanta Journal-Constitution*, July 9, 1992, p. E1.
42. Rosemary O'Leary, "The Impact of Federal Court Decisions on the Policies and Administration of the U.S. Environmental Protection Agency," *Administrative Law Review* 41 (Fall 1989): 565.
43. West and Cooper express the skeptical view toward presidential control of regulation.

> Although it has offered clear and expedient prescriptions, the use of separation of powers to justify presidential hegemony within the administrative process has proved intellectually unsatisfying to many. The heart of the problem is that the concept itself becomes extremely arbitrary without a functional basis for differentiating institutional roles. Given that agency rulemaking often involves balancing important social interests subject to few if any substantive constraints, for example, the formalistic argument that all power automatically becomes executive once delegated becomes an appeal to blind faith in which governmental activities are defined according to who performs them.

West and Cooper, "Legislative Influence v. Presidential Dominance," p. 593.

44. Rosenberg notes that judicial decisions may be most sweeping in their impact in separation of powers cases that take a "rigid" approach centering on "one dominant feature of the relationship" between branches. But we also know that courts are cognizant of the merits of judicial restraint, which is a disincentive to the courts to make "tough calls" in separation of powers cases. Apparently, the court is capable of delivering a decision of extensive consequences, but may know enough to pick its issues carefully. Rosenberg, "Congress's Prerogative Over Agencies and Agency Decisionmakers," p. 30, and McLain interview.
45. An example is the report of the Brownlow Committee, cited in chapter 5.
46. See James L. Sundquist, *The Decline and Resurgence of Congress* (Washington, D.C.: Brookings Institution, 1981), pp. 66–67. Tabulating the cognitive approach and policy-making behavior of the three branches of the national government, David H. Rosenbloom recognizes that only the executive branch is guided by the rational-scientific approach and rational-comprehensive behavior. Patricia W. Ingraham and David H. Rosenbloom, "Political Foundations of the American Federal Service: Rebuilding a Crumbling Base," *Public Administration Review* 50 (March/April 1990): 211–12. The other two branches may have recognized the special capacity of the executive branch.

CHAPTER 8

1. National Materials Advisory Board, *Pneumatic Dust Control in Grain Elevators: Guidelines for Design Operation and Management* (Washington, D.C.: National Academy Press, 1982), p. v.

2. Quoted in written testimony by Deborah Berkowitz, director of safety and health, Food and Allied Services Trade Department, AFL-CIO, in U.S., *Hearing on Oversight of the Office of Management and Budget Regulatory Review and Planning Process.* See also *Through the Corridors of Power: A Guide to Federal Rulemaking* (Washington, D.C.: OMB Watch, 1987), p. 38.
3. *Through the Corridors of Power*, p. 37.
4. Ibid., p. 38.
5. W. Kip Viscusi, "Reforming OSHA Regulation of Workplace Risks," in *Regulatory Reform: What Actually Happened*, ed. Leonard W. Weiss and Michael W. Klass (Boston: Little, Brown and Company, 1986), p. 252.
6. Berkowitz testimony in U.S., *Hearing on Oversight of the Office of Management and Budget Regulatory Review and Planning Process*, p. 49.
7. *Through the Corridors of Power*, p. 38.
8. Quoted in testimony by Dr. Kendall W. Keith, National Grain and Feed Association, OSHA hearing, Kansas City, Mo., June 1984, p. 8.
9. W. Kip Viscusi, *Risk By Choice: Regulating Health and Safety in the Workplace* (Cambridge: Harvard University Press, 1983).
10. Testimony by Larry Jackson, secretary/treasurer of the International Union of the American Federation of Grain Millers, in U.S., *Hearing on Oversight of the Office of Management and Budget Regulatory Review and Planning Process*, p. 6.
11. Berkowitz testimony, ibid., pp. 3–4, 49.
12. Quoted in Keith testimony, p. 8.
13. [Keith Mestrich], Food and Allied Services Trades Department, AFL-CIO, "Grain Dust Fires and Explosions," undated (written May 1989), pp. 4–8.
14. *Federal Register* 52 (December 31, 1987): 49592.
15. *National Grain and Feed Association v. Occupational Safety and Health Administration*, 858 F. 2d 1019 (5th Cir. 1988), amended and superseded, 866 F. 2d 717 (5th Cir. 1989).
16. NGFA *v.* OSHA, 858 F. 2d 1019 (5th Cir. 1988).
17. NGFA *v.* OSHA, 866 F. 2d 717 (5th Cir. 1989).
18. Interview by the author with Keith Mestrich, director of safety and health, AFL-CIO's Foods and Allied Services Trades (FAST) Department, August 16, 1989.
19. NGFA *v.* OSHA, 903 F. 2d 308 (5th Cir. 1990).
20. Interview with Thomas H. Seymour, September 4, 1990.
21. Interview with David C. Vladeck, attorney, Public Citizen Litigation Group, August 27, 1990.
22. Seymour interview, September 4, 1990.
23. Data as of August 16, 1989, provided to the author by the USDA's Federal Grain Inspection Service for the period 1981–1989 showed a decreasing rate of explosions and casualties. The improvement is attributed to industry's own program of improved operations and safer equipment.
24. *U.S. Code* [U.S.C.], title 42, §§9601–9657 (1982 & Supp. III 1985).
25. CERCLA §221, 42 U.S.C. §9631.

26. Executive Orders 12286 and 12316, rpt. in 3 C.F.R., 1981 comp., pp. 119, 168.
27. 40 C.F.R. 300, 47 Fed. Reg. 31180 (July 16, 1982), later revised.
28. See 40 C.F.R. part 300, App. B (1985). See also William Funk, "Federal and State Superfunds: Cooperative Federalism or Federal Preemption," *Environmental Law* 16 (Fall 1985): 1–2, 9.
29. 52 Fed. Reg. 11513 (April 9, 1987).
30. 53 Fed. Reg. 51961–52082 (December 23, 1988).
31. 55 Fed. Reg. 51532 (December 14, 1990), at 51567–69.
32. 42 U.S.C. §§1857–1857l (1976).
33. 42 U.S.C. §1857c-6.
34. Don R. Goodwin, memorandum to Sheldon Myers, "NSPS Meeting at Office of Management and Budget on November 19, 1982," EPA, December 3, 1982.
35. Rourke, "Executive Responsiveness to Presidential Policies," p. 7.
36. Lettie M. Wenner, *The Environmental Decade in Court* (Bloomington: Indiana University Press, 1982).

CHAPTER 9

1. U.S., Office of Management and Budget, *Regulatory Program of the United States Government, April 1, 1988–March 31, 1989* (Washington, D.C.: GPO, September 1988), pp. 16–22.
2. U.S., Office of Management and Budget, *Regulatory Program of the United States Government, April 1, 1990–March 31, 1991* (Washington, D.C.: GPO, Aug. 3, 1990), p. 6.
3. Elizabeth Sanders, "The Presidency and the Bureaucratic State," in *The Presidency and the Political System*, ed. Michael Nelson (Washington, D.C.: Congressional Quarterly Press, 1988), p. 400.
4. Hugh Heclo, "Issue Networks and the Executive Establishment," in *The New American Political System*, ed. Anthony King (Washington, D.C.: American Enterprise Institute for Public Policy Research, 1978), pp. 88, 102–05.
5. The term has been used by R. Shep Melnick, "The Politics of Partnership," *Public Administration Review* 45 (November 1985): 658.
6. Paul R. Verkuil, "Welcome to the Constantly Evolving Field of Administrative Law," *Administrative Law Review* 42 (Winter 1990): 2.
7. Hubert Treiber defends the assertion that regulatory policy is generally in a state of crisis in "Crisis in Regulatory Policy?" *Contemporary Crises* 9 (July 1985): 256.
8. Goodman and Wrightson, *Managing Regulatory Reform*, p. 210.
9. Martin Mayer, *The Greatest-Ever Bank Robbery: The Collapse of the Savings and Loan Industry* (New York: Charles Scribner's Sons, 1990), p. 1.
10. Howard Kurtz, "Asleep at the Switch: How the Media Bungled the Story and Contributed to the S&L Crisis," *Washington Post National Weekly Edition*, December 21–27, 1992, p. 7.

11. Catherine England, "Lessons from the Savings and Loan Debacle: The Case for Further Financial Deregulation," *Regulation* 15 (Summer 1992): 37–38.
12. Mayer, *The Greatest-Ever Bank Robbery*, pp. 136, 144.
13. Ibid., p. 190.
14. Ibid., p. 197.
15. Kurtz, "Asleep at the Switch," p. 9.
16. Quoted in Mayer, *The Greatest-Ever Bank Robbery*, p. 32.
17. Quoted in Kurtz, "Asleep at the Switch," p. 8.
18. Quoted in Mayer, *The Greatest-Ever Bank Robbery*, p. 259.
19. See, e.g., Tom R. Tyler, *Why People Obey the Law* (New Haven: Yale University Press, 1990), pp. 37–38, 58–59. But notice that the *most* compelling reason for compliance is consistency between the content of a law or rule and the individual's moral code. "The most important normative influence on compliance with the law is the person's assessment that following the law accords with his or her sense of right and wrong; a second factor is the person's feeling of obligation to obey the law and allegiance to legal authorities.... Personal morality is clearly a more important influence on compliance than legitimacy." Ibid., pp. 64, 68.
20. "The Public View of Regulation," *Public Opinion*, (January/February 1979), cited by Mark Green and Nancy Drabble in U.S., *Hearings on Regulation Reform Act of 1979*, part 1, p. 333.
21. Cited by Kathleen F. O'Reilly in U.S., *Hearings on Regulatory Reform Legislation*, part 1, 1233.
22. Quoted in Eads and Fix, *Relief or Reform?*, p. 7.
23. Edwards, "Director or Facilitator?" pp. 218–219. Edwards cites the following sources: William Schneider, "The Voters' Mood 1986: The Six-Year Itch," *National Journal*, December 7, 1985, p. 2758; "Supporting a Greater Federal Role," *National Journal*, April 18, 1987, p. 924; "Opinion Outlook," *National Journal*, April 18, 1987, p. 964; Seymour Martin Lipset, "Beyond 1984: The Anomalies of American Politics," *PS* 19 (Spring 1986): 223; and "Federal Budget Deficit," *Gallup Report*, August 1987, pp. 25, 27.
24. Gallup Organization survey for the Times Mirror Company, May 13–22, 1988, cited in Everett Carll Ladd, *The American Polity*, 5th ed. (New York: W. W. Norton and Co., 1993), p. 277.
25. NBC News/*Wall Street Journal* survey, January 13–16, 1990, cited in Ladd, *The American Polity*, p. 277.
26. U.S., Advisory Commission on Intergovernmental Relations, *Changing Public Attitudes on Government and Taxes: 1992*. See also "ACIR Probes Public Views on Regulation," *PA Times*, September 1, 1992, pp. 3, 12.
27. See chapter 3.
28. Presentation by Marshall R. Goodman, related to his paper, "A Kinder and Gentler Regulatory Reform." OIRA deputy administrator Tozzi boasted that he could "tell in about four minutes if a rule made sense." Quoted in Bryner, *Bureaucratic Discretion*, pp. 82–83.

29. Some improvements were made, such as a decline in the "bypassing" of states in federal-local relationships and the delegation of more administrative authority in environmental programs. David B. Walker, "American Federalism from Johnson to Bush," *Publius: The Journal of Federalism* 21 (Winter 1991): 112.
30. Ibid., p. 113.
31. U.S., *Regulatory Federalism: Policy, Process, Impact and Reform*, p. 258.
32. Gregory B. Christiansen and Robert H. Haveman, "The Reagan Administration's Regulatory Relief Effort: A Mid-Term Assessment," in *The Reagan Regulatory Strategy*, ed. Eads and Fix, p. 80.
33. Goodman and Wrightson, *Managing Regulatory Reform*, p. 114.
34. George Steiner, quoted in Murray L. Weidenbaum, "Regulatory Reform: A Report Card for the Reagan Administration," *California Management Review* 26 (Fall 1983): 23.
35. Richard A. Harris and Sidney M. Milkis, *The Politics of Regulatory Change: A Tale of Two Agencies* (New York: Oxford University Press, 1989).
36. Goodman and Wrightson, *Managing Regulatory Reform*, pp. 207–08.
37. The "zone of twilight" was described in the concurring opinion of Justice Jackson in *Youngstown v. Sawyer*.

CHAPTER 10

1. Larry Berman and Bruce W. Jentleson, "Bush and the Post-Cold-War World: New Challenges for American Leadership," in *The Bush Presidency*, ed. Campbell and Rockman, p. 99.
2. Aberbach, "The President and the Executive Branch," pp. 231–32.
3. Ibid., p. 223.
4. Michael Duffy and Dan Goodgame, *Marching in Place: The Status Quo Presidency of George Bush* (New York: Simon and Schuster, 1992), pp. 58, 64–66.
5. Christine Triano and Nancy Watzman, "Immoral, Illegal And Deadly," *The Nation*, March 23, 1992, p. 381.
6. Goodman, "A Kinder and Gentler Regulatory Reform," pp. 10–11.
7. Bert A. Rockman, "The Leadership Style of George Bush," in *The Bush Presidency*, ed. Campbell and Rockman, p. 3.
8. Jones, "Meeting Low Expectations," p. 51.
9. Quoted in Duffy and Goodgame, *Marching in Place*, p. 70.
10. Ibid., p. 58.
11. Aberbach, "The President and the Executive Branch," p. 240.
12. William A. Niskanen, "Small Change," *Regulation* 15 (Winter 1992): 10.
13. Burt Solomon in *National Journal*, quoted in Aberbach, "The President and the Executive Branch," p. 237.
14. Aberbach, "The President and the Executive Branch," p. 223.
15. President George Bush, "Remarks to Members of the American Retail Federation,"

May 17, 1989, in U.S., Office of the Federal Register, *Weekly Compilation of Presidential Documents* 25, 20 (May 22, 1989): 729.

16. President George Bush, "Remarks at the Annual National Legislative Conference of the Independent Insurance Agents of America," March 14, 1989, in U.S., Office of the Federal Register, *Weekly Compilation of Presidential Documents* 25, 11 (March 20, 1989): 346.
17. Eastland, *Energy in the Executive*, p. 164.
18. Observers believed from the beginning of his presidency that Bush had assigned regulatory relief a low priority. "I don't expect much deregulatory initiative from the Bush Administration," said William A. Niskanen, a former Reagan adviser. "Deregulation seems to be one of those things where the political costs are higher than the payoffs." Quoted in Richard L. Berke, "Deregulation Has Gone Too Far, Many Telling New Administration," *New York Times*, December 11, 1988, p. 1. In any event, Reagan launched his program at a time when regulatory reform had an honorable reputation. Bush may have recognized reform's soiled reputation and had a compelling reason to move cautiously.
19. Michael Richards, "Regulatory Tide Ebbs and Flows," *Christian Science Monitor*, September 19, 1991, p. 8.
20. Steven Waldman and Mary Hager, "A Quayle Hunts the Watchdogs," *Newsweek*, January 6, 1992, p. 34. See also Jonathan Rauch, "The Regulatory President," *National Journal*, November 30, 1991, p. 2905, and Niskanen, "Small Change," p. 10.
21. "The Reregulation President" [editorial], *Wall Street Journal*, June 17, 1991, p. A10.
22. Peter Brimelow, "A Green Face Instead of a Red Face?" *Forbes*, December 11, 1989, p. 80.
23. The statement in "Building a Better America" was reprinted in U.S., *Regulatory Program of the United States Government, April 1, 1990–March 31, 1991*, p. 5.
24. Gerald M. Boyd, "Quayle Says He'll Play Important Role for Bush," *New York Times*, January 14, 1989, p. 8.
25. Goodman's presentation accompanied the delivery of his paper, "A Kinder and Gentler Regulatory Reform."
26. Triano and Watzman, *All the Vice President's Men: How the Quayle Council on Competitiveness Secretly Undermines Health, Safety, and Environmental Programs* (Washington, D.C.: OMB Watch, September 1991), p. 3.
27. Dana Priest, "Competitiveness Council Suspected of Unduly Influencing Regulators: Secrecy Foils Senate Panel's Attempt to Probe Vice President's Group," *Washington Post*, November 18, 1991, p. A19.
28. Jim Sibbison, "Dan Quayle, Business's Backdoor Boy," *The Nation*, July 29/August 5, 1991, p. 162.
29. Ibid.
30. "FDA Hopes to Speed Drug Approval with Sweeping Changes in Process," *Atlanta Journal*, November 8, 1991, p. A5.
31. Sibbison, "Dan Quayle, Business's Backdoor Boy," front cover and p. 160; and Julia

Malone, "Quayle Panel Under Fire for Bold, Secretive Moves," *Atlanta Journal-Constitution*, November 17, 1991, p. A4.

32. Bob Woodward and David S. Broder, "Quayle's Quest: Curb Rules, Leave 'No Fingerprints,'" *Washington Post*, January 9, 1992, p. A16.
33. Philip J. Hilts, "Questions on Role of Quayle Council," *New York Times*, November 19, 1991, p. B12.
34. Woodward and Broder, "Quayle's Quest," p. A1.
35. Kirk Victor, "Quayle's Quiet Coup," *National Journal*, July 6, 1991, pp. 1676–78.
36. Michael Duffy, "Need Friends in High Places?" *Time*, November 4, 1991, p. 25.
37. Quoted in Victor, "Quayle's Quiet Coup," p. 1678.
38. U.S., Congress, House, Committee on Energy and Commerce, Subcommittee on Health and the Environment, *Hearings on Clean Air Act Implementation*, part 2, 102d Cong., 1st and 2d sess., Nov. 14, Dec. 10, 1991, Feb. 7, 1992, p. 2.
39. Interview by the author with Dr. Cornelius M. Kerwin, July 1, 1992.
40. Testimony in *Hearings on Clean Air Act Implementation*, part 2, pp. 292–93.
41. Richard Fly, "Introducing Dan Quayle, Competitiveness Czar," *Business Week*, February 27, 1989, p. 37.
42. Woodward and Broder, "Quayle's Quest," p. A17.
43. John H. Cushman Jr., "Federal Regulation Growing Despite Quayle Panel's Role," *New York Times*, December 24, 1991, p. A1.
44. Elizabeth A. Palmer, "White House War on Red Tape: Success Hard to Gauge," *Congressional Quarterly Weekly Report*, May 2, 1992, p. 1156.
45. Niskanen, "Small Change," p. 10; Bob Deans, "Freeze on New Rules Extended," *Atlanta Journal*, April 30, 1992, p. A2; Palmer, "White House War on Red Tape," p. 1155.
46. Palmer, "White House War on Red Tape," p. 1156.
47. Deans, "Freeze on New Rules Extended," p. A2.
48. Phillip A. Davis, Mike Mills, and Holly Idelson, "Outcry Greets Bush's Plans to Delay New Rules," *Congressional Quarterly Weekly Report*, January 18, 1992, p. 165.
49. See also Peter M. Shane, "Negotiating for Knowledge: Administrative Responses to Congressional Demands for Information," *Administrative Law Review* 44 (Spring 1992): 200.
50. Hilts, "At Heart of Debate on Quayle Council: Who Controls Federal Regulations?" *New York Times*, December 16, 1991, p. B11.
51. Davis et al., "Outcry Greets Bush's Plans to Delay New Rules," p. 164.
52. See, e.g., Victor, "Quayle's Quiet Coup," p. 1680; and Barbara Rosewicz, "Environmental Chief Clashes With New Foe: Deregulation Troops," *Wall Street Journal*, March 27, 1992, p. A1.
53. Rosewicz, "Environmental Chief Clashes With New Foe," p. A1.
54. Victor, "Quayle's Quiet Coup," p. 1676.
55. Graeme Browning, "Getting the Last Word," *National Journal*, September 14, 1991, p. 2195.

56. Victor, "Quayle's Quiet Coup," p. 1676.
57. Rosewicz, "Environmental Chief Clashes With New Foe," p. A6.
58. Robert A. Anthony, "'Well, You Want the Permit Don't You?' Agency Efforts to Make Nonlegislative Documents Bind the Public," *Administrative Law Review* 44 (Winter 1992): 31–32. In "Memorandum of the Vice President to Heads of Executive Departments and Agencies on the Regulatory Review Process," March 22, 1991, p. 1, Quayle wrote (quoted in ibid., p. 32. n. 4):

> The Administration has consistently interpreted the Executive Order [12291] to include all agency policy guidance that affects the public. Such policy guidance includes not only regulations that are published for notice and comment, but also strategy statements, guidelines, policy manuals, grant and loan procedures, Advance Notices of Proposed Rule Making, press releases and other documents announcing or implementing regulatory policy that affects the public.

59. Rosewicz, "Environmental Chief Clashes With New Foe," p. A1.
60. Ann Devroy, "Bush Between Push and Pull on Clean Air," *Washington Post*, April 26, 1992, p. A18.
61. Ernie Freda, "The Men the Lawmakers Leave Behind," *Atlanta Journal*, December 15, 1992, p. A7.
62. Rauch, "The Regulatory President," p. 2906.
63. Goodman, "A Kinder and Gentler Regulatory Reform," p. 11.
64. Browning, "Getting the Last Word," p. 2194.
65. Idelson, "Glenn Trying to Shed Light on Rule-Making Process," *Congressional Quarterly Weekly Report*, November 23, 1991, p. 3449.
66. Jeffrey H. Birnbaum, "White House Competitiveness Council Provokes Sharp Anger Among Democrats in Congress," *Wall Street Journal*, July 8, 1991, p. A8.
67. Hilts, "Questions on Role of Quayle Council," p. B12.
68. U.S., *Regulatory Review Sunshine Act*, p. 6.
69. Hilts, "House Panel Plans Inquiry on Quayle Council's Staff," *New York Times*, November 22, 1991, p. A14.
70. See *Hearings on Clean Air Act Implementation*, part 2.
71. U.S., Congress, House, Committee on Energy and Commerce, Subcommittee on Oversight and Investigations, *The Superfund National Contingency Plan: Report on a Case Study of* OMB *Involvement in Agency Rulemaking*, 101st Cong., 1st sess., 1989, Committee Print 101-B.
72. Clifford Krauss, "House Votes to Eliminate Money for Regulatory Council Headed by Quayle," *New York Times*, July 2, 1992, p. A16.
73. Quoted in Keith Schneider, "Industries Gaining Broad Flexibility on Air Pollution," *New York Times*, June 26, 1992, pp. A1, A16.
74. Davis et al., "Outcry Greets Bush's Plans to Delay New Rules," p. 164.
75. Broder and Woodward, "Quayle's Quest," p. A1.

76. Duffy and Goodgame, *Marching in Place*, p. 63.
77. Frank Luntz, "Learning From Failure," *Washington Post National Weekly Edition*, November 9–15, 1992, p. 28.
78. Duffy and Goodgame, *Marching in Place*, p. 59.
79. Ibid., p. 62.
80. Kerwin interview, July 1, 1992.
81. Gerald F. Seib and Bob Davis, "Bush and Clinton Joust Over How to Regulate U.S. Business Activity," *Wall Street Journal*, September 23, 1992, p. A6.
82. Ibid.
83. Rose Gutfield and Rosewicz, "Economic Concerns Likely to Dominate Regulation Debate," *Wall Street Journal*, November 5, 1992, p. A18.
84. Devroy and Ruth Marcus, "For Clinton, A Surprising Role Model," *Washington Post*, November 15, 1992, pp. A1, A8.
85. Dan Balz, "How Not To Be President: Clinton Hopes to Learn from Carter's Blunders," *Washington Post National Weekly Edition*, December 7–13, 1992, p. 11.
86. Seib and Davis, "Bush and Clinton Joust," p. A6.
87. David McIntosh, "Breaking the Iron Triangle," *Regulation* 16 (1993): 26.
88. U.S., Office of the Vice President, *Crating a Government That Works Better and Costs Less: Report of the National Performance Review*, September 7, 1993 (rev. September 10, 1993), p. 32. The administration's estimate is remarkable in this respect: as explained in chapter 1, Murray L. Weidenbaum, a Reagan-Bush economist, released a 1979 report estimating compliance costs at about $120 billion per year. As explained in chap. 1, n. 37, Weidenbaum's estimate and similar studies were denounced by the Consumer Federation of America, the Center for Policy Alternatives of the Massachusetts Institute of Technology, and the Congressional Research Service. But the Clinton administration's estimate, which would appear to vindicate Weidenbaum, seems to have attracted little notice from those who excoriated Weidenbaum.
89. *Report of the National Performance Review*, p. 33.
90. Donald F. Kettl, "Are We the Captains of Our Ship?" *Administration and Society* 3 (Winter 1993): 3.
91. William Niskanen, "Clinton Regulation Will Be 'Rational': Interview with Sally Katzen, the New OIRA Administrator," *Regulation* 16 (1993): 38.
92. Ibid., p. 36.
93. Ibid., p. 37.
94. *Report of the National Performance Review*.
95. David Osborne and Ted Gaebler, *Reinventing Government: How the Entrepreneurial Spirit Is Transforming the Public Sector* (Reading, Mass.: Addison-Wesley, 1992).
96. 58 Fed. Reg. 51,735 (1993).
97. Eric Planin and Stephen Barr, "Reinventing Government Savings Projections," *Washington Post National Weekly Edition*, December 6–12, 1993, p. 31.
98. Barr, "The Slow Work of Intervention," ibid.
99. Ibid., p. 32.

CHAPTER 11

1. See, e.g., *Federalist* 51 [James Madison].
2. *Immigration and Naturalization Service v. Chadha*, 462 U.S. 919, 951 (1983), using language appearing in *Buckley v. Valeo*, 424 U.S. 1, 121 (1976).
3. Bowers, "Looking at OMB's Regulatory Review," pp. 331–45.
4. Melnick, "The Politics of Partnership," p. 655.
5. Melnick writes, "Judicial rhetoric about a court-agency partnership is more than just a clever disguise for judicial usurpation of administrative authority. While a few agencies—most notably the Federal Communications Commission and the Nuclear Regulatory Commission—continued to fight with the courts for years, most adapted to the courts' requirements and have even applauded their efforts." Ibid., p. 653.
6. Kenneth A. Shepsle, "Studying Institutions: Some Lessons from the Rational Choice Approach," *Journal of Theoretical Politics* 1, 2 (1989): 133.
7. James G. March and Johan P. Olsen, *Rediscovering Institutions: The Organizational Basis of Politics* (New York: Free Press, 1989), p. 160.
8. [Mathew] D. McCubbins, Roger G. Noll, and Barry R. Weingast, "Structure and Process, Politics and Policy: Administrative Arrangements and the Political Control of Agencies," *Virginia Law Review* 75 (March 1989): 431–82.
9. Ibid., pp. 437–40.
10. Shepsle, "Studying Institutions," pp. 134–35.
11. McCubbins et al., "Structure and Process, Politics and Policy," pp. 432–33.
12. Shepsle, "Studying Institutions," p. 136.
13. Ibid., p. 137.
14. James G. March and Johan P. Olsen, "The New Institutionalism: Organizational Factors in Political Life," *American Political Science Review* 78 (September 1984): 738.
15. Heinz Eulau, *Journeys in Politics* (New York: Bobbs-Merrill, 1964), p. 256.
16. Talcott Parsons, in *Toward a General Theory of Action*, ed. Talcott Parsons and Edward A. Shils (Cambridge: Harvard University Press, 1951), p. 140, emphasis deleted.
17. Richard M. Pious, *The American Presidency* (New York: Basic Books, 1979), p. 12 n. 15.
18. James Bryce, *The American Commonwealth*, rev. ed. (New York: Macmillan Co., 1889), 1:227.
19. *Marbury v. Madison*, 5 U.S. (1 Cranch) 137, 177.
20. Richard M. Emerson, "Power-Dependence Relations," *American Sociological Review* 27 (February 1962): 31–40.
21. S. F. Nadel, *The Theory of Social Structure* (London: Cohen and West Ltd., 1957), pp. 114–21.
22. Seidman and Gilmour, *Politics, Position, and Power*, pp. 50–51.
23. Paul F. Secord and Carl W. Backman, *Social Psychology* (New York: McGraw-Hill Book Company, 1964), p. 277.

24. Edward S. Corwin, *The President: Office and Powers, 1787–1984*, 5th rev. ed. (New York: New York University Press, 1984), p. 201.
25. March and Olsen, *Rediscovering Institutions*, p. 150.
26. Cited in Peter M. Blau, *Exchange and Power in Social Life* (New York: John Wiley and Sons, 1964), p. 170.
27. Ibid.
28. See James D. Thompson, *Organizations in Action: Social Science Bases of Administrative Theory* (New York: McGraw-Hill Book Company, 1967).
29. Quoted in Blau, *Exchange and Power in Social Life*, p. 156.
30. Cited ibid., p. 92.
31. Ibid., p. 93.
32. Ibid., pp. 115–16.
33. Charles E. Lindblom, "The Market as Prison," *Journal of Politics* 44 (May 1982): 324–35.
34. Blau, *Exchange and Power in Social Life*, p. 321.
35. See Mosher, *Democracy and the Public Service.*
36. Blau, *Exchange and Power in Social Life*, p. 288.
37. Richard E. Neustadt, *Presidential Power and the Modern Presidents: The Politics of Leadership from Roosevelt to Reagan* (New York: Free Press, 1990), p. 32.
38. Louis W. Koenig, *The Chief Executive* (New York: Harcourt Brace Jovanovich, 1975), p. 184.
39. James P. Pfiffner, "Political Appointees and Career Executives: The Democracy-Bureaucracy Nexus," in Pfiffner, ed., *The Managerial Presidency*, p. 176.
40. Bernard Gwertzman, "The Shultz Method," *New York Times Magazine*, January 2, 1983, p. 15.
41. Rourke, *Bureaucracy, Politics, and Public Policy*, p. 130.
42. Clinton Rossiter, *The American Presidency* (New York: Harcourt, Brace, and World, 1960), pp. 19–22.
43. Rourke, *Bureaucracy, Politics, and Public Policy*, p. 74. As president-elect, Bill Clinton was given a preview of the recalcitrance that he, too, would encounter. "Led by Chairman Colin Powell, the JCS [Joint Chiefs of Staff] in mid-December [1992] warned Clinton's aides that they would resign as a group if the incoming administration chose an unacceptable plan for legitimizing the military status of gays." The day after Clinton's inauguration, Secretary of Defense Les Aspin "met the chiefs in 'the tank'—the soundproof chamber on the Pentagon's second floor where the JCS meet twice a week—and the result was a stormy, two-hour debate." The chiefs "have steadily leaked their continued opposition to [Clinton's] offers of a deal." "Gays and the Military," *Newsweek*, February 1, 1993, pp. 53, 55.
44. Charles E. Lindblom, *The Intelligence of Democracy: Decision Making Through Mutual Adjustment* (New York: Free Press, 1965).
45. Pfiffner, "Political Appointees and Career Executives," p. 168.
46. Quoted ibid., p. 174.

47. Quoted ibid.
48. Waterman, *Presidential Influence and the Administrative State*, p. 25.
49. *Vermont Yankee v. Natural Resources*, 519, 547.
50. Ibid., 557.
51. *Chevron U.S.A., Inc., v. Natural Resources Defense Council, Inc.*, 467 U.S. 837 (1984).
52. John F. Belcaster, "The D.C. Circuit's Use of the *Chevron* Test: Constructing a Positive Theory of Judicial Obedience and Disobedience," *Administrative Law Review* 44 (Fall 1992): 745, 749, and 750.
53. Ibid., p. 758.
54. Sundquist, *The Decline and Resurgence of Congress*, p. 16.
55. See Waterman, *Presidential Influence and the Administrative State*, pp. 25–26.
56. Edwards, "Director or Facilitator?" p. 216.
57. James T. Patterson, *Congressional Conservatism and the New Deal: The Growth of the Conservative Coalition in Congress, 1933–1939* (Lexington: University of Kentucky Press, 1967), chapter 8.
58. Jimmy Carter, *Keeping Faith: Memoirs of a President* (Toronto: Bantam Books, 1982), p. 80.
59. Quoted in Edwards, "Director or Facilitator?", p. 217.
60. Ibid., p. 224.
61. Mark A. Peterson, "The Presidency and Organized Interests: White House Patterns of Interest Group Liaison," *American Political Science Review* 86 (September 1992): 613.
62. Samuel Kernell, *Going Public: New Strategies of Presidential Leadership* (Washington, D.C.: Congressional Quarterly, 1986).
63. See *Federalist* 51. The author (probably James Madison) offered the memorable prescription, "Ambition must be made to counteract ambition."
64. See also chapter 1.
65. Coldwell Daniel III, "The New Theory of Public Utilities: The Case of the Natural Monopoly," *The Antitrust Bulletin* 26 (Spring 1981): 138.

References

Aberbach, Joel D. *Keeping a Watchful Eye: The Politics of Congressional Oversight.* Washington, D.C.: Brookings Institution, 1990.

Ball, Howard. *Controlling Regulatory Sprawl: Presidential Strategies from Nixon to Reagan.* Westport, Conn.: Greenwood Press, 1984.

———, ed. *Federal Administrative Agencies: Essays on Power and Politics.* Englewood Cliffs, N.J.: Prentice-Hall, 1984.

Becker, Theodore L. *The Impact of Supreme Court Decisions.* New York: Oxford University Press, 1969.

Bernstein, Marver H. *Regulating Business by Independent Commission.* Westport, Conn.: Greenwood Press, 1977 (rpt. of 1955 volume).

Blau, Peter M. *Exchange and Power in Social Life.* New York: John Wiley, 1964.

Braybrooke, David, and Charles E. Lindblom. *A Strategy of Decision.* New York: Free Press, 1963.

Breyer, Stephen. *Regulation and Its Reforms.* Cambridge: Harvard University Press, 1982.

Bryce, James. *The American Commonwealth.* Rev. ed. New York: Macmillan Co., 1889.

Bryner, Gary C. *Bureaucratic Discretion: Law and Policy in Federal Regulatory Agencies.* New York: Pergamon Press, 1987.

Burford, Anne, with John Greenya. *Are You Tough Enough?* New York: McGraw-Hill, 1986.

Campbell, Colin, S.J., and Bert A. Rockman, eds. *The Bush Presidency: First Appraisals.* Chatham, N.J.: Chatham House Publishers, 1991.

Carter, Jimmy. *Keeping Faith: Memoirs of a President.* Toronto: Bantam Books, 1982.

Cater, Douglass. *Power in Washington, D.C.: A Critical Look at Today's Struggle to Govern in the Nation's Capital.* New York: Random House, 1964.

Choper, Jesse H. *Judicial Review and the National Political Process: A Functional Reconsideration of the Role of the Supreme Court.* Chicago: University of Chicago Press, 1980.

Chubb, John, and Paul Peterson, eds. *The New Direction in American Politics.* Washington, D.C.: Brookings Institution, 1985.

Corwin, Edward S. *The President: Office and Powers, 1787–1984.* 5th rev. ed. New York: New York University Press, 1984.

Coser, Lewis A. *The Functions of Social Conflict.* Glencoe, Ill.: Free Press, 1956.

Craig, Barbara Hinkson. *Chadha: Story of an Epic Constitutional Struggle.* New York: Oxford University Press, 1988.

Crovitz, L. Gordon, and Jeremy A. Rabkin, eds. *The Fettered Presidency: Legal Constraints on the Executive Branch.* Washington, D.C.: American Enterprise Institute, 1989.

Curtis, Richard, and Maggie Wells. *Not Exactly a Crime: Our Vice Presidents from Adams to Agnew.* New York: Dial Press, 1972.

Davis, Kenneth Culp. *Administrative Law Treatise.* 2d ed. San Diego, Calif.: By the author, 1978.

———. *1982 Supplement to Administrative Law Treatise.* San Diego, Calif.: K.C. Davis, 1982.

Derthick, Martha, and Paul J. Quirk. *The Politics of Deregulation.* Washington, D.C.: Brookings Institution, 1985.

Dodd, Lawrence C., and Bruce I. Oppenheimer, eds. *Congress Reconsidered.* 1st ed. New York: Praeger Publishers, 1977.

Duffy, Michael, and Dan Goodgame. *Marching in Place: The Status Quo Presidency of George Bush.* New York: Simon & Schuster, 1992.

Eads, George C., and Michael Fix, eds. *Relief or Reform? Reagan's Regulatory Dilemma.* Washington, D.C.: Urban Institute Press, 1984.

———, eds. *The Reagan Regulatory Strategy: An Assessment.* Washington, D.C.: Urban Institute, 1984.

Eastland, Terry. *Energy in the Executive: The Case for the Strong Presidency.* New York: Free Press, 1992.

Eulau, Heinz. *Journeys in Politics.* New York: Bobbs-Merrill, 1964.

Evans, Rowland Jr., and Robert D. Novak. *Nixon in the White House.* New York: Random House, 1971.

Fiorina, Morris P. *Congress: Keystone of the Washington Establishment.* 2d ed. New Haven: Yale University Press, 1989.

Fisher, Louis. *The Politics of Shared Power: Congress and the Executive.* Washington, D.C.: Congressional Quarterly Press, 1981.

Foreman, Christopher H., Jr. *Signals From the Hill: Congressional Oversight and the Challenge of Social Regulation.* New Haven: Yale University Press, 1988.

Freeman, J. Leiper. *The Political Process: Executive Bureau-Legislative Committee Relations.* New York: Random House, 1965.

Frisby, David. *Georg Simmel.* Chichester, England: Horwood Limited, 1984.

Fuchs, Edward Paul. *Institutionalizing Cost-Benefit Analysis: Politics in the Regulatory Process, 1974–1981.* Ph.D. diss., University of Houston, 1983.

———. *Presidents, Management, and Regulation.* Englewood Cliffs, N.J.: Prentice-Hall, 1988.

Goodman, Marshall R., and Margaret T. Wrightson. *Managing Regulatory Reform: The Reagan Strategy and Its Impact.* New York: Praeger Publishers, 1987.

Greenwald, Carol. *Group Power: Lobbying and Public Policy.* New York: Praeger Publishers, 1977.

Harris, Joseph P. *Congressional Control of Administration.* Washington, D.C.: Brookings Institution, 1964.

Harris, Richard A., and Sidney M. Milkis. *The Politics of Regulatory Change: A Tale of Two Agencies.* New York: Oxford University Press, 1989.

Hart, John. *The Presidential Branch.* New York: Pergamon Press, 1987.

Heclo, Hugh. *A Government of Strangers: Executive Politics in Washington.* Washington, D.C.: Brookings Institution, 1977.

Heffron, Florence, with Neil McFeeley. *The Administrative Regulatory Process.* New York: Longman 1983.

Jacobs, Donald P., ed. *Regulating Business: The Search for an Optimum.* San Francisco, Calif.: Institute for Contemporary Studies, 1978.

Jones, Charles O., ed. *The Reagan Legacy: Promise and Performance.* Chatham, N.J.: Chatham House Publishers, 1988.

Katz, Daniel, and Robert L. Kahn, *The Social Psychology of Organizations.* New York: John Wiley, 1966.

Kaufman, Herbert. *The Administrative Behavior of Federal Bureau Chiefs.* Washington, D.C.: Brookings Institution, 1981.

———. *The Forest Ranger: A Study in Administrative Behavior.* Baltimore: Johns Hopkins University Press, 1960.

Kernell, Samuel. *Going Public: New Strategies of Presidential Leadership.* Washington, D.C.: Congressional Quarterly Press, 1986.

King, Anthony, ed. *The New American Political System.* Washington, D.C.: American Enterprise Institute, 1978.

Kirst, Michael W. *Government Without Passing Laws: Congress's Nonstatutory Techniques for Appropriations Control.* Chapel Hill: University of North Carolina Press, 1969.

Koenig, Louis W. *The Chief Executive.* New York: Harcourt Brace Jovanovich, 1975.

Kolko, Gabriel. *The Triumph of Conservatism: A Reinterpretation of American History, 1900–1916.* Glencoe, Ill.: Free Press, 1963.

Kurland, Philip B., and Gerhard Casper, eds. *The Supreme Court Review, 1978*. Chicago: University of Chicago Press, 1978.

Ladd, Everett Carll. *The American Polity*. 5th ed. New York: W. W. Norton, 1993.

Light, Paul C. *Vice-Presidential Power: Advice and Influence in the White House*. Baltimore: Johns Hopkins University Press, 1984.

Lindblom, Charles E. *The Intelligence of Democracy: Decision Making Through Mutual Adjustment*. New York: Free Press, 1965.

Litan, Robert E., and William D. Nordhaus. *Reforming Federal Regulation*. New Haven: Yale University Press, 1983.

Lowi, Theodore J. *The End of Liberalism: The Second Republic of the United States*. 2d ed. New York: W. W. Norton & Company, 1979.

McGraw, Thomas K., ed. *Regulation in Perspective: Historical Essays*. Cambridge: Harvard University Press, 1981.

Mackenzie, G. Calvin, ed. *The In-and-Outers: Presidential Appointees and Transient Government in Washington*. Baltimore: Johns Hopkins University Press, 1987.

March, James G., and Johan P. Olsen. *Rediscovering Institutions: The Organizational Basis of Politics*. New York: Free Press, 1989.

Mayer, Martin. *The Greatest-Ever Bank Robbery: The Collapse of the Savings and Loan Industry*. New York: Charles Scribner's Sons, 1990.

Meier, Kenneth J. *Regulation: Politics, Bureaucracy, and Economics*. New York: St. Martin's Press, 1985.

Meiners, Roger E., and Bruce Yandle, eds. *Regulation and the Reagan Era: Politics, Bureaucracy and the Public Interest*. New York: Holmes & Meier, 1989.

Miller, James C., and Bruce Yandle. *Benefit-Cost Analysis of Social Regulations*. Washington, D.C.: American Enterprise Institute, 1979.

Morgan, Ruth P. *The President and Civil Rights: Policymaking by Executive Order*. New York: St. Martin's Press, 1970.

Mosher, Frederick C. *Democracy and the Public Service*. 2d ed. New York: Oxford University Press, 1982.

Nadel, S. F. *The Theory of Social Structure*. London: Cohen & West Ltd., 1957.

Nader, Ralph. *Unsafe at Any Speed: The Designed-in Dangers of the American Automobile*. New York: Grossman Publishers, 1965.

Nathan, Richard. *The Administrative Presidency*. New York: John Wiley, 1983.

———. *The Plot That Failed: Nixon and the Administrative Presidency*. New York: John Wiley, 1975.

Nelson, Michael, ed. *The Presidency and the Political System*. Washington, D.C.: Congressional Quarterly Press, 1988.

Neustadt, Richard E. *Presidential Power and the Modern Presidents: The Politics of Leadership from Roosevelt to Reagan*. New York: Free Press, 1990.

Noll, Roger G. *Reforming Regulation: An Evaluation of the Ash Council Proposals*. Washington, D.C.: Brookings Institution, 1971.

Ogul, Morris S. *Congress Oversees the Bureaucracy: Studies in Legislative Supervision*. Pittsburgh: University of Pittsburgh Press, 1976.

Osborne, David, and Ted Gaebler. *Reinventing Government: How the Entrepreneurial Spirit Is Transforming the Public Sector*. Reading, Mass.: Addison-Wesley, 1992.

Owens, Henry, and Charles Schultze, eds. *Setting National Priorities*. Washington, D.C.: Brookings Institution, 1976.

Parsons, Talcott, and Edward A. Shils, eds. *Toward a General Theory of Action*. Cambridge: Harvard University Press, 1951.

Patterson, James T. *Congressional Conservatism and the New Deal: The Growth of the Conservative Coalition in Congress, 1933–1939*. Lexington: University of Kentucky Press, 1967.

Petersen, H. Craig. *Business and Government*. 3d ed. New York: Harper & Row, Publishers, 1989.

Pfiffner, James P., ed. *The Managerial Presidency*. Pacific Grove, Calif.: Brooks/Cole Publishing Company, 1991.

Pfiffner, James P., and R. Gordon Hoxie, eds. *The Presidency in Transition*. New York: Center for the Study of the Presidency, 1989.

[Plocher, David.] OMB *Control of Rulemaking: The End of Public Access*. Washington, D.C.: OMB Watch, 1985.

Pyle, Christopher H., and Richard M. Pious. *The President, Congress, and the Constitution*. New York: Free Press, 1984.

Quirk, Paul J. *Industry Influence in Federal Regulatory Agencies*. Princeton: Princeton University Press, 1981.

Reagan, Michael D. *Regulation: The Politics of Policy*. Boston: Little, Brown, 1987.

Reich, Robert B., ed. *Public Management in a Democratic Society*. Englewood Cliffs, N.J.: Prentice-Hall, 1990.

Rossiter, Clinton. *The American Presidency*. New York: Harcourt, Brace, and World, 1960.

Rourke, Francis E. *Bureaucracy, Politics, and Public Policy*. 3d ed. Boston: Little, Brown and Company, 1984.

Salamon, Lester M., and Michael S. Lund, eds. *The Reagan Presidency and the Governing of America*. Washington, D.C.: Urban Institute Press, 1984.

Secord, Paul F., and Carl W. Backman. *Social Psychology*. New York: McGraw-Hill Book Company, 1964.

Seidman, Harold, and Robert Gilmour. *Politics, Position, and Power: From the Positive to the Regulatory State*. 4th ed. New York: Oxford University Press, 1986.

Sethi, S. Prakash, ed. *Up Against the Corporate Wall*. 4th ed. Englewood Cliffs, N.J.: Prentice-Hall, 1982.

Starling, Grover. *Strategies for Policy Making*. Chicago: Dorsey Press, 1988.

Steiner, George A., and John F. Steiner. *Business, Government, and Society: A Managerial Perspective*. 3d ed. New York: Random House, 1980.

Stockman, David A. *The Triumph of Politics: How the Reagan Revolution Failed*. New York: Harper & Row, Publishers, 1986.

Sundquist, James L. *The Decline and Resurgence of Congress*. Washington, D.C.: Brookings Institution, 1981.

Thompson, James D. *Organizations in Action: Social Science Bases of Administrative Theory*. New York: McGraw-Hill, 1967.

Tolchin, Susan J., and Martin Tolchin. *Dismantling America: The Rush to Deregulate*. New York: Oxford University Press, 1985.

Truman, David B. *The Governmental Process: Political Interests and Public Opinion*. 2d ed. New York: Albert A. Knopf, 1971.

Tyler, Tom R. *Why People Obey the Law*. New Haven: Yale University Press, 1990.

U.S. Advisory Commission on Intergovernmental Relations. *Regulatory Federalism: Policy, Process, Impact and Reform*. Washington, D.C.: GPO, February 1984.

U.S. Congress. House. Committee on Energy and Commerce. *Presidential Control of Agency Rulemaking: An Analysis of Constitutional Issues That May Be Raised by Executive Order 12291*. Report prepared for the use of the House Committee on Energy and Commerce. 97th Cong., 1st sess., June 15, 1981.

U.S. Congress. House. Committee on Energy and Commerce. Subcommittee on Oversight and Investigations. *Hearing on EPA's Asbestos Regulations: A Case Study of Interference in Environmental Protection Agency Rulemaking by the Office of Management and Budget*. 99th Cong., 1st sess., April 16, 1985.

U.S. Congress. House. Committee on Energy and Commerce. Subcommittee on Oversight and Investigations. *Hearing on Role of OMB in Regulation*. 97th Cong., 1st sess., June 18, 1981.

U.S. Congress. House. Committee on Energy and Commerce. Subcommittee on Oversight and Investigations. *The Superfund National Contingency Plan: Report on a Case Study of OMB Involvement in Agency Rulemaking*. 101st Cong., 1st sess., 1989.

U.S. Congress. House. Committee on Government Operations. Subcommittee on Manpower and Housing. *Hearings on Office of Management and Budget Control of OSHA Rulemaking*. 97th Cong., 2d sess., March 11, 18, and 19, 1982.

U.S. Congress. House. Committee on Interstate and Foreign Commerce. Subcommittee on Oversight and Investigations. *Federal Regulation and Regulatory Reform*. 94th Cong., 2d sess., October 1976.

U.S. Congress. House. Committee on the Judiciary. Subcommittee on Administrative Law and Government Relations. *Regulation Reform Act of 1979*. Parts 1 and 2. 96th

Cong, 1st and 2d sess., Nov. 7, 13, 16, 28, 1979; Dec. 3, 5, 10, 1979; Jan. 29, 1980; Feb. 1 and 5, 1980.

U.S. Congress. House. Committee on the Judiciary. Subcommittee on Administrative Law and Government Relations. *Hearings on Regulatory Procedures Act of 1981*. 97th Cong., 1st sess., March 24, April 2, 7, and 30, May 5, 7, 14, and 19, Sept. 10, 1981.

U.S. Congress. Senate. Committee on Environment and Public Works. *Office of Management and Budget Influence on Agency Regulations*. 99th Cong., 2d sess., May 1986.

U.S. Congress. Senate. Committee on Governmental Affairs. *Federal Management Reorganization and Cost Control Act of 1986*. Calendar No. 744, S.Rept. 99-347, July 31 (legislative day July 28), 1986.

U.S. Congress. Senate. Committee on Governmental Affairs. *Hearing on Regulatory Reform Legislation of 1981*. 97th Cong., 1st sess., May 12 and June 23, 1981.

U.S. Congress. Senate. Committee on Governmental Affairs. *Hearings on Reauthorization of* OMB*'s Office of Information and Regulatory Affairs*. 101st Cong., 2d sess., Feb. 21, 22, 1990.

U.S. Congress. Senate. Committee on Governmental Affairs. *Hearings on Regulatory Reform Legislation*. Part 1. 96th Cong., 1st sess., March 20; April 6 and 24; May 3, 4, 16, and 18, 1979.

U.S. Congress. Senate. Committee on Governmental Affairs. *Office of Management and Budget: Evolving Roles and Future Issues*. 99th Cong., 2d sess., February 1986.

U.S. Congress. Senate. Committee on Governmental Affairs. *Paperwork Reduction Act of 1980*. 96th Cong., 2d sess., 1980.

U.S. Congress. Senate. Committee on Governmental Affairs. *Regulatory Review Sunshine Act*. 102d Cong., 2d sess., Feb. 25 (legislative day Jan. 30), 1992, S.Rept. 102-256.

U.S. Congress. Senate. Committee on Governmental Affairs. *Study on Federal Regulation*. Vol. 5. *Regulatory Organization*. 95th Cong., 1st sess., December 1977.

U.S. Congress. Senate. Committee on Governmental Affairs. Subcommittee on Energy, Nuclear Proliferation, and Governmental Processes. *Hearing on Federal Regulation*. Part 1. *Effect on the Automobile Industry*. 97th Cong., 1st sess., April 16, 1981.

U.S. Congress. Senate. Committee on Governmental Affairs. Subcommittee on Energy, Nuclear Proliferation, and Governmental Processes. *Hearing on Federal Regulation*. Part 3. 97th Cong., 1st sess., July 2, 1981.

U.S. Congress. Senate. Committee on Governmental Affairs. Subcommittee on Intergovernmental Relations. *Hearing on Oversight of the Office of Management and Budget Review and Planning Process*. 99th Cong., 2d sess., January 28, 1986.

U.S. Congress. Senate. Committee on Governmental Affairs. Subcommittee on Oversight of Government Management. *Hearings on Oversight of Agency Compliance With Executive Order 12044 "Improving Government Regulations"*. 96th Cong., 1st sess., October 10, 1979.

U.S. Congress. Senate. Committee on Labor and Public Welfare. *Hearings on the Establishment of a Commission on Ethics in Government.* 82d Cong., 1st sess., June–July 1951.

U.S. Congress. Senate. Committee on the Judiciary. *Hearings on Regulatory Reform.* Part 1, 96th Cong., 1st sess., May 10 and 15, 1979.

U.S. Congress. Senate. Committee on the Judiciary. Subcommittee on Administrative Practice and Procedure. *Administrative Procedure Act Amendments of 1978.* 95th Cong., 2d sess., Sept. 12, 13, 20, and 21, 1978.

U.S. Congress. Senate. Committee on the Judiciary. Subcommittee on Administrative Practice and Procedure. *Hearings on Regulatory Reform.* Part 2. 96th Cong., 1st sess., June 13, July 18, 20, 25, and 26, 1979.

U.S. Office of Management and Budget. *Regulatory Program of the United States Government, April 1, 1987–March 31, 1988.* Washington, D.C.: GPO, June 1987.

U.S. Office of Management and Budget. *Regulatory Program of the United States Government, April 1, 1988–March 31, 1989.* Washington, D.C.: GPO, September 1988.

U.S. Office of Management and Budget. *Regulatory Program of the United States Government, April 1, 1990–March 31, 1991.* Washington, D.C.: GPO, August 3, 1990.

U.S. Office the the Vice President. *Creating a Government That Works Better and Costs Less: Report of the National Performance Review.* Washington, D.C.: GPO, September 7, 1993 (rev. September 10, 1993).

U.S. White House. *Economic Report of the President and the Annual Report of the Council of Economic Advisers.* Washington, D.C.: GPO, 1982.

U.S. White House. President's Committee on Administrative Management. *Administrative Management in the Government of the United States.* January 8, 1937.

Viscusi, W. Kip. *Risk By Choice: Regulating Health and Safety in the Workplace.* Cambridge: Harvard University Press, 1983.

Waterman, Richard W. *Presidential Influence and the Administrative State.* Knoxville: University of Tennessee Press, 1989.

Wayne, Stephen J. *The Legislative Presidency.* New York: Harper & Row, Publishers, 1978.

Weidenbaum, Murray L. *Business, Government, and the Public.* 2d ed. Englewood Cliffs, N.J.: Prentice-Hall, 1981.

———. *Business, Government, and the Public.* 3d ed. Englewood Cliffs, N. J.: Prentice-Hall, 1986.

———. *The Future of Business Regulation: Private Action and Public Demand.* New York: AMACOM, 1979.

Weiner, David L., and Aidan R. Vining. *Policy Analysis: Concepts and Practice,* 2d ed. Englewood Cliffs, N.J.: Prentice-Hall, 1992.

Weiss, Leonard W., and Michael W. Klass, eds. *Regulatory Reform: What Actually Happened.* Boston: Little, Brown, 1986.

Welborn, David M. *The Governance of Federal Regulatory Agencies*. Knoxville: University of Tennessee Press, 1977.

Wenner, Lettie M. *The Environmental Decade in Court*. Bloomington: Indiana University Press, 1982.

Wildavsky, Aaron. *The New Politics of the Budgetary Process*. New York: HarperCollins, 1992.

Wilson, James Q., ed. *The Politics of Regulation*. New York: Basic Books, 1980.

Index